T0295580

ia ≠ ai

**INVESTMENT ANALYTICS
IN THE DAWN OF
ARTIFICIAL INTELLIGENCE**

ia ≠ ai

INVESTMENT ANALYTICS
IN THE DAWN OF
ARTIFICIAL INTELLIGENCE

Bernard Lee

HedgeSPA, USA

World Scientific

NEW JERSEY · LONDON · SINGAPORE · BEIJING · SHANGHAI · HONG KONG · TAIPEI · CHENNAI · TOKYO

Published by

World Scientific Publishing Co. Pte. Ltd.

5 Toh Tuck Link, Singapore 596224

USA office: 27 Warren Street, Suite 401-402, Hackensack, NJ 07601

UK office: 57 Shelton Street, Covent Garden, London WC2H 9HE

British Library Cataloguing-in-Publication Data
A catalogue record for this book is available from the British Library.

INVESTMENT ANALYTICS IN THE DAWN OF ARTIFICIAL INTELLIGENCE

ISBN 978-981-4725-35-4
ISBN 978-981-4730-45-7 (pbk)

For any available supplementary material, please visit
https://www.worldscientific.com/worldscibooks/10.1142/9823#t=suppl

Desk Editor: Sandhya Venkatesh

Printed in Singapore

Contents

Preface xi

1 Introduction 1

1.1 The Fourth Industrial Revolution   2

1.2 Unhealthy Myths   3

1.3 New Regulatory Framework   4

1.4 Defining a Road Map   5

1.4.1 Nature of Financial Services 5

1.4.2 What AI and FinTech Cannot Accomplish 6

2 Navigation and Vocabulary 9

2.1 Use Case   9

2.2 Platform Navigation   10

2.2.1 Investment Categories 10

2.2.2 Product Attributes 12

2.2.3 Long and Short Exposure 12

2.2.4 Portfolio Gauges 12

2.2.5 Product Statistics 22

I CONSTRUCT PORTFOLIOS   **25**

3   Understanding Risk 27

3.1   Use Case   27

3.2   A Brief History of Risk Management   28
3.2.1   Evolving from Insurance to Risk Management 28

3.3   Extreme Risk Measures   29

3.4   Related Risk Modeling Techniques   32
3.4.1   Fat Tails 32
3.4.2   Uniform Margins 34
3.4.3   Arrival Times 34
3.4.4   Empirical Observations 35

4   Objective Functions in Portfolio Construction 40

4.1   Use Case   40

4.2   Seven Objective Functions   41
4.2.1   Minimum Absolute Residual 41
4.2.2   Minimum Variance 41
4.2.3   Minimum Peak-to-Trough MDD 42
4.2.4   Minimum 95% Value-at-Risk 44
4.2.5   Minimum 95% Conditional Value-at-Risk 46
4.2.6   Maximum Sharpe Ratio 48
4.2.7   Maximum Alternative Sharpe Ratio 49
4.2.8   Assumption 51

5   Risk and Return Attribution 52

5.1   Use Case   52
5.1.1   A Graph to Illustrate the Point 52

5.2   Risk Attribution   53

5.3   Ex-Ante Return Attribution   54

5.4   Difference between Return Attribution & Risk Attribution   60

5.5   Conclusion   60

6   Portfolio-Level Factor Analysis 61

6.1   Use Case   61

6.2　**Portfolio-Level Factor Exposure**　62

6.3　**Conclusion**　64

7　**A Hedging Use Case** 66

7.1　**Use Case**　66

7.1.1　Controlling Extreme Risks through Volatility Derivatives 67

7.2　**Methodology**　68

7.2.1　VIX Futures 68

7.2.2　Variance Futures 71

7.2.3　OTM Put Options on SPX 80

7.3　**Hedging Performance**　85

7.3.1　1-Month VIX Futures 85

7.3.2　3-Month Variance Futures 88

7.3.3　1-Month OTM Put Options on SPX 91

7.4　**Overall Comparison of Choices of Objective Functions**　98

7.5　**Step-by-Step Walk Through**　100

II　SELECT ASSETS　105

8　**Alpha Selection Using Factors** 107

8.1　**Use Case**　107

8.2　**Methodology**　108

8.2.1　Balance Sheet 101 108

8.2.2　Fundamental Factors 109

8.3　**Factors**　119

8.3.1　Compound Factors 119

8.3.2　Factor Set Definition 121

8.4　**Statistical Criteria**　123

8.5　**Implementation**　124

8.5.1　Reviewing Fundamental Data 126

8.5.2　Default Settings 128

9　**Standard Derivative Instruments** 129

9.1　**Use Case**　129

9.2   **Options Pricing Model**   **129**
9.2.1   Options Implied Volatility   130

9.3   **Interest Rate Term Structure**   **132**

9.4   **Commodity Term Structure**   **132**

III   DECIDE AND EXECUTE   **135**

10   **Rebalancing** **137**

10.1   **Use Case**   **137**

10.2   **Goals in a Typical Portfolio Rebalancing Process**   **137**

10.3   **Methodology for Capital Adequacy**   **140**
10.3.1   SCR Ratio and MCR Calculation   140
10.3.2   Risk Modules   140

11   **Forward Scenarios and Historical Simulations** **145**

11.1   **Use Case**   **145**

11.2   **Forward-Looking Scenarios**   **146**

11.3   **Historical Simulation**   **149**

12   **Combining Upside with Black Swan Scenarios** **151**

12.1   **Use Case**   **151**
12.1.1   Defining the Investment Problem   152
12.1.2   Potential Scenarios on Watch   153
12.1.3   Traditional Approach   153
12.1.4   Stochastic Analysis Solution   154
12.1.5   Outcome   155

12.2   **Methodology**   **156**
12.2.1   Objective   156
12.2.2   Overview   157
12.2.3   Formula   157
12.2.4   Computational Process   158

12.3   **Worked Example**   **160**
12.3.1   Overview   160
12.3.2   Definitions   160

12.4   Conclusion   **170**

IV   DELIVER REPORTS   **171**

13   Customary Back Office Reporting **173**

13.1   Use Case   **173**

13.2   Investment Reports   **173**

13.2.1 Investor Summary 174
13.2.2 Transactions 176
13.2.3 Consolidated Positions 177
13.2.4 Portfolio Summary 177
13.2.5 Profit and Loss 178
13.2.6 Allocation 179
13.2.7 Net Asset Value 180
13.2.8 Portfolio Statistics 184
13.2.9 Risk and Return 185
13.2.10 Correlation 187
13.2.11 Exposures 188
13.2.12 Aggregated Reports 188

14   Additional Reporting **194**

14.1   Use Case   **194**

14.2   Maintenance and Accounting Reports   **194**

14.2.1 Custom Benchmark 195
14.2.2 Product Benchmark Mapping 198
14.2.3 Accounting Details 201
14.2.4 Subscription Redemption Details 202
14.2.5 Transactions 205

15   Compliance Analysis **208**

15.1   Use Case   **208**

15.2   Monitoring Compliance Rules   **209**

16   Data Integrity Validation **212**

16.1   Use Case   **212**

16.2   Defining Data Integrity   **212**

16.2.1 A Practical Example   213

16.3   Standard Data Integrity Tests   **216**

16.4   Mitigation Methods   **218**

16.4.1 Sample Algorithm to Fill Missing Data:
        Expectation-Maximization   218

16.4.2 Sample Treatment of Outliers and Influential Cases   219

16.4.3 Sample Data Integrity Validation Process   220

16.5   Conclusion   **221**

V   DEPLOY   **223**

17   Deployment Best Practices **225**

17.1   Use Case   **225**

17.2   Dashboard for Investment Teams   **226**

17.3   API for End-Investor Access   **230**

17.4   Management Approval Panel   **232**

18   Implications of a Post-IA+AI Society **234**

18.1   Winners and Losers   **235**

18.2   Enlarging the Overall Pie in the Fight against Poverty   **235**

18.3   Changing Global Asset Management Landscape   **236**

18.4   More Frauds Initially Until Robust Solutions Stand Out   **237**

18.5   Steady-State Outcomes   **238**

18.5.1 How may the Steady-State Outcome Impact the Industry?   238

18.5.2 How may the Steady-State Outcome Manifest in Time?   239

18.5.3 How may the Steady-State Outcome Manifest Geographically? 241

18.6   Final Conclusion   **243**

Bibliography **245**

Index **249**

Preface

What is the symbolism behind our eye-catching short title *ia* ≠ *ai*?

A class of highly mathematical algorithms that works with three-dimensional (3D) data known as "graphs" can be applied to optimization and machine learning. These 3D data algorithms have a variety of immediate military and civilian applications, and their research has reached a certain maturity. For instance, during the Cold War, the North Atlantic Treaty Organization (NATO) used similar algorithms to reduce a 3D state space describing data collected by remote sensors in the Atlantic Ocean to calculate the most likely locations of Russian submarines. Our research challenge focuses on applying these algorithms to solve more complex problems with higher dimensional data commonly found in finance. In general:

1. Financial data tend to be in higher dimensions (easily over 100) with time subscripts;
2. Financial observations are assumed to be probability distributions instead of static point estimates; and
3. Jumps can be observed in the data, often at much higher frequencies than predicted by the normal distribution.

It is tempting to hyperbolize with catchphrases such as "quantum finance" but let's aim to simplify complications. The 3D research analogy is to train and test routing optimization and machine learning algorithms for navigation when the way-finding coordinates and obstacles such as buildings change dynamically and are expressed in higher dimensions with jumps:

1. One cannot expect any machine to learn from an almost infinite number of

possible scenarios given the larger size and the higher dimensions of the state space (which may mean that we may never collect enough data for robust learning), thus we reduce the dimensionality of the problem by describing the underlying dynamics where feasible, without destroying the information contents of extreme events; and

2. We accept the negative impact of extreme events by choosing an optimal path in the presence of jumps (a.k.a. stochastic optimization) instead of attempting instantaneous course corrections (a.k.a. stochastic control). This is doable and even desirable in finance but not necessarily the case for traditional engineering applications.

Similar problems have been solved many times before with 3D data, so this book divides and conquers. Our eye-catching short title $ia \neq ai$ symbolizes how investment analytics is *not* a simplistic reapplication of artificial intelligence (AI) techniques proven in engineering as the popular press likes to suggest. This book presents best-of-class sophisticated techniques to solve high dimensional problems with properties that go deeper than what is required to solve customary problems in engineering today.

Bernard Lee, Ph.D., CFA
17 June 2019
California, USA

INVESTMENT ANALYTICS IN THE DAWN OF ARTIFICIAL INTELLIGENCE

1. Introduction

In the coming decade, business school case studies will be written on the sheer amount of media coverage on artificial intelligence (AI) and financial technology (FinTech) recently, especially after Bitcoin reached almost US$20,000 by December 2017 and then crashed back to the US$3,000+ level in 2018. Initially, the popular media was preparing the global audience for the second coming of a messiah in finance, and then quickly reversed to reminding them of how those who could not remember financial bubbles were condemned to repeat the past.

Tesla founder Elon Musk told the National Governors Association of a looming AI "threat", which could even spark a war. So, he proposed the creation of a regulatory body to guide its development.[1]

"I was surprised by your suggestion to bring regulations before we know what we are dealing with," Arizona Governor Doug Ducey said in response.

Very few of us doubt that the rapid advance, and the public's growing acceptance of advanced technology in finance, will change the landscape of the global financial industry. AI techniques are not new, and Wall Street has always been searching for better technology and methodologies year after year.

New firms and new players emerge with each generation of new technology. What seems different this time is the public's recognition (and its fear) of the change and the eagerness in proposing a drastic response by overhauling the existing

---

[1]15 July 2017, *The Wall Street Journal*, https://www.wsj.com/articles/elon-musk-warns-nations-governors-of-looming-ai-threat-calls-for-regulations-1500154345.

regulatory framework, which may change the fundamental relationships among the buyers, sellers, and overseers of financial services completely. Compliance departments will find it much more challenging to deny approval "when the customers ask for the solution." This book's publication is timed to create impact.

1.1   The Fourth Industrial Revolution

The term FinTech describes the application of technology to finance, but what exactly is AI-powered FinTech? The defining characteristics of AI-powered technology are that the machine should be able to make some of its decisions autonomously, as in a self-driving car finding its way from downtown to the airport. The sudden acceptance of AI in finance may have less to do with the hard facts of recent technological advances, since certain underlying techniques have been in use for decades, but more to do with the emotional acceptance of letting a Tesla vehicle drive one's family from home to airport on autopilot.

A machine that can learn from its own mistakes is one key to public acceptance, but many useful, day-to-day tasks are deterministic and do not require machine learning. Today's machines still have a long way to go before coming up with insights; at best, machines can emulate known human decision patterns, which is why the best AI-powered investment analytics engine today can only perform basic investment management tasks in an autonomous manner. Such an outcome is not necessarily undesirable because a machine that can perform routine tasks similar to what a human portfolio manager does but on a much large amount of data and with speed and precision can still make a meaningful difference. This observation also means that model parameters should still be set by humans, or that certain analytics that resembles data-mining should be avoided by human operators. The best AI-powered investment analytics should allow an investment professional to use essentially the same front-end user interface today, perhaps without being aware of that AI-powered machine learning algorithms have been added to the back-end – just like today a Tesla driver can still drive with a steering wheel without activating its self-driving features.

Why suddenly the intense media interest about AI and FinTech then? The mass media uses the analogy that AI and FinTech are driving the so-called Fourth Industrial Revolution. Like new technologies in previous industrial revolutions, we expect complaints from those whose skills are being phased out and whose jobs may be put at risk. However, new jobs requiring perhaps different skills will also be created. If the world suddenly finds itself in a situation where all major productive activities are automated, there will be a massive dislocation of the global job market, leading to civil unrest and perhaps even open conflicts, especially when countries cannot agree on a "fair" distribution of new jobs and new economic opportunities.

Thankfully, we are not in that situation today: once again, what is changed today is not the technology *per se* but its social acceptance.

Hence, we should first try to understand how AI and FinTech will impact society, and then work out how best to manage the potential outcomes. Setting up more entities to regulate AI and FinTech is one way to manage the potential outcomes but not the only way. Other obvious and potentially more effective steps may include educating the younger generation on new and relevant skills so that they are ready for new opportunities that may come up, and incentivizing successful technology companies to reinvest earnings in R&D and to allow their technology to be deployed for *pro bono* causes, with one policy goal for them to give back to society.

1.2 Unhealthy Myths

Before any debates on how best to manage the potential outcomes, it may be helpful to set the facts straight and dispute certain unhealthy myths about AI and FinTech:

1. AI, Big Data, and FinTech are not some form of magic. The current state of the art can automate certain repetitive tasks, and analyze a massive amount of data, but AI is still a long way from displacing many financial industry jobs. An article on *The Wall Street Journal* correctly pointed out the excessive hype over AI and FinTech prevalent in today's mainstream media, even though some of its descriptions can be made more technically precise.[2]

2. Despite the AI-driven FinTech hype, finance is still one of the most "backward" industries in adopting modern technology. One plausible explanation is that financial data formats and standards remain highly fragmented even in developed markets today. The amount of integration required by adopting *any* "newer" technology in finance will create immense headcounts. In addition, because no new technology is perfect, a skillful combination of traditional techniques and new technologies can still tackle unsolved or hard-to-solve problems: for example, AI can be used to recognize a high-dimensional pattern from a massive volume of financial data that human brains cannot visualize and are, therefore, less likely to design traditional rule-based algorithms to work with such data. The market's rule of thumb is that AI should produce a clear improvement before being deployed to replace a more traditional modeling technique or decision paradigm.

3. If everyone uses the same techniques, it can be shown by simulation that the chances for system-wide instability will increase dramatically.[3] Diverse

---

[2] 17 July 2017, *The Wall Street Journal*, `https://www.wsj.com/articles/robotic-hogwash-artificial-intelligence-will-not-take-over-wall-street-1500304343`.

[3] See, for instance, [**Lee 2010**] detailed explanations.

parameterization and error feedback mechanisms can be critical to allow a machine to learn and diversify its solutions instead of producing a highly similar solution for every investor. AI can also bring an unintended benefit: If every investor in the market relies on low-fee indexing (therefore free riding on someone else's research), eventually, society may no longer be allocating capital in the most efficient manner.[4] AI/FinTech can address that specific problem as a still cost-effective alternative to ETFs today. Fees can still be lowered, but assets can be chosen based on each investor's specific criteria and preferences to encourage market diversity.

1.3 New Regulatory Framework

A new regulatory body as suggested by Elon Musk may not be the right solution. As a practical thought experiment, let's ask whether and how such a new regulatory body can work:

1. Who will staff such a regulatory body? A new agency as such tends to attract compliance officers and lawyers who are unlikely to have deep technical training and first-hand experience working with the underlying technology. There is a well-known challenge among those who talk about rapidly advancing technology to come up with effective policies. The handful of experts with both technical and regulatory backgrounds can expect to fill the (usually) better-paying jobs in the industry instead of taking public policy roles.

2. Given today's internet speed, if one country decides to put in place more stringent regulations, researchers and suppliers can simply deploy the same technology and service using servers hosted at a different country. A classic example is that, after the US restricted the export of certain drone technology, American military allies simply shopped elsewhere. Today's global framework in finance is that most firms are regulated from the jurisdictions where services are hosted and customers are billed. Moving jurisdiction is a relatively straightforward and inexpensive investment. If businesses located in a specific country "miss the boat" because of stringent restrictions unique to one jurisdiction, eventually the regulators there may be forced to give in due to intense business lobbying.

3. Ultimately, even if there is such an agency staffed by competent staff, and we can overcome the enormous challenge to coordinate the many jurisdictions involved globally, exactly what is such a regulator expected to accomplish, as in what rules it should set and when it should intervene?

---

[4]17 August 2017, *The Wall Street Journal*, https://www.wsj.com/articles/worlds-biggest-pension-fund-wants-to-stop-index-trackers-eating-the-economy-1502974668.

1.4 Defining a Road Map

While it is tempting to hypothesize on the potential impact of technology and automation on finance by reading today's mass media, the reality is often more about working through the more precise details instead of prophesying on abstract disruption scenarios. AI and FinTech do not need to mean only the destruction of jobs. They can also mean more employment opportunities. The policy focus should be about to share those opportunities so that the net outcome is a general improvement to most buyers and sellers of financial services. More regulations are no "silver bullet", and they may create more problems than they solve.

In this section, we aim to identify the most relevant topics by making an educated guess on which technology may matter the most to a post-AI financial industry.

1.4.1 Nature of Financial Services

Let's begin with a deeper understanding of financial services because we aim to use AI and FinTech to automate finance. The following is an excerpt from an e-mail providing invited feedback to a government program:

> In order to give a clear explanation of how to apply artificial intelligence (AI) to investing: to the technology-trained crowd, you have to start by explaining how investments are made in the real world, for instance, the difference between retail, high net worth and institutional investments. To the finance-trained crowd, you have to explain what AI does and does not do, by giving some simple examples such as how AI engines can tell the difference between a dog and a wolf. Only then, we can go into a deeper explanation of why AI investing is not just mechanical pattern recognition, or the computer may simply recommend buying only Government bonds for any risk-averse investor.
>
> It can be ineffective and even misleading to give an oversimplified explanation instead. To give you an analogy, you may have seen recent online postings on how "Facebook killed their AI engine that was inventing a new language".[a] As someone who has been working on machine learning algorithms over the last 30 years, I went back to the original post and read that Facebook engineers merely tried to solve a standard train and test problem in machine learning. There was no surprise. After two or three rounds of rewriting by journalists who did not have the necessary technical knowledge to comprehend the problem at hand, the story was rewritten to read like how "Skynet" from the Terminator movies was about to conspire against the human race by inventing its own secret language!
>
> ─────────────────────
> [a]15 June 2017, *The Atlantic*, https://www.theatlantic.com/technology/archive/2017/06/artificial-intelligence-develops-its-own-non-human-language/530436/.

All financial markets aim to solve matching problems for buyers and sellers of financial assets. The entire financial market cannot outperform itself. Unless your next door neighbor is someone who has exceptionally better insights on public equities or bonds, like a Mr. Warren Buffet, to most investors investing is primarily coming up a collection of investments with suitable statistical properties to match future assets against estimated liabilities or future spending. According to the Berk-Green argument in [**Berk 2004**],[5] there are limits on the ability to add value by selecting superior assets because:

1. First, performance on larger institutional portfolios tends to be heavily driven by allocating to the "right" region, country and/or sector;
2. Then, by finding misunderstood companies (e.g., over-hyped companies that are expected to fall in value, or vice versa); and
3. Finally, by finding "home run" investments that require domain expertise to pick let's say the next Google or Facebook, which is few and far in between statistically.

By comparison, the following elements of institutional investing that are likely to take a long time to, or may never, be automated:

1. Face-to-face relationship management;
2. Initial public offerings, since the public listing of securities has legal and regulatory implications; and
3. Selecting novel investment ideas (e.g., a new technology, a potential medical cure) where there may not be sufficient data available for any AI engine to crunch numbers on and/or compare to.

1.4.2   What AI and FinTech Cannot Accomplish

What will happen to the financial industry with more new and emerging technologies? Will new and emerging technologies in finance create unintended outcomes? As explained earlier in this chapter, new technology should not mean automatic job losses. By comparison, the old world of supermarkets is gradually replaced by the new world of Amazon and Google Express. Has digital shopping led to any instant monopoly? Does ordering and delivering become fully automated overnight? Are consumers stuck with fewer choices or blessed with more choices? While Walmart (best known for its strategy of driving down prices by buying bulk) is hurt by automation, volume discounter Costco is enjoying significantly higher revenues per square feet. This observation shows that the issue is not about technology but how best to manage and deploy the technology, and that new technology does not need to imply immediate negative outcomes such as monopoly or job losses. Technology

---

[5]Berk, JB and RC Green, Mutual Fund Flows and Performance in Rational Markets, *Journal of Political Economy*, Volume 112, Number 6, December 2004.

can also mean more choices and better services: JP Morgan CEO Jamie Dimon said that he expected headcount to go up after the further implementation of AI.[6]

We must first understand AI's strengths and its limitations. AI's most fundamental limitation is that machines need to learn from large volumes of past data. Most AI engines start by "emulating" how humans make simplistic decisions. When the computer can do so with speed and over an immense volume of data, it may still be able to come up with decisions that human decision makers cannot have foreseen. However, human intelligence does give us some ability to tackle new and novel situations without first learning from a large volume of past data. Those decisions are called insights. For instance, there are well-known limitations in sentiment scores in interpreting sarcastic comments as well as phrases with "double meanings." Moreover, short sellers of financial assets are known for their habit to promote biased articles and/or fake news to many websites. Despite these well-known shortcomings, if a computer can scan a massive number of news and social media sentiment scores on all relevant stocks for end investors to review, there is still obvious value to most portfolio managers in doing that, instead of scanning bad news of investee companies manually and be surprised only when the asset sponsors call. This observation is one example of focusing on the strengths of AI.

This book aims to discuss investment analytics (IA), one specific area of Fintech, that has already been automated by computers in the industry or most likely the case soon. We will focus on what is likely to get approved today in a typical compliance process, and then explain how some of the current technologies may be enhanced by AI. To give more specific examples:

1. Traditional portfolio theory often leads to corner solutions that can accept only around 20 30 investments, which is simply not how institutional investments are run today. With 25 or so investments, institutions will run out of financial assets with sufficient liquidity that they can invest in.

2. Traditional technology tends to fit pre-selected financial products in pre-computed asset allocation buckets, commonly known as "two-stage" optimization. Such a process may force a less interesting Emerging Market stock to be included in a portfolio at the expenses of a promising Developed Market stock. A helpful feature to investors that can work around this known problem is single-stage asset selection and allocation by grinding through as many data as computers can crawl from the internet about all possible investments.

3. The replacement technology must provide some ability to diversify the outputs by specifying customized parameters for each investor, without which everyone is solving for roughly the same solution to outperform, which is log-

---

[6]26 June 2017, Dimon Says JP Morgan Headcount to Keep Rising Despite Automation, *Bloomberg*, https://www.bloomberg.com/news/articles/2017-06-26/dimon-says-jpmorgan-headcount-to-keep-rising-despite-automation.

ically infeasible based on the Berk-Green argument cited earlier. Any failure to diversify views and inputs, and therefore outputs, may lead to systematic failures, as in everyone buying the same financial assets when markets are up and then rushing for exits at the same time, with predictable adverse market outcomes.

The basic analysis, synthesis, and documentation in finance today have been and will stay automated. This book aims to explain what that state of the art is, what IA and AI can and cannot do, how they can help to address some of the issues above, and finally the pros and cons of relevant approaches. We propose that the most effective way to do so is by following the typical rebalancing cycle of a professional investor:

Part I – Construct Portfolios;
Part II – Select Assets;
Part III – Decide and Execute; and
Part IV – Deliver Reports.

In **Part V – Deploy**, we will tie these discussions together with an analysis of the foreseeable implications of the post-IA+AI financial industry after these or similar technologies are widely adopted. We will discuss potential policy and social issues from such adoption and take an objective approach in our analysis: AI, IA and other types of FinTech can help, but no new technology provides a perfect solution to every society, nor can they solve everyone's investment problems overnight. Our policy analysis will also reference objective evidence presented by the relevant simulations. We will conclude by suggesting ways by which more effective policy and financial regulations can encourage innovation, more efficient allocation of capital, global growth, and ultimately better overall quality of life for humanity.

INVESTMENT ANALYTICS IN THE DAWN OF ARTIFICIAL INTELLIGENCE

2. Navigation and Vocabulary

2.1 Use Case

Christine is the investment manager of a pension fund. Right now her pension fund is not doing particularly well in meeting its liabilities. Since her fund sponsors are extremely risk-aversive, she seeks to take a conservative approach towards asset selection despite a keen interest to outperform. On the other hand, she expects a bull market to come in one year and decides to take advantage of that opportunity to build up the reserve for rainy days.

Her goal is to outperform a "balanced" benchmark by asset allocation but also by asset selection. She understands that she needs to invest in different asset classes to diversify the portfolio. After all, diversification is just another name for the old adage, "You shouldn't put all your eggs in one basket." However, by adding more and more assets into each asset class, the portfolio performs increasingly like an unexciting index. The volatility of the portfolio decreases while the portfolio struggles to outperform. She needs to avoid over-diversification.

So, what is the best way for Christine's portfolio to target a reasonable level of diversification with well-focused bets? Before deep-diving into the analytical techniques, we need to help Christine learn the basic vocabulary of investment analytics used by professional investors. Although Christine has not decided whether she wants to subscribe to an existing platform or build her own customized solution, she feels that as the first step of her learning journey she can familiarize herself with the navigation of the HedgeSPA core investment platform.

2.2   Platform Navigation

Upon logging onto the HedgeSPA platform, there is a "Selection Panel" on the left-hand side. The default selection under "Selection Panel" is **Portfolio Tree**, where there is a list of portfolios listed in a tree. Other choices to select from include "Products", "Analytics", and "Library". The top half of the right-hand side shows the portfolio or product tabs that have been opened, and the bottom half shows the analytics tabs that are opened for each portfolio or product. Figure 2.1 shows how the "Asian HNW" portfolio is selected in the **Portfolio Tree** on the left-hand side, the positions of the "Asian HNW" portfolio on the upper half of the right-hand side and the "Performance Chart" of the portfolio shown on the lower half of the right-hand side.

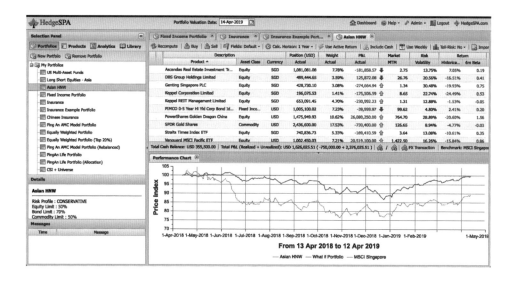

Figure 2.1: Platform Default Panels after Logging In

2.2.1   Investment Categories

Please choose "Products" in the "Selection Panel". The **Product Tree** area shows a typical universe of investment products available to investors organized in a tree hierarchy. When you enter the HedgeSPA Investment Analytics Platform, "Selection Panel" is on the left side of the platform. You can click "Products" and then "Tree" to see asset classes. After that, you can click on the "+" box to look for specific products or click on the "-" box to collapse the branch as shown in Figure 2.2.

This tree structure lets the user very quickly browse through their product universe without having to recall specific keywords, as shown below:

Figure 2.2: "Products → Tree" under "Selection Panel"

The default organization of this hierarchy is as follows:

- Asset Class
- Primary Reference (for the asset class above)
- Alphabetical Order
- Product

System administrators can modify the order of the tree hierarchy to better reflect their institution's investment processes.

2.2.2   Product Attributes

Product Attributes allows users to review selected product-specific attributes and analytical statistics. To show **Product Attributes**, you first need to choose one product by using the "Product Tree" as shown in Figure 2.2 or clicking "Products" and then "Filter" to use the text filters and keywords. In this case, you can choose the product by specifying its asset class, sub-region, or the product type, or typing its name in "Product Name" directly. Next, you should click on the "Search" button, and you will see the products of interest under the "Product" column as shown in Figure 2.3. Finally, you can double-click on the product to let its information appear on the right side of the platform, as shown in Figure 2.4.

After selecting one product, you can click on "Analytics" under "Selection Panel" to look for "Product Attributes", which is under "Asset Selection" in Figure 2.5. Then, you can double-click on "Product Attributes" to access this analytic tool. Some common attributes in fixed income may include convexity, bond type, and maturity date, but the use of this analytic tool is not limited to fixed income assets.

2.2.3   Long and Short Exposure

The **Long/Short Exposures** portfolio analytic tool gives investment managers a quick way to review their portfolios' Long, Short, Net and Gross exposures by asset class and at the full portfolio level. To access **Long/Short Exposures**, you should select and double click one specific portfolio from a list of portfolios after you click "Portfolios", which is under "Selection Panel", shown as Figure 2.7. Like the selected product, the chosen portfolio will appear on the right side of the platform as Figure 2.8.

Then, you should click on "Analytics" and look for "Long/Short Exposures" under "Exposures". After that, you can double-click on "Long/Short Exposures" to access the **Long/Short Exposures** portfolio analytic tool as shown in Figure 2.10.

2.2.4   Portfolio Gauges

There are many standard statistics used to measure any specific portfolio's investment risk and return, such as 6-month beta, volatility, value at risk (VaR), conditional value at risk (CVaR), Sharpe Ratio (SR), Alternative Sharpe Ratio (ASR), historical return, skewness, kurtosis, semi-deviation, and maximum drawdown (MaxDD). They can

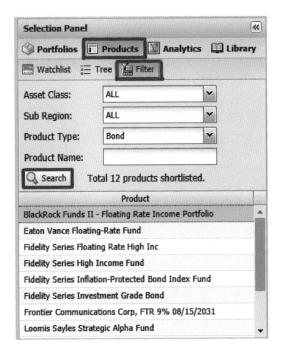

Figure 2.3: "Products → Filter" under "Selection Panel"

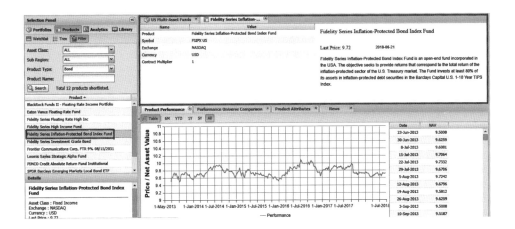

Figure 2.4: Selected Product

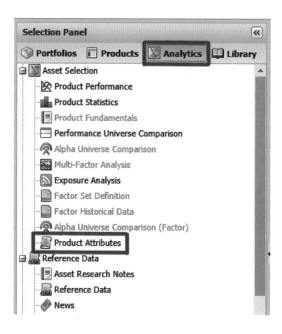

Figure 2.5: "Analytics → Product Attributes"

Figure 2.6: Product Attributes

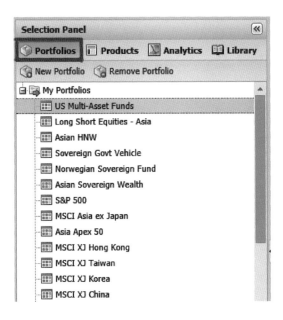

Figure 2.7: "Portfolios" under "Selection Panel"

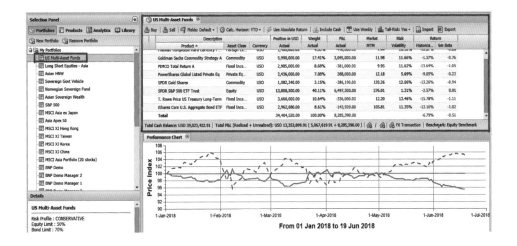

Figure 2.8: Selected Portfolio

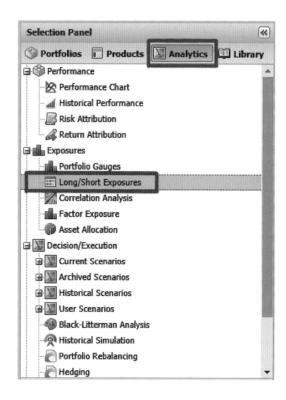

Figure 2.9: "Analytics → Long/Short Exposures"

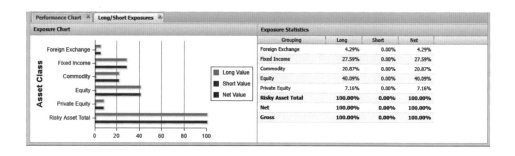

Figure 2.10: Long/Short Exposures

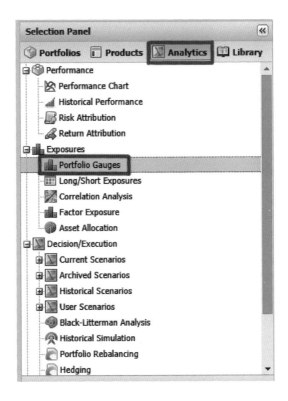

Figure 2.11: "Analytics → Portfolio Gauges"

Portfolio	Historical Return	Volatility	VaR	cVaR	MaxDD	Beta	SR	ASR	Skewness	Kurtosis	Treynor Ratio	Jensen's Measure	Semi-Deviation
Actual Portfolio	-6.79%	5.91%	11.39%	13.21%	14.47%	-0.51	-1.4875	-1.6841	0.80	4.86	0.1727	-0.0472	5.27%
Hypothetical Portfolio	-6.79%	5.91%	11.39%	13.21%	14.47%	-0.51	-1.4875	-1.6841	0.80	4.86	0.1727	-0.0472	5.27%

Figure 2.12: Portfolio Gauges

be found in **Portfolio Gauges** as shown in Figure 2.12 by clicking "Analytics" and then "Portfolio Gauges" under "Exposures". In addition, a precise explanation and description of these statistical measurements have been given below.

6-month Beta

6-month Beta is used to measure the sensitivity of the expected excess portfolio return to the expected excess benchmark returns, which is defined as:

$$E(R_\pi) = R_f + \beta_\pi(E(R_m) - R_f)$$

where $E(R_\pi)$ denotes the portfolio expected return,
R_f denotes the risk-free market return,
$E(R_m)$ denotes the expected return of the market,
$E(R_m) - R_f$ measures the market premium,
β_π can be calculated according to

$$\beta_\pi = \frac{Cov(R_\pi, R_m)}{Var(R_m)}$$

$Cov(R_\pi, R_m)$ denotes the covariance between the portfolio return and market return, and
$Var(R_m)$ denotes the variance of the market return.

Volatility

Volatility is the standard deviation of the portfolio return, defined as:

$$volatility = \sqrt{E[(R_pf - \overline{R_pf})^2]} = \sqrt{\frac{\Sigma(R_pf - \overline{R_pf})^2}{n-1}}$$

where R_{pf} denotes the return of the target portfolio,
$\overline{R_{pf}}$ denotes the mean return of the target portfolio, and
n denotes sample size.

Value at Risk

A portfolio's value-at-risk (VaR) is defined as the maximum loss in the portfolio value over a specified period of time, at a given level of confidence. The traditional VaR is defined as:

$$VaR_{\pi,\alpha} = -F^{-1}(\alpha),$$

where $F(y) = \int_{-\infty}^{y} \frac{1}{\sigma_\pi \sqrt{2\pi}} e^{-\frac{1}{2}\left(\frac{x-\mu}{\sigma_\pi}\right)^2} dx$. The VaR using Cornish-Fisher expansion is defined as:

$$VaR_{\pi,\alpha} = -(\mu_{\pi,A} + Z_{cf,\pi} * \sigma_{\pi,A}) = -\mu_{\pi,A} - Z_{cf,\pi} * \sigma_{\pi,A}$$

where the Cornish-Fisher Expansion is defined as:

$$Z_{cf,\pi}(Z_\alpha) = Z_\alpha + \tfrac{1}{6}(Z_\alpha^2 - 1)S_\pi + \tfrac{1}{24}(Z_\alpha^3 - 3Z_\alpha)(K_\pi - 1) - \tfrac{1}{36}(2Z_\alpha^3 - 5Z_\alpha)S_\pi^2$$

with S denoting Skewness and K denoting Excess Kurtosis, or "plain vanilla" Kurtosis minus 3.

CVaR

The Conditional Value at Risk (known as the expected shortfall) is the expected loss over a specified time horizon under the normal distribution given that the loss is greater or equal to the value at risk (VaR). The portfolio CVaR at $\alpha\%$, denoted by $CVaR_{\pi,\alpha}$ can be computed as:

$$CVaR_{\pi,\alpha} = E(VaR_{\pi,\gamma} \mid 0 < \gamma \leq \alpha).$$

Cornish-Fisher CVaR is the case where $\alpha = 0.05$, $cVaR_{\pi,0.05}$ is computed by taking the average of VaR at discrete α from 0.005 to 0.045 with increments step of 0.005, as defined by:

$$
\begin{aligned}
CVaR_{\pi,0.05} &= E(VaR_{\pi,\gamma} \mid 0 < \gamma \leq 0.05) \\
&= \frac{1}{0.05} \int_0^{0.05} VaR_{\pi,\gamma}d\gamma \\
&\simeq \frac{1}{9}(VaR_{\pi,0.005} + VaR_{\pi,0.010} + \ldots + VaR_{\pi,0.045})
\end{aligned}
$$

Sharpe Ratio

Sharpe Ratio (SR) measures the risk-adjusted performance of a portfolio. The portfolio's Sharpe Ratio (SR) can be computed as:

$$SR = \frac{\mu_{\pi,A} - R_f}{\sigma_{\pi,A}}$$

where $\mu_{\pi,A}$ is expected portfolio return,
R_f is the risk-free rate, and
$\sigma_{\pi,A}$ is the standard deviation of the portfolio.

Alternative Sharpe Ratio

The Alternative Sharpe Ratio (ASR) is similar to the Sharpe Ratio but incorporates the appropriate cross-moment information for tail behavior including skewness and excess kurtosis, and provides a robust departure from the assumption of normality in portfolio returns. The Alternative Sharpe Ratio (ASR) can be computed as:

$$ASR = \frac{\Sigma_i(R_{i,A} - R_f)w_i}{Z_\pi \, \sigma_{\pi,A}} + \frac{1}{2}\frac{\Sigma_i w_i(Z_i^+ \sigma_{i,A})^2}{Z_\pi \, \sigma_{\pi,A}} - \frac{1}{2}Z_\pi^- \, \sigma_{\pi,A}$$

where:

$$Z_\pi^+ = \frac{max(Z_{cf\pi}(Z_\alpha^+),0)}{Z_\alpha^+}$$

$$Z_\pi^- = \frac{min(Z_{cf\pi}(Z_\alpha^-),0)}{Z_\alpha^-}$$

$$Z_{cf\pi}(Z_\alpha) = Z_\alpha + \frac{1}{6}(Z_\alpha^2 - 1)S_\pi + \frac{1}{24}(Z_\alpha^3 - 3Z_\alpha)(K_\pi - 1) - \frac{1}{36}(2Z_\alpha^3 - 5Z_\alpha)S_\pi^2$$

S denotes Skewness, and

K denotes Excess Kurtosis, or "plain vanilla" Kurtosis minus 3.

If there is no non-normality, *ASR* reverts back to *SR*, since $S = 0$ and $K = 0$.

Historical Return

This statistic shows the average historical annual return of the product. Annualized returns are reported under the Year-To-Date (YTD) and One-Year (1YR) periods of measurement.

Skewness

Skewness measures the asymmetry of a return distribution from normal distribution and the skewness of the portfolio or an asset can be computed as:

$$\text{Portfolio Skewness } S_\pi = \frac{\frac{1}{T}\Sigma_{t=1}^{T}(R_{\pi,t}-\mu_\pi)^3}{(\frac{1}{T-1}\Sigma_{t=1}^{T}(R_{\pi,t}-\mu_\pi)^2)^{3/2}}$$

$$\text{Asset Skewness } S_i = \frac{\frac{1}{T}\Sigma_{t=1}^{T}(R_{i,t}-\mu_i)^3}{(\frac{1}{T-1}\Sigma_{t=1}^{T}(R_{i,t}-\mu_i)^2)^{3/2}}$$

where:

$R_{\pi,t}$ denotes the portfolio return (usually measured based on a 1-year moving window) at time t,

$R_{i,t}$ denotes the ith asset return (usually measured based on a 1-year moving window) at time t,

$t = 1,...,T$,

T denotes the total number of days considered,

μ_π denotes the portfolio's annualized mean, and

μ_i denotes the ith asset's annualized mean.

Kurtosis

Kurtosis measures the peakedness of a return distribution and the kurtosis of the portfolio or an asset can be computed as:

$$\text{Portfolio Kurtosis: } K_\pi = \frac{\frac{1}{T}\Sigma_{t=1}^{T}(R_{\pi,t}-\mu_\pi)^4}{(\frac{1}{T-1}\Sigma_{t=1}^{T}(R_{\pi,t}-\mu_\pi)^2)^2}$$

$$\text{Asset Kurtosis: } K_i = \frac{\frac{1}{T}\Sigma_{t=1}^{T}(R_{i,t}-\mu_i)^4}{(\frac{1}{T-1}\Sigma_{t=1}^{T}(R_{i,t}-\mu_i)^2)^2}$$

where:

$R_{\pi,t}$ denotes the portfolio return (usually measured based on a 1-year moving window) at time t,

$R_{i,t}$ denotes the ith asset return (usually measured based on a 1-year moving window) at time t,

$t = 1,...,T$,

T denotes the total number of days considered,

μ_π denotes the portfolio's annualized mean, and

μ_i denotes the ith asset's annualized mean.

Typically, kurtosis is compared to the kurtosis of a normal distribution, which has the kurtosis value of 3. Excess Kurtosis is the Plain Kurtosis minus 3.

Semi-Deviation

Semi-Deviation measures the standard deviation of the difference between the portfolio return and the mean return, sampled only when the former is lower. The semi-deviation can be calculated as follows:

$$\text{Semi-Deviation} = \sqrt{\frac{1}{n}\sum_{R_\pi < \overline{R_\pi}}^{n}(\overline{R_\pi} - R_\pi)^2}$$

where:

n is the total number of returns less than the mean return,

R_π is the portfolio return, and

$\overline{R_\pi}$ is the mean return.

Maximum Drawdown (MaxDD)

The percentage Maximum Drawdown (MaxDD%) of a portfolio is the measure of the decline of the portfolio's Net Asset Value (NAV) from "peak to trough" in its time series from time 0 to time T. The percentage maximum drawdown as measured from the peak is defined as:

$$MaxDD_\pi\% = Max_{(0 \leq t \leq T)}Drawdown_\pi\%(t)$$

The drawdown% at any time t $(0 \leq t \leq T)$ is defined as:

$$Drawdown_\pi\%(t) = \frac{Drawdown_\pi(t)}{NAV_{\pi,0 \leq \tau \leq t}^{peak}}$$

where:
$$Drawdown_\pi(t) = NAV^{peak}_{\pi,0 \le \tau \le t} - NAV_{\pi,t}$$
$$NAV_{\pi,t} = w^T NAV_t = [w_1...w_n].$$

2.2.5   Product Statistics

The **Product Statistics** tool shown in the bottom right of the platform as in Figure 2.14 also gives users a quick overview of the standard statistical measurements of investment risk and return for the selected asset, such as Volatility, Maximum Drawdown, Value at Risk (VaR), Conditional Value at Risk (CVaR), Sharpe Ratio, Alternative Sharpe Ratio, Historical Return, Skewness, Kurtosis, and Semi-Deviations. The **Product Statistics** tool could be found by clicking "Analytics" and then "Product Statistics" under "Asset Selection".

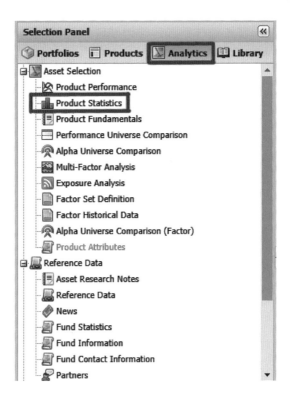

Figure 2.13: "Analytics → Product Statistics"

Product Statistics	
Name	**Value**
Volatility (%)	5.56
Maximum Drawdown (%)	22.71
VaR (95%)	9.18
CVaR (95%)	10.58
Sharpe Ratio (rf = 2%)	-0.7984
Alternate Sharpe Ratio (rf = 2%)	0
Historical Return (%)	-4.44
Skewness	0.04
Kurtosis	2.11
Semi-Deviation (%)	5.28

Figure 2.14: Product Statistics

Part I

CONSTRUCT PORTFOLIOS

INVESTMENT ANALYTICS IN THE DAWN OF ARTIFICIAL INTELLIGENCE

3. Understanding Risk

3.1 Use Case

After trying the navigation of the HedgeSPA platform as part of her learning journey and getting a refresher on the vocabulary of investment analytics, Christine starts to think about finding the right signals to buy or to sell in a portfolio. However, we will fully discuss asset selection only from Chapter 8 onward. This may seem counter-intuitive at first, but the flow will become clear as we continue. The buy and sell signals should come from within the portfolio first. Only when an asset "switch" is required, we will look for assets not already included in the portfolio.

If an investor is born with the perfect foresight to choose out-performing assets, and the amount of out-performance always exceeds the borrowing cost for him/her to invest, then it no longer matters how he/she combines his/her investments into a portfolio. The investor can make almost unlimited profits simply by applying leverage.

Most experienced investors learn from experience that there is no such a thing as perfect foresight no matter how successful your asset selection skills are. Logically, risk-free profits can be problematic. If a group of investors is able to identify such "sure win" investments, then they will either invest so much that prices of the investments will be driven up, thus negating any profits. Alternatively, the leverage providers will find out what they are trying to do and demand higher interest rates and/or a share of their profits. Either way, risk-free profits will turn into risky profits, and such a portfolio will come with a risk profile that must be managed by the investors.

Portfolio rebalancing is the art of managing the risk of a portfolio when new investment ideas are introduced to the portfolio and successful investment ideas or stop-loss positions are sold off. Therefore, in order to understand portfolio rebalancing, Christine must first start with a better understanding of the techniques to analyze the risk of a portfolio, starting with a review of risk management as a discipline.

3.2   A Brief History of Risk Management

3.2.1   Evolving from Insurance to Risk Management

Risk management is a relatively young corporate function. The discipline has been associated with market crises since the Dutch tulip mania in the 1600's. Table 3.1 is included to illustrate the key milestones showing the important dates in the evolution of risk management and related practices:[1]

Table 3.1: Historical Milestones in Risk Manamgement

1730	First futures contracts on the price of rice in Japan
1864	First futures contracts on agricultural products at the Chicago Board of Trade
1900	Louis Bachelier's thesis "Théorie de la Spéculation"; Brownian motion
1932	First issue of the Journal of Risk and Insurance
1946	First issue of the Journal of Finance
1952	Publication of Markowitz's article "Portfolio Selection"
1961-1966	Treynor, Sharpe, Lintner, and Mossin develop the CAPM
1963	Arrow introduces optimal insurance, moral hazard, and adverse selection
1972	Futures contracts on currencies at the Chicago Mercantile Exchange
1973	Option valuation formulas by Black and Scholes and Merton
1974	Merton's default risk model
1977	Interest rate models by Vasicek and Cox, Ingersoll and Ross (1985)
1980	Sydney Futures Exchange introduced first futures contract in the world with cash settlement
1980-1990	Exotic options, swaptions, and stock derivatives
1979-1982	First OTC contracts in the form of swaps: currency and interest rate swaps.
1985	Creation of the Swap Dealers Association, which established the OTC exchange standards
1987	First risk management department in a bank (Merrill Lynch)
1989	Sydney Futures Exchange first to extend "floor trading" hours with introduction of after-hours electronic trading platform
1988	Basel I
Late 1980s	Value at risk (VaR) and calculation of optimal capital
1992	Article by Heath, Jarrow, and Morton on the forward rate curve Integrated Risk Management
1992	RiskMetrics
1993	World's first overnight options on futures launched by Sydney Futures Exchange
1994-1995	First bankruptcies associated with misuse (or speculation) of derivatives
1997	CreditMetrics
1997-1998	Asian and Russian crisis and LTCM collapse
2001	Enron bankruptcy
2002	New governance rules by Sarbanes-Oxley and NYSE
2004	Basel II
2007	Beginning of the financial crisis
2009	Solvency II (Actual implementation dates vary country by country)
2010	Basel III

[1]Source: [**Dionne 2013**], page 6 and industry sources.

Although some insurers, the most traditional providers of risk management services, have been operating for close to 200 years, modern risk management started only in the 1950's. Since the early 1970's, risk management has grown beyond a discipline focused on insurance as its only practical application and evolved into a protection tool that complements other financial functions. Initially, large corporations with diversified portfolios of assets self-insured against either the losses from an accident or the financial consequences of an unfavorable event, using a pool of liquid reserves that can be used to cover financial losses resulting from a negative market event and an accident.[2]

As one can see from the table above, the use of financial derivatives in banking and finance arose during the 1970's and expanded rapidly during the 1980's, as banking and finance companies intensified their risk management activities. By the 1990's, international risk regulations began to emerge. As a result, leading financial firms developed internal risk management models and capital calculation methodologies to hedge their earning results against unanticipated market risks and to reduce regulatory capital requirements. Naturally, the industry began to develop risk governance framework, introduced independent risk management functions, and created chief risk officer positions. Nonetheless, these developments still failed to prevent and mitigate the impact of the Global Financial Crisis that began in 2007.[3]

3.3 Extreme Risk Measures

Pundits blamed the failures of risk models to correctly capture extreme events as one major cause of the Global Financial Crisis. Thus, the central problems in risk management involve the estimation of extreme quantiles, or assessing how the value of a given variable with a (typically non-normal) distribution may exceed a low (or extreme) probability confidence. A typical example of such tail risk measures is the estimation of losses in insurance, and Value-at-Risk (VaR) calculations in finance. Other related measures included expected shortfall, return level, and maximum drawdown. They are described below:

1. **Value-at-Risk (VaR)** – Value-at-Risk, also known as VaR, is a financial industry tool for measuring and managing risk. The layman's definition of VaR is the risk capital sufficient to cover losses of a portfolio over a specified holding period at a certain level of statistical confidence. Suppose a random variable with distribution function F models the profits and losses (P&L) or

---

[2]See Isaac Ehrlich, Gary S. Becker, "Market Insurance, Self-Insurance, and Self-Protection", *The Journal of Political Economy*, Vol. 80, No. 4 (Jul - Aug, 1972), pp. 623-648 and Georges Dionne and Louis Eeckhoudt, "Self-insurance, self-protection and increased risk aversion", *Economics Letters*, 1985, vol. 17, issue 1-2, pp. 39-42.

[3]Source: see [**Dionne 2013**] for details.

returns on a certain financial asset over a certain time horizon. VaR is the p-th quantile of the distribution of portfolio profits & losses:

$$VaR_p = F^{-1}(1-p)$$

where F^{-1} is the inverse function of the distribution function F. The following graph illustrates the concept of measuring value-at-risk at 95% confidence or 5% significance:

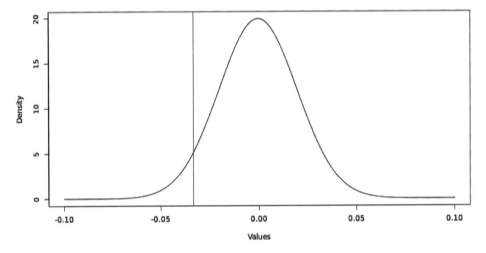

Figure 3.1: Value-at-Risk at 95% Confidence or 5% Significance

2. **Conditional Value at Risk (CVaR)** – Another common measure of risk is the Conditional Value-at-Risk all, or CVAR, defined as the conditional expectation of the potential size of any tail loss exceeding VaR. Mathematically, CVaR is defined as:

$$CVaR_p = E[X|X > VaR_p]$$

3. **Return Level** – The return level R_n^k is the level which is expected to exceed, on average, only once in a sequence of k periods of length n. Thus, R_n^k is a

quantile-based measure:

$$R_n^k = H^{-1}(1-p)$$

of the distribution function H. What we are looking for is an event which occurs only once every k periods and which therefore has probability $1/k$. Thus we have $p = 1/k$ and

$$R_n^k = H^{-1}(1-1/k)$$

4. **Maximum Drawdown** – Drawdown is the measure of a variable's decline from its most recent historical peak. Typically, the drawdown is compared to the cumulative profit. This ensures there is sufficient equity available to finance a portfolio strategy. The Maximum Drawdown (*MDD*) up to time *T* is the maximum of the peak-to-trough loss in the variable's value over time interval $(0, T)$, or:

$$MDD(0, T) = \max_{t \in (0,T)} \left\{ \max_{\tau \in (0,T)} [X(t) - X(\tau)] \right\}$$

The classic variance-covariance VaR method uses the assumption of a normal distribution of returns for both the assets and portfolios. Those return distributions are well known to exhibit non-normal skewness and excess kurtosis, and the assumption of normality will lead to significant underestimation of the risk associated with the target portfolio.

It will be helpful to provide an intuitive explanation of Value-at-Risk. If the VaR on a US$ 20 million asset is US$ 2 million at a one-week, 95% confidence level, there is a 5% chance that the value of this asset will drop more than US$ 2 million (i.e., its value dropping below US $18 million from the current value of US $ 20 million) in any given week or its value can drop by more than 10% in roughly 5 weeks in a two-year period. Typically, VaR is defined to measure the possible loss in value from "normal market risk", as opposed to all possible risk, such as non-normal market shocks as well as non-market risks such as "unexpected" credit and liquidity events.

Today, Value-at-Risk is used by many financial institutions to measure the potential losses in their trading books. The VaR on a trading portfolio can be compared to the capital set aside by the institutions to ensure that any losses will not put the firms' liquidity at risk. However, statistical evidence shows that most asset prices are not normally distributed. This is the most problematic assumption because the non-normality of assets has the strongest impact on the tail ends of a portfolio's return distribution, something that asset sponsors and regulators are most concerned about.

Other risk measures such as Conditional Value-at-Risk (CVaR) or Entropic Value-at-Risk (EVaR), as defined below, are known to show certain desirable mathematical properties as compared to VaR. VaR is not known as a coherent risk measure since it violates the sub-additivity property, which is defined as:

$$\text{If } X, Y \in L, \text{ then } \rho(X+Y) \leq \rho(X) + \rho(Y).$$

Finally, we should note that VaR is upper bounded by other coherent risk measures like Conditional Value-at-Risk (CVaR) or Entropic Value-at-Risk (EVaR):

$$VaR_{1-\alpha}(X) \leq CVaR_{1-\alpha}(X) \leq EVaR_{1-\alpha}(X)$$

where

$$VaR_{1-\alpha}(X) := \inf_{t \in R}\{t : Pr(X \leq t) \geq 1 - \alpha\}$$

$$CVaR_{1-\alpha}(X) := \frac{1}{\alpha} \int_0^\alpha \{VaR_{1-\gamma}(X)\} d\gamma$$

$$EVaR := \inf_{z \leq 0}\{z^{-1} ln(\frac{M_X(z)}{\alpha})\}$$

3.4   Related Risk Modeling Techniques

3.4.1   Fat Tails

Following the 2008 Global Financial Crisis, conventional financial theories have been challenged for their inability to explain extreme, or once-in-a-decade, events in a manner that reflects the much higher frequency at which those events take place in reality. Traditional strategies of asset pricing often rely on the normal distribution curve to make market assumptions, primarily as a result of its mathematical convenience, but real-life markets simply don't behave in such a way. Under the normal distribution 99.7% of asset variations should fall within 3 standard deviations of their mean. Not surprisingly, market practitioners understated the risk of assets and the volatility of portfolios based on this incorrect assumption.

Statistical evidence suggests that the distributions of major financial market variables exhibit tail behavior that is significantly "fatter" than the shape of the tail in the normal distribution. Such fat tails are the result of a statistical phenomenon known as leptokurtosis, which means a significantly greater likelihood of extreme loss events occurring than the level suggested by the normal distribution. Since the magnitude of fat tails is difficult to predict and the number of fat-tail observations available for "model calibration" is small by definition, unforeseen left-tail events can result in devastating effects on portfolio returns. Assuming that the portfolio manager has already chosen good assets as we will discuss starting from chapter 8, the key to protecting portfolio return is to construct the portfolio in such a way that minimizes its tail risk exposure from unexpected market events. The distribution of a random variable X is described to have a fat tail if:

$$Pr[X > x] \sim x^{-\alpha}, \alpha > 0$$

i.e., if X has probability density function $f_X(x)$ described as:

$$f_X(x) \sim x^{-(1+\alpha)}, \alpha > 0$$

Here the tilde notation "$\sim$" refers to the asymptotic equivalence of functions.

In order to understand the significance of tail risk, we must first understand the normal distribution and its well-studied shortcomings. A normal distribution assumes that, given enough observations, all values in the sample will be distributed equally above and below the mean. About 99.7% of all variations fall within three standard deviations of the mean and therefore there is only a 0.3% chance of any extreme event occurring. This property is mathematically convenient which is why many financial models such as the Modern Portfolio Theory, the Efficient Market Hypothesis and the Black-Scholes option pricing model all assume normality. However, the marketplace does not fit perfect mathematical assumptions and is influenced by irrational human behavior that cannot predictable by rigid and simplistic mathematical models. These are some of the reasons why we consistently observe fat-tail behavior in markets.

The 2008 Global Financial Crisis has been caused by a series of events including sub-prime mortgages, credit default swaps, and high leverage ratios. As a result, major financial institutions such as Bear Sterns and Lehman Brothers went bankrupt, financial markets crashed and many of the foundations of the global economic system were undermined. Prior to the 2008 Global Financial Crisis, financial institutions appeared to be operating without any concerns for large potential downside risks. So, they overlooked the shortcomings of normally distributed models. Since 99.7% of variations fall within three standard deviations of its mean under the assumption of normality, the notion of visible profits and invisible losses created a financial system that was much riskier than predicted. Future models must focus on how the behavior of assets relates and contributes to fat-tail behavior in order to adequately manage financial tail risk.

In the post-Crisis era, it is generally accepted that financial asset returns exhibit fatter tails than normal distributions. Since normally distributed models are still used throughout the financial industry, the downside risk of a portfolio tends to be understated. Simply being aware of fat tails is not enough to protect against extreme financial turmoils. Constructing a portfolio with tail-risk reduction techniques, while costly in the shorter term, can have the longer-term benefits for portfolios that are expected to outlive a major crisis in the future. The ideal portfolio should not only generate a good return for each unit of risk taken, but should also provide some protection against tail risk exposure and be constructed in such a way to offer some defense against tail events.

3.4.2 Uniform Margins

The prediction or estimation of extreme events that may occur in the future is difficult and involves a wide range of variables. Even though a probabilistic approach is adopted, the corresponding prediction is likely to be less accurate as the prediction time horizon lengthens. Under current practice, simple extrapolation – assuming all risk variables are distributed in the uniform margins – is known to decrease accuracy in predicting the future. We have seen how correlation breaks down when random variables are not normally distributed. The breakdown of correlation is still manageable in market risk, but credit and operational risk are usually estimated with more skewed distributions because losses are less frequent but more extreme. When an extreme event does happen, one event has a tendency to lead to another event, which is why the use of copula is preferred over correlation.

The marginal distribution function of a time series $X_t, t = 1, ..., T$ can be described as follows:

$$F_t(x) = P(X_t \leq x) = F(\infty, ..., \infty, x, \infty, ..., \infty)$$

where $F(x_1, ..., x_t, ..., x_T)$ is the joint probability distribution function of the time series. In practice, the marginal distribution of a time series is often approximated by ignoring the dependence structure that may exist in the data. However, there is no reason to believe that this assumption of independence is empirically valid.

3.4.3 Arrival Times

Poisson distribution can be used to model operational risk. It is a discrete distribution that is used to model the probability of n number of events that can happen in a particular time interval, provided we know what the average is. For example, if we know that the average number of accidents that happen on a stretch of road is 5 per day, then the Poisson distribution can answer questions such as "what is the probability of having 6 accidents in one hour".[4] Thus, it seems reasonable to

---

[4]See https://riskprep.com/all-tutorials/36-exam-22/
63-distributions-in-finance for details.

approximate discrete events based on such a distribution. However, in insurance, extreme events do not necessarily follow standard Poisson assumptions. One of its standard assumptions suggest that the occurrence of one event does not affect the probability that a second event will occur, i.e., events are supposed to occur independently, when in reality extreme events (especially those in finance such as credit events) have ripple or domino effects across an entire industry or an entire economy. Also, the number of extreme events that will arrive every decade is unlikely to follow a Poisson distribution, because of the observation that the occurrence rate is not constant (lower rate during the boom time, higher rate during recession periods).

3.4.4 Empirical Observations

The following charts confirm the discussions above with two of the most actively traded securities, the S&P 500 index, and the spot price of West Texas Intermediate (WTI):

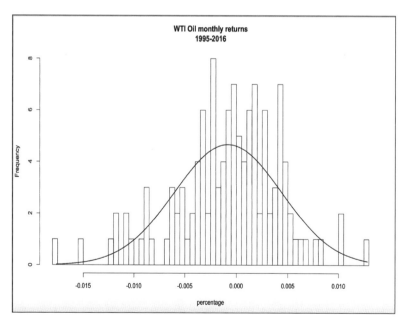

Figure 3.2: Fat-tail Distribution of WTI

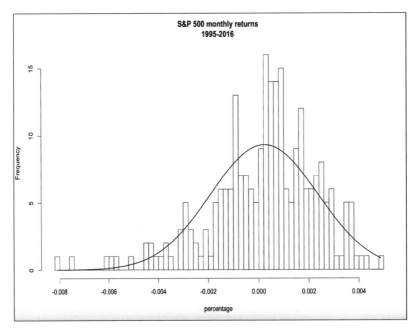

Figure 3.3: Fat-tail Distribution of S&P 500 Index

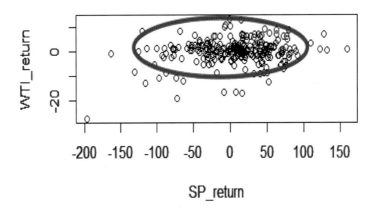

Figure 3.4: Observations Outside a Bi-variate Normal Distribution of S&P 500 and WTI Monthly Returns Between 1995 and 2016

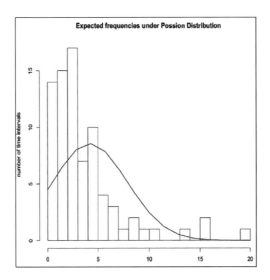

Figure 3.5: Sample Poisson Distribution

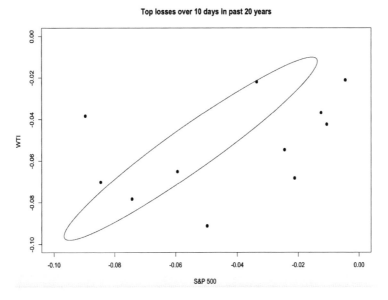

Figure 3.6: Top 11 Losses over 10 Days on Both S&P and WTI and 8 Losses as Outliers Outside the Bi-variate Normal Distribution

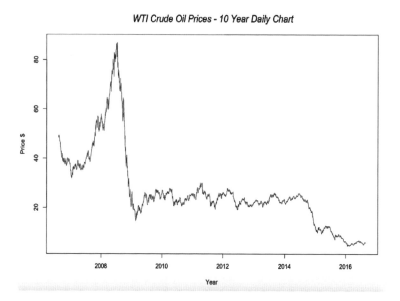

Figure 3.7: WTI 10-Year Daily Charts

Figure 3.8: S&P500 10-Year Daily Charts

Date	S&P 500	WTI Oil
Jul 2012	-0.0212	**-0.0682**
Jan 2013	-0.0125	**-0.0568**
Mar 2013	-0.0045	**-0.0783**
Apr 2013	**-0.0743**	-0.0283
Jun 2013	**-0.0897**	-0.0384
Oct 2013	-0.0106	**-0.0424**
Nov 2013	**-0.0498**	**-0.0912**
Dec 2013	**-0.0846**	**-0.0702**
Jun 2014	**-0.0370**	-0.0651
Nov 2014	-0.0164	**-0.590**
May 2015	**-0.0381**	**-0.0612**
Nov 2015	**-0.0594**	-0.0302
Apr 2016	-0.0245	**-0.046**
May 2016	**-0.0670**	-0.0384
Jun 2014	-0.0106	**-0.0448**
Jul 2015	**-0.346**	-0.431
Aug 2015	**-0.0412**	-0.032

Table 3.2: Top 10 Losses (**bolded**) over One Month on Both the S&P 500 Index and WTI, Illustrating How the Uniform Fat Tail Assumption is Inadequate because these Bolded Outliers (Over 3 Standard Deviations Away from their Mean in Normal Distribution) Can Skew Results Significantly

	S&P 500	WTI Oil
Skewness	-0.8291669	-0.4874761
Kurtosis	14.276701	0.6996997

Table 3.3: Skewness and Kurtosis on Both the S&P 500 Index and WTI, Illustrating Again How the Uniform Fat Tail Assumption is Inadequate

INVESTMENT ANALYTICS IN THE DAWN OF ARTIFICIAL INTELLIGENCE

4. Objective Functions in Portfolio Construction

4.1 Use Case

As a professional investment manager, Christine is proposing a solution to another pension plan that is dissatisfied with its current external investment manager. Like most pension plans, her prospective client has specific long-term targets on the portfolio's risk and returns, and wants to better understand how Christine can deliver a potential improvement on the portfolio's upside return relative to downside risk. "Anyone can use leverage to double up on portfolio volatility, and that is precisely the type of haphazard risk-takers that we want to avoid," said one of the pension trustees. Thus, Christine needs to meet the requirements of the trustees in a skillful and intelligent way.

She has read the previous chapters and understands that she needs to diversify her portfolio by allocating her investments among multiple asset classes and assets. She has selected stocks such as Apple, Tesla, ExxonMobil, Southwest Airlines and a bunch of other stocks that are relatively uncorrelated and are expected to rise in value in the long run. Nonetheless, Christine is not sure how best to combine a collection of separately selected assets together into a portfolio that can deliver superior risk-to-return *ex-ante* statistics. What is the most effective way to predict the dynamics among individual assets under a market meltdown? How best to establish a reliable relationship between *ex-ante* risk on a portfolio and its realized returns?

This chapter will talk about key portfolio objective functions and related analytics tools in order to better equip Christine with the right tools to meet her prospective client's investment requirements.

4.2 Seven Objective Functions

In this chapter, we will discuss the seven most commonly used statistics to illustrate what can be achieved based on these statistics and how to form appropriate objective functions based on them. The seven statistics discussed are Absolute Percentage Change, Variance, Maximum Drawdown (MDD), Value-at-Risk (VaR), Conditional Value-at-Risk (CVaR), Sharpe Ratio (SR) and Alternative Sharpe Ratio (ASR).

In all the equations below:
1. Let $A(t)$ be the day-t mark-to-market value of the existing portfolio. In Christine's case, this is her client's portfolio.
2. Let $X_{cumP\&L}(t)$ be the cumulative P&L of the target assets on day t, assuming $X_{cumP\&L}(0) = 0$ in general. In Christine's case, this will be the profit and loss of the portfolio combined with the buy and sell recommendations that she intends to propose to her client.
3. Let h be the recommended position of a specific asset in the rebalancing basket. Naturally, we can assume the positions to be zero before the recommendations are made.

In the following examples, historical data of stocks are extracted for the period from 5 July 2013 to 8 July 2016 from Yahoo Finance (finance.yahoo.com).

4.2.1 Minimum Absolute Residual

The minimum absolute residual recommendation is computed by minimizing the sum of absolute percentage changes in the mark-to-market value of the recommended portfolio, $pherr(t)$, or

$$\min_{h} \sum_{1 \leq t \leq T} |pherr(t)|$$

where $pherr(t) = \frac{MTM(t)}{MTM(t-1)} - 1 = \frac{A(t)+hx_{cumP\&L}(t)}{A(t-1)+hx_{cumP\&L}(t-1)} - 1$; $A(t)$ is the day-t mark-to-market value of the existing portfolio, and; $x_{cumP\&L}(t) = x(t) - x(0)$ is the cumulative P&L of the rebalancing basket on day t, assuming $x(0) = 0$ in general.

While conceptually simple, this objective function is currently not deployed on the HedgeSPA platform due to the lack of clear user interest.

4.2.2 Minimum Variance

The minimum variance recommendation is computed by minimizing the sum of squared percentage changes in mark-to-market value of the recommended portfolio,

$pherr(\cdot)$, or

$$\min_{h} \sum_{1 \leq t \leq T} (pherr\,(t))^2$$

Example

Suppose Christine decides to construct a portfolio of Apple Inc. (AAPL), Alphabet Inc. (GOOG) and Starbucks Corporation (SBUX). She decides to minimize variance as an indicator of the volatility of the portfolio over a specified historical period. She downloads the historical market data of these three stocks and calculates portfolio variance using the formula:

$$\text{Variance} = \frac{\Sigma(x - \mu)^2}{N}$$

where X is the annualized return of the portfolio observations,

μ is the mean of the annualized return of the portfolio, and

N is the number of observations.

Then, Christine changes the weights of these three stocks in the portfolios. She selects 14 levels of averaged portfolio returns and finds the respective minimum variance at each level. These points connect to form the variance efficient frontier as shown in Figure 4.1. Point M is where the portfolio achieves the minimum variance among all possible portfolios of different weight distributions based on historical data. Thus, point M is the goal of this objective function.

4.2.3   Minimum Peak-to-Trough MDD

This objective function aims to minimize the peak-to-trough maximum drawdown of the mark-to-market value of the recommended portfolio, or:

$$\min_{h} MaxDD\left(T; \{A(t) + hx_{cumP\&L}(t)\}_{t=0}^{T}\right)$$

The drawdown is the measure of the peak-to-trough loss in the historical mark-to-market time series of a financial asset. Let $MTM(t) = A(t) + hx_{cumP\&L}(t)$ be the dollar mark-to-market value of the brokerage account representing the recommended portfolio at the end of the period $[0,t]$, and $MTM_{cum,0 \leq \tau < t}^{peak} = \max_{0 \leq \tau \leq t}[MTM(\tau)]$ be the maximum cumulative dollar mark-to-market value in the $[0,t]$ period. The drawdown $DD(t)$ at time t is defined as:

$$DD(t) = MTM_{0 \leq \tau \leq t}^{peak} - MTM(t)$$

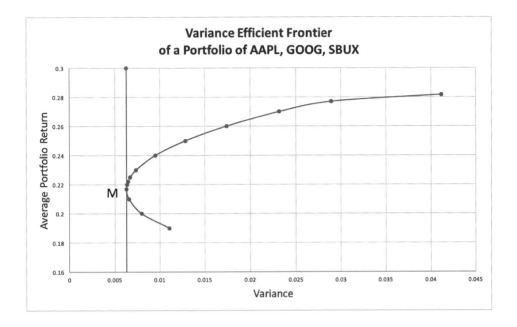

Figure 4.1: Minimizing Variance

The Maximum Drawdown (*MaxDD*) from time 0 to time T is the maximum of the drawdown over the MTM history from time 0 to time T, or:

$$MaxDD\left(T;\{MTM(t)\}_{t=0}^{T}\right) = \max_{0 \leq t \leq T}\{DD(t)\}$$

Alternatively, *MaxDD%* is also used to describe the percentage drop from the peak to the trough as measured from the peak. Using *MaxDD* as a measure of risk, the optimization procedure will find an estimate of the hedge ratio h that can achieve the lowest possible *MaxDD*.

Example

Christine decides to construct a portfolio of Apple Inc. (AAPL), Alphabet Inc. (GOOG) and Starbucks Corporation (SBUX). This time, she decides to use MDD as a measure of downside risk over a historical period. She calculates MDD as expressed in percentage terms based on the formula:

$$MDD\% = (\text{Trough Value} \div \text{Respective Peak Value}) - 1$$

The efficient frontier of this portfolio is drawn as below, which connects the feasible points based on minimum MDD at 18 levels of portfolio returns. Then Christine only keeps half of the observations above the horizontal line where the minimally required portfolio return is achieved. On the graph as shown in Figure 4.2., the point is where the portfolio achieves the minimum MDD among all the MDDs at the minimally required portfolio return. Thus, the red point on the graph achieves the goal of this objective function.

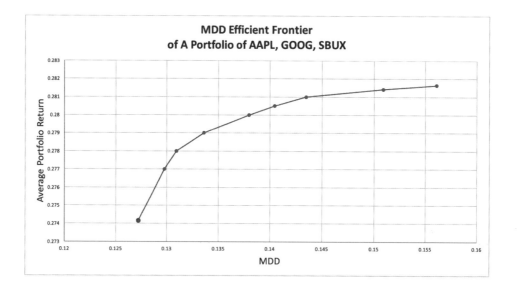

Figure 4.2: Minimizing Maximum Drawdown

Many asset sponsors will not tolerate a 20% or even deeper drawdown in any account. It is not uncommon to see the activation of automatic liquidation procedures when the drawdown of a portfolio exceeds 20%, as well as a formal warning if a 15% drawdown is reached.[1]

4.2.4   Minimum 95% Value-at-Risk

The minimum potential loss, or Value-at-Risk at 95% computed from the daily P&L of the recommended portfolio is defined as:

$$\min_{h} VaR \left(A_{P\&L}(t) + h x_{P\&L}(t) \right)$$

[1]See Chekhlov, Alexei and Uryasev, Stanislav P. and Zabarankin, Michael, "Portfolio Optimization with Drawdown Constraints", April 8, 2000. *Research Report #2000-5.* https://ssrn.com/abstract=223323.

with $A_{P\&L}(t) = A(t) - A(t-1)$ and $x_{P\&L}(t) = x(t) - x(t-1)$. $VaR_{95\%}(\cdot)$ is the value which is higher than 5% of the daily P&L and lower than the other 95%. To put it into a more mathematical form:

$$VaR_{95\%}(X) = min\left(z \mid F(z) \geq 95\%\right)$$

Example

To shape the loss distribution function based on $VaR_{95\%}$ for a portfolio constructed from Apple Inc (AAPL), Alphabet Inc. (GOOG) and Starbucks Corporation (SBUX), Christine first calculates the daily P&L of each portfolio composed of different weights. Although some investment managers use annualized moving-window returns instead of daily returns, Christine chooses daily P&L to conform to client requirements. She then sorts the historical returns in the ascending order and finds the threshold where $index = integer\,[5\% * count\,(observations)]$. This threshold is the value of a simple historical $VaR_{95\%}$. Besides 95%, two other commonly used confidence levels are 99% and 99.5%.

Christine then plots out the efficient frontier of $VaR_{95\%}$ against different levels of portfolio returns as shown in Figure 4.3. The line that goes through point M, which is the lowest level of $VaR_{95\%}$ the portfolio could achieve based on historical data. This point on the graph achieves the goal of this objective function.

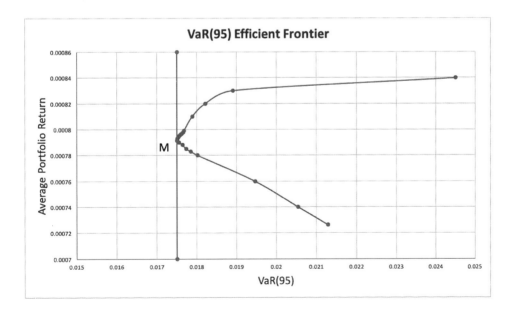

Figure 4.3: Minimizing VaR 95%

4.2.5   Minimum 95% Conditional Value-at-Risk

The minimum Expected Shortfall or Conditional Value-at-Risk at 95% as computed from the daily P&L of the recommended portfolio is defined as:

$$\min_{h} CVaR \left(A_{P\&L}(t) + h x_{P\&L}(t) \right)$$

with $A_{P\&L}(t) = A(t) - A(t-1)$ and $x_{P\&L}(t) = x(t) - x(t-1)$. CVaR is computed using the Cornish-Fisher expansion, where

$$CVaR_{95\%}(\cdot) \;=\; -[\mu(\cdot) + \sigma(\cdot)\mathbb{E}\left(z_{cf,1-\kappa} \mid \kappa > 95\%\right)]$$

$$= \; -\mu(\cdot) - \sigma(\cdot)\mathbb{E} \left[\begin{array}{c} z_{C(1-\kappa)} + \frac{1}{6}\left(z^2_{C(1-\kappa)} - 1\right)S(\cdot) \\[2mm] + \frac{1}{24}\left(z^3_{C(1-\kappa)} - 3z_{C(1-\kappa)}\right)K(\cdot) \\[2mm] - \frac{1}{36}\left(2z^3_{C(1-\kappa)} - 5z_{C(1-\kappa)}\right)S(\cdot)^2 \end{array} \;\middle|\; \kappa > 95\% \right]$$

with $z_{C(1-\kappa)}$ being the critical value for probability $1 - \kappa$ with standard normal distribution (e.g. $z_{C(1-\kappa)} = -1.64$ at $\kappa = 95\%$), and μ, σ, S and K following the standard definitions of mean, volatility, skewness and excess kurtosis, respectively, as computed from the daily P&L of the hedged portfolio. Practically, the expected value of the tail of $z_{cf,1-\kappa}$ at and above 95% estimated numerically by using the discrete average of $z_{C(1-\kappa)}$ taken at 95.5%, 96.5%, 97.5%, 98.5% and 99.5% (e.g. $z_{C(1-\kappa)} = -1.70$ at $\kappa = 95.5\%$, $z_{C(1-\kappa)} = -1.81$ at $\kappa = 96.5\%$, $z_{C(1-\kappa)} = -1.96$ at $\kappa = 97.5\%$, $z_{C(1-\kappa)} = -2.17$ at $\kappa = 98.5\%$, and $z_{C(1-\kappa)} = -2.58$ at $\kappa = 99.5\%$, while their average is -2.04), as at a sampling frequency higher than 1%, as required.

The Choice between VaR and CVaR:

Both VaR and CVaR are measures of possible worst losses based on a certain confidence interval. The only difference is that VaR does not account for scenarios exceeding the threshold, while CVaR takes the weighted average of all the data beyond the threshold and thus gives a more comprehensive worst-case loss scenario. CVaR always gives an expected value of loss at or exceeding VaR. The mathematical relationship between VaR and CVaR is defined as the following:

$$CVaR_{\alpha}(X) = \frac{1}{\alpha} \int_{0}^{\alpha} VaR_{\beta}(X)\, d\beta$$

The following graph imposes VaR and CVaR on a histogram:

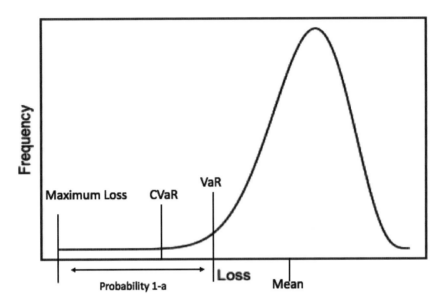

Figure 4.4: VaR, CVaR and Maximum Loss Imposed on a Histogram

In practice, the industry has not been using CVaR as much as VaR due to the general difficulty in obtaining robust observation points beyond the 95% threshold. However, CVaR has proven to be mathematically superior. CVaR is a coherent risk measure in that it is normalized, monotonic, sub-additive, positive homogeneous, and translation invariant, while VaR is not a coherent risk measure because it fails the sub-additivity test. In addition, CVaR is usually continuous with respect to the confidence interval while VaR can be discontinuous depending on the estimation method, especially historical simulation.

Example

Once again, Christine decides to construct a portfolio of Apple Inc. (AAPL), Alphabet Inc. (GOOG) and Starbucks Corporation (SBUX). In order to find an allocation of weights that minimize conditional value-at-risk or CVaR, Christine finds the minimum and maximum possible portfolio returns and select 19 levels of returns in between. Then she calculates the minimum $CVaR_{95\%}$ at each level of daily P&L and connects those points to get the efficient frontier.

She finds the vertical line that is tangent to this efficient frontier. The point M is where Christine finds the minimum CVaR at 95% confidence interval. This point on the graph as shown in Figure 4.5 achieves the goal of this objective function.

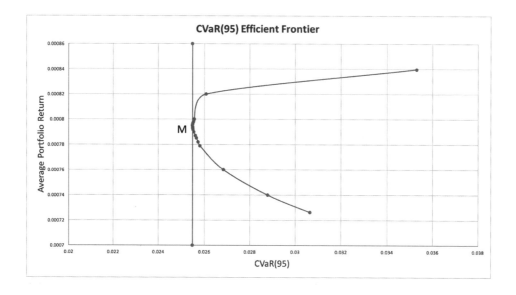

Figure 4.5: Minimizing 95% CVaR

4.2.6 Maximum Sharpe Ratio

The above objective functions are primarily risk measures. It is not uncommon that minimizing the risk measures will result in minimizing both the downside *and* the upside of its associated profit and loss stream. As an alternative, we maximize the traditional portfolio Sharpe Ratio, as defined as:

$$SR \equiv \frac{\sum_i e_i \pi_i}{\sigma_\pi}$$

where: e_i = excess return rate of the i-th asset of the portfolio π;

Example

To illustrate this with an example, suppose Christine is constructing a portfolio with Alphabet Inc. (GOOG), Apple Inc. (AAPL) and IBM Corporation (IBM) common stocks and she wants to find the combination that gives the portfolio as high a traditional Sharpe Ratio as possible.

First, she calculates the minimum Standard Deviation at 14 selected levels of average portfolio returns. Then she connects them to get the efficient frontier as shown in the graph below. The point M is where the portfolio achieves its maximum Sharpe Ratio, which is also the intercept point on the efficient frontier where a tangent line could be drawn to the intercept representing the risk-free rate of return, which is assumed to be 2% in this example. This point on the graph as shown in Figure 4.6 achieves the goal of this objective function.

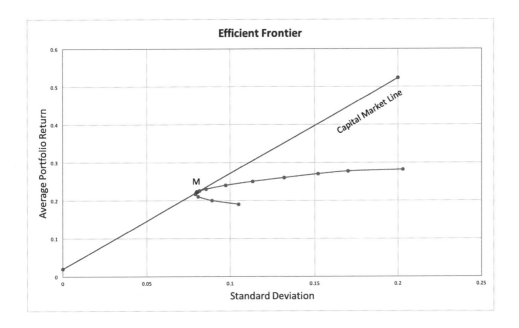

Figure 4.6: Maximizing Sharpe Ratio

4.2.7 Maximum Alternative Sharpe Ratio

The well-known shortcoming of the Sharpe Ratio is that it does not reward the presence of upside behavior for individual assets or penalize downside portfolio tail risk behavior which is generally considered undesirable. Moreover, an improved ratio should automatically revert to the traditional Sharpe Ratio in the absence of any non-normal behavior.

The portfolio problem is essentially one of combining long assets, we will have defined an Omega-function-like measure (Omega functions are functions based on ratios of a measure of upside cumulants to a measure of downside cumulants) known as the Alternative Sharpe Ratio (ASR), which has been shown mathematically to behave as described above in [**Lee 2004**].

This is a more "balanced" approach to optimal hedging from the perspective of not only minimizing risk (which also tends to minimize returns) but also achieving an optimal balance between "upside moments" and "downside risk", and is generally consistent with real-world practice in that investment managers tend to "under hedge" or avoid minimizing downside in order to preserve upside. This objective function is defined as:

$$ASR \equiv \frac{\sum_i e_i \pi_i}{\overline{z_\pi} \, \sigma_\pi} + \frac{1}{2} \frac{\sum_i \pi_i \left(z_i^+ \sigma_i\right)^2}{\overline{z_\pi} \, \sigma_\pi} - \frac{1}{2} \overline{z_\pi} \, \sigma_\pi$$

where:

e_i = excess return rate of the i-th asset of the portfolio π; given that our use case starts with a single rebalancing asset, the i-th asset in the portfolio itself, which is calculated as the percentage changes in the mark-to-market value of the recommended portfolio, $pherr(t)$

π_i = i-th position of the portfolio π

$$z_i^+ = \frac{max\left(z_{cf}\left(z_C^+(i)\right),0\right)}{z_C^+}$$ where z_C^+ is the critical value for probability κ and

$$z_\pi^- = \frac{min\left(z_{cf}\left(z_C^-(\pi)\right),0\right)}{z_C^-}$$ where z_C^- is critical value for probability $1 - \kappa$

(e.g. $z_C^+ = 2.33$ at 1%, $z_C^- = -2.33$ at 99%)

Example

Suppose this time Christine is constructing a portfolio with Alphabet Inc. (GOOG), Apple Inc. (AAPL) and IBM Corporation (IBM) common stocks with as high an Alternative Sharpe Ratio as possible. First, she calculates all the inputs of the model, i.e., the Cornish-Fisher expansion at 99% confidence level for both the portfolio and individual stocks, the standard deviations of both the portfolio and individual stocks, and the average return of both the portfolio and individual stocks. Next, she plugs other parameters into the formula and calculates the portfolio ASR.

In order to draw the graph of ASR vs. return, Christine chooses 13 levels of return and calculates the maximum ASR at each return level. The line that connects these 13 points is shown in Figure 4.7. This right most point on the graph as shown in the graph, denoted by M, achieves the goal of this objective function.

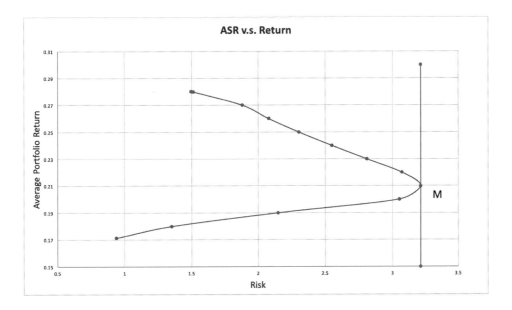

Figure 4.7: Maximizing Alternative Sharpe Ratio

4.2.8 Assumption

In all the examples provided above, we use historical data to calculate the objective functions. This is valid only under the assumption that no fundamental changes have happened to the underlying statistics, or, in technical terms, no regime shift. However, this assumption is not always correct. In the presence of regime shifts, investment managers may merge these methods with forecasted returns in order to produce more robust portfolio rebalancing recommendations, a technique that we will discuss in the next few chapters.

INVESTMENT ANALYTICS IN THE DAWN OF ARTIFICIAL INTELLIGENCE

5. Risk and Return Attribution

5.1 Use Case

Christine just showed a proposed portfolio to her client. Her client's primary concern is the risk of an extremely large loss primarily driven by a few wrong-way bets. The market started plunging at the beginning of 2016 due to the uncertain global economy such as Chinese economic slowdown and bad economic performance in Japan as well as the European Union. Her client lost a significant amount of money during that period and this time he wants a portfolio that will not give him nasty surprises when similar market events happen again.

How should Christine identify positions in her portfolio with potential exposure to extreme risk and make sure that her recommended portfolio will not be needlessly harmed by similar extreme scenarios? How does she determine which positions contribute the most to portfolio tail risk? How can she review objectively calculated break-even returns for each investment to make sure that it stands a reasonable chance of contributing to her portfolio return target? How will those break-even returns compare to their actual performance histories?

5.1.1 A Graph to Illustrate the Point

In order to understand why portfolio managers need to identify positions with potential exposure to extreme tail risks, let's look at how the British Pound did in the two months leading up to the UK's referendum to leave the European Union. The following histogram is constructed from the time series of GBP/USD exchange rate collected from 5 May 2016 to 4 July 2016 from the foreign exchange broker Onada:[1]

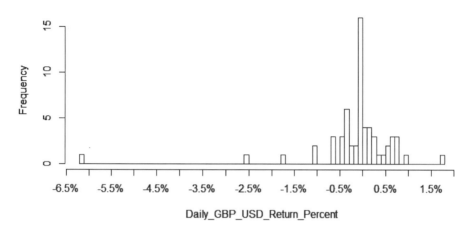

The skewness of the distribution is -3.93 and its standardized kurtosis with the subtraction of the constant of 3 is 22.46. This means the graph is highly skewed towards the negative, and its shape is leptokurtic. Its central peak is much higher and pointier than the normal distribution.

When any portfolio manager has a negatively skewed distribution similar to this, he/she needs to find out which specific positions contribute the most to the negative fat tail of the portfolio return distribution.

5.2 Risk Attribution

Risk Attribution compares the position weight of each investment to its Percentage Contribution to Tail Risk (PCTR), defined as

$$\%RC_i = \frac{w_i}{R(\vec{w})} \cdot \frac{\partial R(\vec{w})}{\partial w_i},$$

which let investors explore which investments contribute disproportionately to portfolio tail risk relative to their weights. Mathematically, R is only required to be a risk measure that is first-order homogenous, i.e. $R(\lambda w) = \lambda R(w)$.

---

[1] See https://www.oanda.com/currency/converter/.

Risk Attribution Layout

A typical **Risk Attribution** panel displays Portfolio Weight, PCTR (Percentage Contribution to Tail Risk), Net Weight vs. PCTR, and a graphical comparison for each Group, Subgroup and individual position within the portfolio.

As shown in Figure 5.1, the Net Weight vs PCTR column is designed to provide a quick visual guide to the results, with a green up arrow indicating the position is contributing less risk than its weight, whereas a red down arrow indicates the position is contributing more risk than its weight. The color scheme can be customized by the user. For instance, a rational investor should prefer a 10%-weighted investment that contributes to 5% of portfolio risk over one that contributes to 20% of portfolio risk. Therefore, investors are advised to look for "large down arrows" as potential positions to reduce weights.

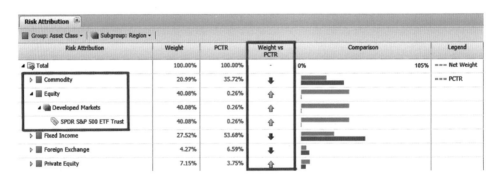

Figure 5.1: Risk Attribution

The **Risk Attribution** tree shown in Figure 5.1 is structured in three levels based on the primary group (e.g. asset class), the second subgroup (e.g. region), and the tertiary level on individual investments. Clicking on the arrow next to each node in the tree can expand on that node and drill down to the next level. The aggregation helps investors identify regions and countries with a disproportional concentration in portfolio tail-risk contributions. To get **Risk Attribution**, you should first select a portfolio and then click "Analytics" to find "Risk Attribution", which is under "Performance".

5.3 Ex-Ante Return Attribution

Ex-ante Return Attribution performs roughly the same calculation, except that everything is displayed in return space instead of risk space. For instance, the break-even or implied return for an asset, or how much return the asset has to make in order to pay for its tail risk contribution, is given by

$$\sum_i w_i e_i \cdot \frac{\%RC_i}{w_i} = \frac{\sum_i w_i e_i}{R(\vec{w})} \cdot \frac{\partial R(\vec{w})}{\partial w_i}$$

where e_i can be either the historical return of an asset, or its forward-looking econometric projection, also known as Scenario Return. Investors can then compare the Scenario Return of each asset, region, or asset class to its Implied Return to find out which asset is not contributing a return proportional to its risk.

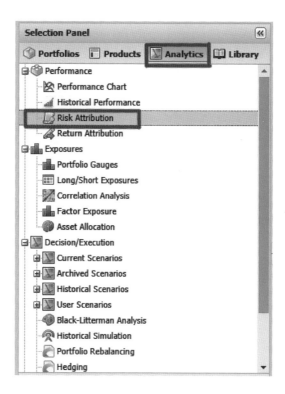

Figure 5.2: "Analytics → Risk Attribution"

Return Attribution Layout

Return Attribution compares an investment's Historical Return with its Implied Return, or the return required to justify the risk it contributes to the portfolio. A typical *Ex-ante* **Return Attribution** panel displays Scenario Return, Implied Return, Scenario vs. Implied, and a graphical comparison for each Group, Subgroup and individual position within the portfolio. To get **Return Attribution**, you should click "Analytics" first and double-click "Return Attribution" in Figure 5.3.

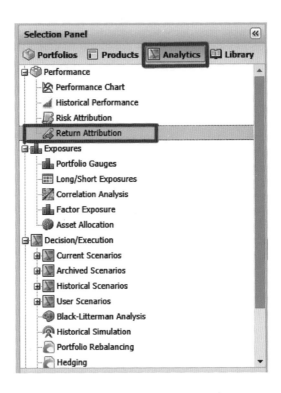

Figure 5.3: "Analytics → Return Attribution"

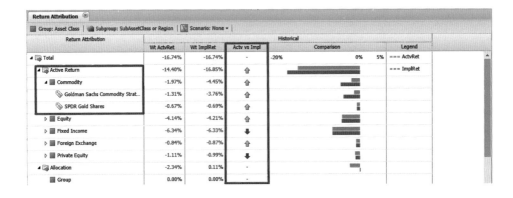

Figure 5.4: Return Attribution

Return Attribution						
■ Group: Asset Class | ■ Subgroup: SubAssetClass or Region | ▨ Scenario: US Economic Recovery ▾						
Return Attribution				Scenario		
	Wt ActvScenRet	Wt ScenImplRet	Scen vs Impl	Scenario Comparison		Scenario Legend
▲ ⊞ Total	-9.67%	-9.67%	-	-10% 0% 5%		=== ScenRet
▲ ⊞ Active Return	-8.07%	-9.78%	⬆			=== ImplRet
▲ ■ Commodity	-2.13%	-1.98%	⬇			
◈ Goldman Sachs Commodity Strat...	-1.38%	-1.68%	⬆			
◈ SPDR Gold Shares	-0.76%	-0.30%	⬇			
▷ ■ Equity	-0.18%	-4.10%	⬆			
▷ ■ Fixed Income	-4.50%	-2.57%	⬇			
▷ ■ Foreign Exchange	-0.49%	-0.41%	⬇			
▷ ■ Private Equity	-0.76%	-0.71%	⬇			
▲ ⊞ Allocation	-1.61%	0.10%	-			

Figure 5.5: Return Attribution under the US Economic Recovery Scenario

As shown in Figure 5.4, a green up arrow in the "Actv vs Impl" column indicates that Historical Return > Implied Return, making it potentially desirable to increase the weight in this asset class. A red down arrow indicates that Historical Return < Implied Return, making it potentially desirable to decrease the weight in this asset class.

Also, the **Return Attribution** tree as shown in Figure 5.4 is structured on three levels – the primary group, the secondary subgroup, and the tertiary individual investment positions. By clicking on the arrow next to each node in the tree you can expand that node and drill down to the next level. Once you drill down to the individual product level, you cannot drill down any further.

In addition, **Return Attribution** can be used in tandem with Scenario Analysis to see which investments may justify their risks under the projected market scenario. Click on the drop-down arrow on the Scenario button and a list of different scenarios will appear for users to select. Once a scenario (such as *US Economic Recovery*) is selected, the tool changes to compare the forward-looking Scenario Active Return with the forward-looking Scenario Implied Active Return shown in Figure 5.6. Then you can review whether the scenario return of a specific asset will exceed its implied return so that it is a solid candidate for increasing its weight or vice versa.

Brinson Attribution

Ex-ante Return Attribution is typically complemented by a traditional Brinson Attribution for *ex-post* return attribution. Brinson Attribution is an approach to performance attribution used to explain the difference between the portfolio's performance and benchmark and evaluate the performance of the manager who runs the investment portfolio, based on asset allocation, stock selection, and interaction. **Brinson Attribution** can be accessed by clicking on "Selection Panel" and then "Analytics". A typical example of the Brinson Attribution screen is given by Figure 5.6:

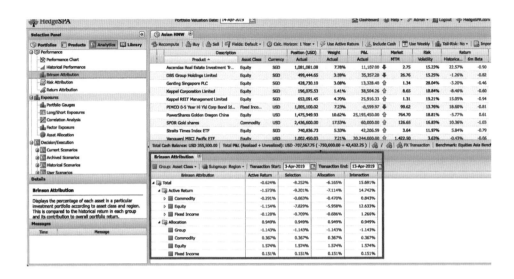

Figure 5.6: Brinson Attribution

Suffice it to say that the Brinson Attribution screen can be quite complex. For the ease of illustration, the following is a simpler worked example of Brinson Attribution:

Month to Date	2018-01-31	2018-02-07		Quarter to Date	2017-12-29	2018-02-07	
Region	**ATTRIBUTION**			**Region**	**ATTRIBUTION**		
	Selection	Allocation	Interaction		Selection	Allocation	Interaction
CN	-0.92%	-0.56%	-0.17%	CN	-1.51%	0.23%	-0.28%
HK	0.08%	-0.12%	0.01%	HK	-0.11%	-0.04%	-0.02%
IN	-0.14%	0.36%	0.09%	IN	-0.33%	0.16%	0.20%
KR	0.00%	-0.55%	0.01%	KR	-0.51%	-0.32%	-0.13%
Other (SG, MY)	0.22%	0.62%	-0.19%	Other (SG, MY)	0.31%	-0.05%	-0.26%
TW	-0.08%	-0.18%	-0.03%	TW	0.04%	0.03%	0.00%
Total	-0.84%	-0.43%	-0.27%	**Total**	-2.11%	0.01%	-0.48%
		Active return	-1.54%			**Active return**	-2.58%

Figure 5.7: Brinson Attribution Worked Example

Let's say our portfolio's benchmark is composed of 60% MSCI World and 40% Barclays Aggregate Indices. The manager adds value by allocating assets and selecting stocks. In this case, this manager chooses to allocate 65% of his assets to the shares of Apple Inc. (AAPL) and 35% of his assets into iShares Barclays Aggregate Bond Fund (AGG). His first bet is on asset selection from Apple's out-performance relative to the MSCI World Index. His second bet is on asset allocation based on his 5% overweight to equities.

According to Table 1 as shown in Figure 5.8, Total Out-performance = Total Portfolio Return - Total Benchmark Return = 18.426% - 5.628% = 12.798%. To get

		Table 1					
	Benchmark				Portfolio		
	Weight		Return			Weight		Return
MSCI World	60%	9.94%	Apple		65%	28.80%
Barclays Aggregate	40%	-0.84%	AGG		35%	-0.84%
Total	100%	5.62800%	Total		100%	18.42600%
					Outperformance	12.79800%

		Table 2					
	Benchmark				Portfolio		
	Weight		Return			Weight		Return
MSCI World	65%	9.94%	Apple		65%	28.80%
Barclays Aggregate	35%	-0.84%	AGG		35%	-0.84%
Total	100%	6.16700%	Total		100%	18.42600%
					Asset Selection	12.25900%
MSCI World	60%	9.94%	MSCI World		65%	9.94%
Barclays Aggregate	40%	-0.84%	Barclays Aggregate		35%	-0.84%
Total	100%	5.62800%	Total		100%	6.16700%
					Asset Allocation	0.53900%
					Outperformance	12.79800%

Figure 5.8: Worked Example in Brinson Attribution

Total Benchmark Return and Total Portfolio Return, we need to use the method of weighted mean. For example, Total Benchmark Return = 60% * 9.94% + 40% * (-0.84%) = 5.628%; Total Portfolio Return = 65% * 28.80% + 35% * (-0.84%) = 18.426%.

To better explain the Total Out-performance, Table 2 in Figure 5.8 shows the out-performance of Asset Selection and Asset Allocation. The sum of them is the Total Out-performance. Here are the step-by-step calculations:

- Firstly, Apple performs better than the MSCI World index, in order to calculate the performance of asset selection, we assume that the weights of MSCI World index (65%) and Barclays Aggregate indices (35%) are the same as the weights of Apple (65%) and AGG (35%) correspondingly. Therefore, Total Adjusted Benchmark Return = 65% * 9.94% + 35% * (-0.84%) = 6.167% and Total Portfolio Return = 65% * 28.80% + 35% * (-0.84%) = 18.426%. Finally, Asset Selection = Total Portfolio Return - Total Adjusted Benchmark Return = 18.426% - 6.167% = 12.259%.
- Then, there is asset allocation based on the 5% overweight to apple. We compare the return in the case of 60% MSCI World and 40% Barclays Aggregate with the return in the case of 65% MSCI World and 35% Barclays Aggregate. Therefore, Asset Allocation = [65% * 9.94% + 35% * (-0.84%)] - [60% * 9.94% + 40% * (-0.84%)] = 6.167% - 5.628% = 0.539%.

- Finally, in Table 2, Total Out-performance = Asset Selection + Asset Allocation = 12.259% + 0.539% = 12.798%, which is the same as the Total Out-performance in Table 1.

5.4   Difference between Return Attribution & Risk Attribution

Return Attribution and **Risk Attribution** use different contrast factors. **Return Attribution** compares historical returns and implied returns to recommend which group or product is desirable to increase its weight because of its potential return, such as interest, dividend, and other forms. **Risk Attribution** compares each group or product's net weight and PCTR (Percentage Contribution to Tail Risk) to recommend which group or product is less risky than its weight and is beneficial to increase.

Both **Return Attribution** and **Risk Attribution** give "large down or up arrow" to directly advise you to decrease or increase weights. They help investors to find a proper asset that the investor could receive more return and experience less risk.

5.5   Conclusion

This chapter describes techniques that will help investors find the strongest signals in a portfolio for a potential increase or decrease in position as compared to either its historical or forecasted returns. Using this analytic tool can produce more robust portfolio rebalancing recommendations at the asset, region, or asset class levels.

INVESTMENT ANALYTICS IN THE DAWN OF ARTIFICIAL INTELLIGENCE

6. Portfolio-Level Factor Analysis

6.1 Use Case

The market conditions have changed. After one year, the risk tolerance, time horizon, and institutional priorities of Christine's clients have changed quite a bit. For example, due to the rising cost of employee medical insurance, her client wants to make less risky and shorter-term investments. The U.S. market is recovering and the Chinese economy is slowing down and is expected to continue to do so, with a trade conflict brewing in the horizon after the U.S. presidential election. Thus, the allocation of assets within the portfolio Christine constructed a year ago is no longer appropriate.

While the client is satisfied by Christine's performance in the past year, the client wants to understand the risk and factors that her portfolio is exposed to, before making adjustments to the portfolio. Moreover, the client wants to have confidence that Christine's performance was not driven primarily by picking "momentum" stocks, or by following the herd, but she has done the necessary research to find "value" stocks. She needs an analytic tool to show the client her portfolio's different exposure to the value and momentum factors.

This chapter discusses how Christine may analyze her portfolio with factor exposure models, with potential adjustments to her rebalancing strategies based on the results.

6.2 Portfolio-Level Factor Exposure

The **Factor Exposure** panel shows the portfolio's exposures to a set of market factors. Analysis can be carried out with either single-factor or multi-factor regression models and on historical returns as well as forward-looking scenarios. This analysis can help use the assets' relationships with single factors, or a set of multiple factors to explain the portfolio's historical or forward-looking performance. "Factor Exposure" can be found under "Exposures" after clicking on "Analytics".

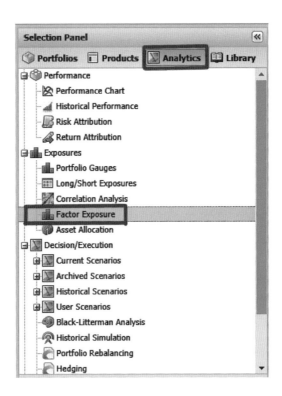

Figure 6.1: "Analytics → Factor Exposure"

As one example shown in the picture below, using a single-factor model, Franklin Templeton Hard Currency Fund is positively correlated to SPDR S&P 500 ETF Trust (SPY) with a beta of 0.1188. Its portfolio-weighted beta is 0.0051. The total beta of this "US Multi-Asset Funds" portfolio is 0.4876.

The user can also perform a traditional multi-factor analysis by clicking on "Model: Single-factor" as shown in Figure 6.2 and then choosing "Model: Multi-factor". The multi-factor analysis shows the summation of the beta coefficients of two factors: namely, M1APJ00V (MSCI AC Asia Pacific ex-Japan Value Net Total Return Index) and M1CXJPI (MSCI AC Asia ex-Japan Momentum Net Return USD Index). For this particular portfolio, one can see from Figure 6.3 its exposure is roughly evenly distributed between Value and Momentum:

Factor Exposure				
Model: Single-factor ▾ Exposures View: Grid ▾				
Product Name	Factor	Beta	SPY	Total
Franklin Templeton Hard Currency FUND	United States	0.1188	0.0051	0.0051
Goldman Sachs Commodity Strategy A	United States	0.2394	0.0426	0.0426
iShares Core U.S. Aggregate Bond ETF	United States	-0.0208	-0.0018	-0.0018
PIMCO Total Return A	United States	-0.0466	-0.0040	-0.0040
PowerShares Global Listed Private Eq	United States	0.7548	0.0539	0.0539
SPDR Gold Shares	United States	0.0464	0.0015	0.0015
SPDR S&P 500 ETF Trust	United States	1.0000	0.4008	0.4008
T. Rowe Price US Treasury Long-Term	United States	-0.1005	-0.0105	-0.0105
Total		-	0.4876	0.4876

Figure 6.2: Factor Exposure Grid (Single-factor)

Factor Exposure			
Model: Multi-factor ▾ Exposures View: Grid ▾			
Product Name	System Factor Universe	M1APJ00V	M1CXJPI
Industrial Bank Co., Ltd.	Asian Value & Momentum	-0.0142	0.0219
Olam International Limited	Asian Value & Momentum	0.0312	0.0385
OZ Minerals Limited	Asian Value & Momentum	-0.0214	-0.0103
PetroChina Co. Ltd.	Asian Value & Momentum	-0.0571	-0.0318
Samsung Electronics Co Ltd	Asian Value & Momentum	0.0158	0.0608
Telstra Corp Ltd	Asian Value & Momentum	-0.0128	0.0162
User		0.0000	0.0000
System		0.5399	0.4724
Portfolio		0.5399	0.4724

Figure 6.3: Factor Exposure Grid (Multi-factor) under "Asian Value and Momentum"

The analysis shown above is frequently requested by asset sponsors as one way to demonstrate how an investment manager is not merely "chasing momentum", a practice that many asset sponsors are not big fans of since there are more cost-effective alternatives available simply by buying a basket or ETF on a momentum index. Users can also change the exposures view from Grid to Chart for a quick review of the overall portfolio's performance to different factors by clicking "Exposures view" as shown in Figure 6.4. In this case, the multi-factor analysis shows the beta coefficients of multiple factors, including HSI, UUP, BNSDS, CWI, SPY, DJP, CSI, EUE, EEM, EWJ, and ISF (these being ticker symbols of the corresponding indices):

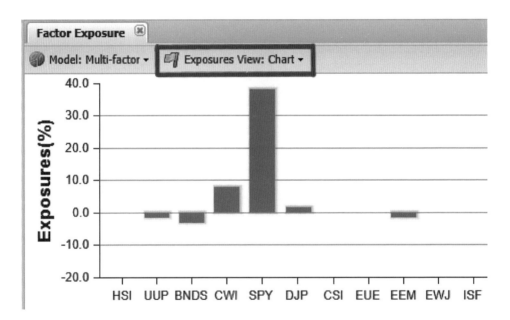

Figure 6.4: Factor Exposure Chart (Multi-Factor)

6.3 Conclusion

One common use of this tool is the identification of possible "momentum chasing" by the investment manager. "Momentum" investing refers to the practice by some investment managers to invest in assets that have shown recent good performance. Asset sponsors are not big fans of such investment strategies because they can achieve similar outcomes with a lower-cost basket or ETF. With our analytic tool, the asset sponsor can objectively determine whether a portfolio has significant exposure to a "momentum" factor, meaning that the portfolio is simply replicating a simplistic "momentum" strategy, as supposed to introducing other factors such as "quality" and "value" to the portfolio. That helps both the asset sponsors and the investment manager, who may not want to be surprised in an investment review meeting. This seemingly simple tool is also one of the most popular on the HedgeSPA platform.

INVESTMENT ANALYTICS IN THE DAWN OF ARTIFICIAL INTELLIGENCE

> ## 7. A Hedging Use Case

7.1 Use Case

Once Christine understands her portfolio's factor exposure, she is now trying to minimize the exposure her portfolio faces in the market in anticipation of a major market downturn, but it's only a temporary solution to avoid the steep transaction costs associated with selling and then buying back her long positions. She understands that it is impossible to hedge the full risk of her portfolio by derivatives alone, primarily because of the potentially high premium costs and the large notional amount of shorts that might induce the very crash of the market that she is trying to avoid. Also, it is impossible for her to predict the exact timing of the market crash and its eventual recovery. To minimize the cost of hedging, instead of putting on a full hedge on her portfolio mechanically, Christine wants to test out a variety of hedging techniques and compares them based on costs and effectiveness. This chapter shows Christine how to use the hedging tools on the HedgeSPA core investment platform to achieve a different exposure profile of her portfolio through a cost-effective hedging strategy.[1]

---

[1]The chapter is excerpted from [**Lee 2012**]. Comments from peer reviewers at the 25th Australasian Finance & Banking Conference, related commenters and idea contributors, including one who graciously declined the offer of second authorship, as well as the able research assistance of Srikanthan Natarajan and Peter Zheng for the coding, running and checking of each and every simulation from raw data in the piece (as supported by the MAS-FGIP scheme) are gratefully acknowledged.

7.1.1 Controlling Extreme Risks through Volatility Derivatives

We will use the specific example of hedging long equity exposure through the use of volatility derivatives, a difficult problem of hedging extreme risks that cannot be solved using customary techniques, so that it can be used to illustrate the power of the HedgeSPA core investment platform.

Futures and options on VIX allow investors to take directional long or short positions on the VIX Index (which measures the SPX's implied volatility over 30 days), whereas VT allows investors to trade the difference between the implied and realized variance of the SPX over three months. There is minimal difference between variance futures and variance swaps, since both contracts are almost identical. However, there are well-known problems associated with using variance futures in trading as well as empirical analyses:

1. Variance futures are illiquid – Trading on the VT contracts has significantly less liquidity than trading on the VIX futures.[2] For example, the average daily trading volume of the VIX futures was 47,744 contracts in 2011, as compared to the single-digit level of open interests traded on the VT or the VA contracts during 2011.[3]

2. VT has a maturity of three months – There have been only 29 non-overlapping VT observations during the December 2004 to March 2012 period covered by our use case. Given the high volatility of returns on variance futures, there is not enough data to determine if the mean return is statistically significant. As a result, where the data may be too sparse to be credible, this use case also explores using the so-called "VIX squared" (which corresponds to the 1-month S&P500 variance swap rate) if and when appropriate.

From an investor's point of view, it seems attractive that the negative correlation between volatility and stock index returns is particularly pronounced in stock market downturns, thereby offering protection against stock market losses when it is needed the most. Empirical studies, however, indicate that this kind of downside or crash protection can be quite expensive because of its constant negative carries. It is also unrealistic to pay for protection during a market downturn by timing the market perfectly.

We begin by using volatility and variance futures as extreme downside hedges. We simulate hedging techniques as they are used in real-life trading, using rolling methods that are generally consistent with market practice – we approach this analysis from the perspective of real-life trading in order to come up with realistic estimates on true hedging effectiveness. These contracts are not liquid, so a dealer

---

[2] See [**Huang 2010**] for details.

[3] Volume information on the VIX futures is available from http://www.cboe.com/micro/vix/pricecharts.aspx, while open interest information on VT and VA is available from http://cfe.cboe.com/data/historicaldata.aspx#VADL.

must be willing to take the opposite side of the trade on an exchange for an investor to buy the position. When the dealers quote the contract, they are replicating their customers' VIX or VT exposures with underlying positions. In theory, there is no obvious explanation as to how using the VIX and variance futures can be more efficient than using the underlying options, since dealers are likely to charge defensive margins due to imperfect replication unless significant trading liquidity native to the VIX future or variance futures markets distorts typical cost to replicate. To objectively analyze the effectiveness of using VIX or variance futures in times of market crisis, we use a long SPX portfolio and compare various hedging strategies using: (i) VIX futures; (ii) variance futures, (iii) 5% out-of-the-money (OTM) SPX put options, and (iv) 10% out-of-the-money (OTM) SPX put options.

This use case is organized as follows. We will describe each of the hedging strategies implemented, followed by an analysis of the hedging results. Finally, we will conclude with an illustration of the actual mechanics on the platform.

7.2   Methodology

7.2.1   VIX Futures

In order to test out the various hedging strategies, our use case uses the daily settlement prices on VIX futures from December 2004 to March 2012, a period covering the Global Financial Crisis. The notional of VIX futures is $1,000 times the value of the VIX Index. Price data on the VIX futures are obtained from the transaction records provided by the Chicago Futures Exchange (CFE).

The settlement date for the VIX futures is the "Wednesday that is 30 days prior to the third Friday of the calendar month immediately following the month in which the contract expires," according to contract specification.[4] This use case chooses to roll on the fifth business day prior to the expiration date for the monthly VIX futures, in order to avoid well-known liquidity problems associated with the last week of trading. More specifically, on the first day of rolling to a contract, we want to take long positions on the second-nearby monthly VIX contracts based on its closing price. The daily cumulative payoffs are calculated using daily settlement prices. The contracts are then closed at the closing prices. On the same day, we buy back the second-nearby contract at the closing price, and so on.

Since an investor is not required to pay upfront cash for the futures positions[5], his mark-to-market value (MTM) at the end of the day is the market value of his futures contract plus the cash balance of any financing required. The act of finally closing the futures in itself is expected to create cash receivable/payable. The daily

---

[4]See http://cfe.cboe.com/cfe-products.

[5]Technically, any initial margin money is good-faith money that still belongs to the investor, so it is not a form of "payment".

P&L is the sum of the change in mark-to-market values of the assets, any margin balance borrowed/received to finance the positions, as well as cash balance received from any final settlement. For the purpose of this calculation, we have ignored the potential financing cost required to meet the investor's margin requirements. Then, we initiate a new contract on the next day to maintain the hedge. If the futures contracts close in the money, one should receive the exercise value of the contracts as cash, or pay cash if the contracts close out of the money. To simplify the analysis, we will ignore any interest charges (accruals) on a negative (positive) balance. The cumulative P&L as given below can be used as our mark-to-market value of the futures contracts starting from time t:

$$Cumulative\ P\&L\,(t+l\triangle t)\ \ in\ the\ first\ rolling\ month$$
$$= \begin{cases} \$1000 \times fvixfut_{cum}\,(t+l\triangle t), & l=0,1,2,\ldots,M_1-1 \\ cash\,(t+l\triangle t), & l=M_1 \end{cases}$$

where $M_1 \equiv (T_1-t)/\triangle t$ is the number of trading days between the current day t and position closing day T_1; $fvixfut_{cum}(t+l\triangle t) = vixfut_{settle}(t+l\triangle t) - vixfut_{open}(t)$ is the cumulative value of the futures contract at daily settlement on day $t+l\triangle t$, taking the difference between the daily settle futures price, $vixfut_{settle}(t+l\triangle t)$, and the day-$t$ futures price at the initiation of the contract, $vixfut_{open}(t)$.

On day T_1 we close out the first VIX futures and keep any resulting net cash flow in a cash account. Since the contract size of VIX futures is \$1,000 multiplied by the VIX Index points, the value of the day-T_1 cash account is:

$$cash\,(T_1) = \$1000 \times fvixfut_{cum}\,(T_1) = \$1000 \times \left[vixfut_{close}(T_1) - vixfut_{open}(t)\right]$$

In theory, the cumulative P&L for VIX futures initiated on day $(T_1+\triangle t)$ in the second rolling month depends on whether interest charges from the first period become part of the P&L for the second period:

$$Cumulative\ P\&L\ (T_1+\xi\triangle t)\ \ in\ the\ second\ rolling\ month$$
$$= \$1000 \times fvixfut_{cum}(T_1+\xi\triangle t) + cash(T_1+\xi\triangle t), \quad for\ \xi = 1,2,\ldots,M_2$$

where $M_2 \equiv (T_2-(T_1+\triangle t))/\triangle t$; $fvixfut_{cum}(T_1+\xi\triangle t) = vixfut_{settle}(T_1+\xi\triangle t) - vixfut_{open}(T_1+\triangle t)$ is the cumulative value of the contract on day $T_1+\xi\triangle t$ with the opening price, $vixfut_{open}(T_1+\xi\triangle t)$, of the second VIX futures, initiated on day $T_1+\triangle t$. The cash balance account, $cash(T_1+\xi\triangle t)$, is given by

$$cash\,(T_1+\xi\triangle t)\ \ in\ second\ rolling\ month = cash\,(T_1) \times e^{R(T_1)\xi\triangle t}$$

where $R(T_1)$ is the continuously compounded zero-coupon interest rate on day T_1. Similar cumulative P&L calculations are used for subsequent periods.

Typically, investors gain exposure to the SPX Index by trading ETF on the SPX.[6] Depositary receipts on the SPX, such as SPDRs, represent ownership in unit trusts designed to replicate the underlying index. SPDRs replicate movements in the underlying stock index almost perfectly. One of the most popular SPDRs, the SPY, is valued at 1/10th the value of the Index.[7] Like other equities, SPDRs are typically transacted in 100-lot (or "round-lot") increments.[8] Further, the notional size of VIX futures is $1,000 per index point. In order to compute the number of VIX futures contracts required for one unit of the SPX index, we apply the appropriate multipliers for adjusting the unit size and the unit dollar values in the hedged portfolio.

In this use case, we assume that a typical investor holds the long asset already, but it will be atypical for any fully-invested portfolio to set aside surplus cash to pay for the cost of hedging, except for realized P&L already captured by a cash account at time t. Any ongoing margin funding requirement is assumed to be minimal. The total amount realized for the asset, when the profit or loss on the hedge is taken into account, is denoted by mark-to-market value (MTM), so that for, $\varsigma = 0, 1, 2, \ldots, M = (T - t)/\triangle t$,

$$
\begin{aligned}
MTM(t + \varsigma \Delta t) &= \$10 \times SPX(t + \varsigma \Delta t) + \\
&\quad h \times [\$1000 \times fvixfut_{cum}(t + \varsigma \Delta t)] + cash(t)
\end{aligned}
$$

The corresponding cumulative P&L of the portfolio from time t is given by

$$
\begin{aligned}
MTM_{cumP\&L}(t + \varsigma \Delta t) &= MTM(t + \varsigma \Delta t) - MTM(t) \\
&= \$10 \times SPX_{cumP\&L}(t + \varsigma \Delta t) + \\
&\quad h \times [\$1000 \times fvixfut_{cum}(t + \varsigma \Delta t)]
\end{aligned}
$$

where $fvixfut_{cum}(t + \varsigma \Delta t)$ is the cumulative value of the futures contract on day $t + \varsigma \Delta t$ for $\forall \varsigma$; $cash(t + \varsigma \Delta t)$ is the cash balance account; $MTM(t) = \$10 \times SPX_{open}(t)$; and $SPX_{cumP\&L}(t + \varsigma \Delta t) = [SPX_{close}(t + \varsigma \Delta t) - SPX_{open}(t)]$.

When hedging is used, the portfolio manager chooses a value for the hedge ratio h that minimizes an objective function of the value of the hedged portfolio, such as

---

[6]An ETF represents fractional ownership in an investment trust, or unit trusts, patterned after an underlying index and is a mutual fund that is traded much like any other fund. Unlike most mutual funds, ETFs can be bought or sold throughout the trading day, not just at the closing price of the day.

[7]A single SPDR was quoted at $78.18, or approximately 1/10th the value of the S&P 500 at 778.12, on March 17, 2009.

[8]If a single unit of SPDRs was valued at $78.18 on March 17, 2009, a 100-lot unit of SPDRs would be valued at $7,818 on that day.

its variance. It is important to use the percentage changes in the cumulative P&L as input, i.e., $MTM_{cumP\&L}(t + \varsigma \Delta t)/MTM_{cumP\&L}(t + (\varsigma - 1)\Delta t) - 1$, because doing so avoids unstable and even non-sensical numerical values when there are massive market shocks in the market, and because that is the most natural quantity to hedge against as seen from the investor's perspective. Figure 7.1 presents an example of the computed hedging ratios times 100 for one unit of the S&P index under all hedging models. All hedging ratios are lower-bounded by zero, for the reason being that most real-life traders are likely to face strict compliance restrictions against "shorting volatility".

7.2.2 Variance Futures

Our use case uses the daily VT futures prices from December 2004 to March 2012, a period covering the Global Financial Crisis. The VT contract's multiplier is $50 per variance point. In the following, we describe the algorithm for the rolling strategies of variance futures at five business days prior to the expiration date. Whenever trading data may be missing or prices appear to be "stale", missing values are "filled" by synthetic VT data replicated from using *VIXTerm* observations. The contracts are rolled quarterly, but hedging can occur monthly.

7.2.2.1 Algorithm for Monthly Rolls of Synthetic 1-month Variance Futures

VT contracts are forward starting three-month variance swaps. The realized variance is calculated as soon as as the front-quarter VT contract enters its front-quarter three-month window. Because VT is based on the realized variance of the SPX, the price of the front-month contract is the sum of the realized variance (*RUG*) and the implied forward variance (*IUG*). *RUG* indicates the realized variance of the SPX corresponding to the front-quarter VT contract.

Using martingale pricing theory with respect to a risk-neutral probability measure Q, the time-t VT price in terms of variance points is the annualized forward integrated variance, $F_t^{VT}(T) = \frac{1}{\tau_1} E_t^Q(v_{T-\tau_1,T})$ for τ_1=3 months = 1/4 year. The value of a forward-starting VT contract is the implied forward variance ($IUG_{T-\tau_1,T}$), given by:

$$F_t^{VT,fs}(T) = \frac{1}{\tau_1} E_t^Q(v_{T-\tau_1,T}) = IUG_{T-\tau_1,T} \tag{7.1}$$

where $0 < t < T - \tau_1 < T$. The analytical pricing formula for front-month VT is given by

$$F_t^{VT,fm}(T) = \frac{1}{\tau_1} E_t^Q(v_{T-\tau_1,T})$$

$$= \left(1 - \frac{T-t}{\tau_1}\right) RUG_{T-\tau_1,t} + \left(\frac{T-t}{\tau_1}\right) IUG_{t,T}, \tag{7.2}$$

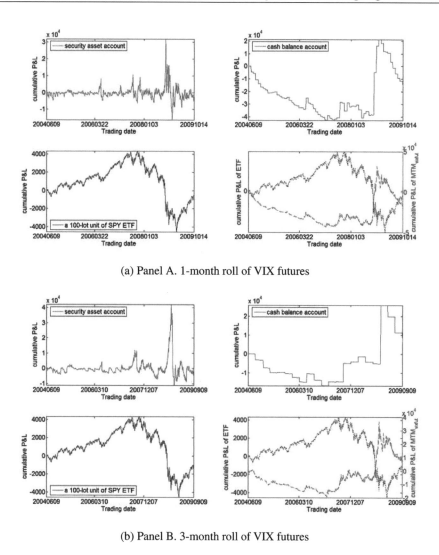

(a) Panel A. 1-month roll of VIX futures

(b) Panel B. 3-month roll of VIX futures

Figure 7.1: **Cumulative dollar P&Ls summing the Long ETF, Short VIX Futures and the Cash Account** – The 1-month rolling strategy in Panel A covers the period from June 10, 2004, to October 14, 2009, while the 3-month rolling strategy in Panel B is from June 10, 2004, to September 9, 2009. SPY ETFs are valued at one-tenth of the value of the SPX and are typically transacted in 100-lot (or "round-lot") increments. Since the study tries to figure out how many contracts of VIX futures are required to hedge a 100-lot unit of SPY ETF, a multiplier for adjusting the unit size and the unit dollar value is applied in the hedged portfolio. The notional size of the VIX futures is $1,000 per index point. MTM_{vixfut} is the sum of asset value and cash accounts on the VIX futures. The fourth subplot of each panel plots trading dates versus cumulative P&L of ETF with y-axis labeling on the left, and trading dates versus cumulative P&L of MTM_{vixfut} with y-axis labeling on the right.

where τ_1 is the total number of business days in the original term to expiration of the VT contract, t is current time, T is the final expiration date of the VT contract, and $0 < \frac{T-t}{\tau} < 1$. The annualized realized variance (RUG) is calculated as follows:[9]

$$RUG = 252 \times \left(\sum_{i=1}^{N_a-1} R_i^2 / (N_e - 1) \right), \tag{7.3}$$

where $R_i = \ln(P_{i+1}/P_i)$ is daily return of the S&P 500 from P_i to P_{i+1}; P_{i+1} is the final value of the S&P500 used to calculate the daily return, and; P_i is the initial value of the S&P 500 used to calculate the daily return.

Since the square of VIX (denoted by $VIX_{t,T}^2$) is defined as the variance swap rate, we are able to evaluate $VIX_{t,T}^2$ by computing the conditional expectation under the risk-neutral measure Q, as follows:

$$VIX_{t,T}^2 \equiv \frac{1}{T-t} E_t^Q (v_{t,T}) \tag{7.4}$$

Based on Eqs. (7.1)–(7.4), the IUG portion of a front-quarter VT contract can be replicated by $VIX_{t,T}^2$ extracted from $VIXTerm$ with identical days to maturity. In other words, we can synthesize the front-quarter VT with the following using notations from above:

$$F_t^{VT,fm} (T) = \left(1 - \frac{T-t}{\tau_1} \right) \times RUG_{T-\tau_1,t} + \left(\frac{T-t}{\tau_1} \right) \times VIX_{t,T}^2 \tag{7.5}$$

Since the market price of a forward-starting VT future completely attributes to IUG, this use case takes the initial *forward VIX* (denoted $fVIX$) curve implicit in $VIXTerm$ to synthesize the forward-starting VT price, i.e., for $\forall t \in [0, T - \tau_1]$,

$$F_t^{VT,fs} (T) = fVIX_{T-\tau_1,T}^2(t) \tag{7.6}$$

Specifically, the following equation uses historic $VIXTerm$ observations to compute a time series history of *forward VIX*^{2}:

$$fVIX_{T-\tau_1,T}^2 (t) = \frac{1}{\tau_1} \left[VIX_{t,T}^2 \times (T-t) - VIX_{t,T-\tau_1}^2 \times (T - \tau_1 - t) \right] \tag{7.7}$$

where $0 < t < T - \tau_1 < T$.

The following steps are used to construct the monthly rolling of VT. On day t, we take a long position of the synthetic forward-starting 1-month variance futures

---

[9]The RUG used in Eq. (7.2) is the RUG data available in the Chicago Futures Exchange website (http://cfe.cboe.com/education/VT_info.aspx), but divided by 10,000.

at the ask (where available) or synthetic ask price. For forward-starting contracts, the daily cumulative payoffs are calculated using midpoints of $fVIX^2_{T-\tau_1,T}(t)$ for $t < T - \tau_1$ based on Eq. (7.6), while for synthetic front-month contracts, we use $RUG_{T-\tau_0,t}$ and midpoints of $VIX^2_{t,T}$ for $T - \tau_1 \leq t < T$ based on Eq. (7.5). The contracts are then closed at their bid prices (where available) or synthetic bid prices on the second Friday of the contract month. On the next day, we buy back the next synthetic forward-starting 1-month variance futures at the asking price, and so on. The primary reason to roll the synthetic 1-month variance futures one week before expiration (on the third Friday of the contract month) is to ensure consistency with other rolling strategies used in this study. Figure 7.2 represents the *spot* and *forward* surfaces of *VIXTerm* midpoints with the axes representing the trading date and day to maturity over the period from June 14, 2004, to October 9, 2009.

Given the growth of the futures and options markets on the VIX, the CBOE has calculated daily historical values for *VIXTerm* dating back to 1992. *VIXTerm* is calculated by applying the VIX formula to specific SPX options to construct a term structure model of fair-value volatility. The generalized VIX formula has been modified to use the actual business days to expiration, allowing investors to track the SPX implied volatility using *VIXTerm* all the way back to 1992. *VIXTerm* of various maturities allows one to infer a complete initial term structure of *IUG* that is contemporaneous with the prices of variance futures of various maturities.

Figure 7.3 represents the price errors (PEs) between market VT and synthetic VT constructed from daily returns of the SPX and *VIXTerm* across the market close dates and VT maturities over the period from June 18, 2004, to October 21, 2009.

Detailed results, as tabulated in Table 7.1, give the summary statistics for the PEs. The median Midpoint value is -1.4238, with a standard deviation of 40.18 and t value of -1.29, which is not significantly different from zero at 95% confidence interval. By analyzing the distribution of the PEs on synthetic VT, the synthetic VT contracts were within 1.5 VIX-point PEs in 96.37% out of the 1,323 trading days for *VIXTerm* bid quotes, 99.02% for *VIXTerm* midpoints and 94.18% for *VIXTerm* ask quotes. This suggests that the synthetic VT contracts as computed from SPX options are generally consistent with the VT traders' thinking.

We observe pricing errors of up to 5.82% from *VIXTerm* ask quotes, which can be caused by the inaccuracy of synthetic *RUG* calculation from the lack of S&P 500 Special Opening Quotation ("SOQ") data.[10] In addition, for simplicity, N_e, or the number of expected S&P 500 values needed to calculate daily returns during the three-month period, is approximated by N_a, the actual number of S&P 500 values

---

[10]For purposes of calculating the settlement value, CFE calculates the three-month realized variance from a series of values of the S&P 500 beginning with the Special Opening Quotation ("SOQ") of the S&P 500 on the first day of the three-month period, and ending with the S&P 500 SOQ on the last day of the three-month period. All other values in the series are closing values of the S&P 500.

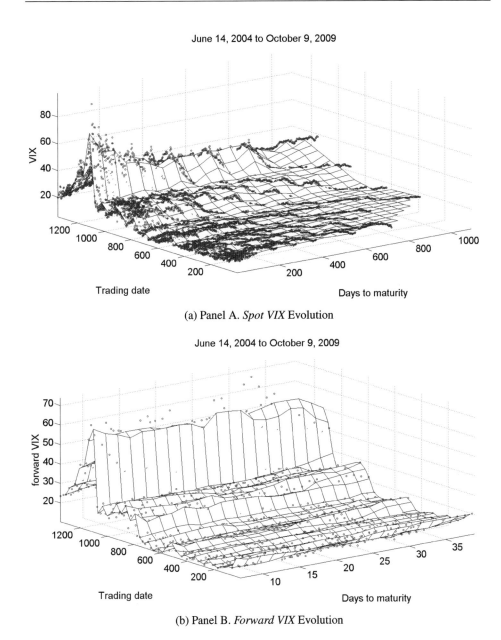

June 14, 2004 to October 9, 2009

(a) Panel A. *Spot VIX* Evolution

June 14, 2004 to October 9, 2009

(b) Panel B. *Forward VIX* Evolution

Figure 7.2: **VIXTerm evolution** – Panel A of this chart represents the *CBOE VIX Term Structure* midpoints as of the market close dates and days to VT maturities over the period from June 14, 2004, to October 9, 2009. The round markers indicate actual observations. Panel B represents the initial *forward* VIX as of the market close dates and days to nearby VT maturities. The round markers indicate actual *forward* VIX observations.

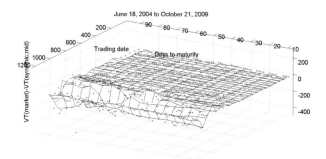

(a) Panel A1. Evolution of price differences between market VT and synthetic VT (Looking *Above* the 3D Surface)

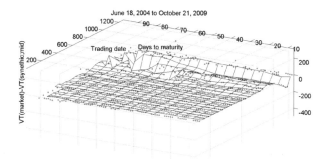

(b) Panel A2. Evolution of price differences between market VT and synthetic VT (Looking *Below* the 3D Surface)

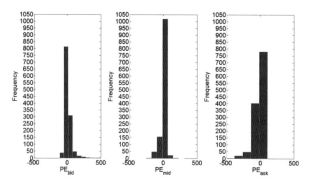

(c) Panel B. Histogram of price differences between market VT and synthetic VT

Figure 7.3: **Price differences between market VT and synthetic VT** – Panel A represents the price differences between market VT and synthetic VT, as constructed from daily returns of the SPX and *CBOE VIX Term Structure* midpoints across the market close dates and VT maturities over the period from June 14, 2004, to September 11, 2009. The round markers indicate actual observations. Panel B shows histograms of those pricing errors across bid, midpoint and ask quotes of CBOE VIX Term Structure.

Table 7.1: **The Distribution of Estimated Bid-Ask Spreads for Futures and Options** – This table provides summary statistics for estimated bid-ask spreads BA_{CS}, based on the high-low spread estimators (as described by [**Corwin 2010**]) for daily settlement prices of VIX futures and the 3-month VT. Daily bid and ask estimators $BA_{VIXTerm}$ of synthetic 1-month VT are constructed from the CBOE VIX Term Structure. Actual bid and ask prices BA_{Actual} for VIX futures, the 3-month VT, and 10% OTM SPX puts are obtained from Bloomberg and CBOE, respectively. Monthly-rolling daily spread estimates are calculated for the full sample period from June 2004, through October 2009, while quarterly-rolling daily spreads are computed for the full sample period from June 2004 through September 2009. The spread estimates for the Financial Crisis period triggered by the bankruptcy of Lehman Brothers are also separately tabulated in Panel B. The VIX futures contract is based on $1,000 times the VIX index. The VT contract's multiplier is $50 per variance point. SPX options are quoted $100 per point. The figure in parentheses is a spread of s%, of which actual/estimated bid-ask spreads equal s% times daily settlement prices of VIX and VT future, or the midpoints of SPX puts.

Bid-ask spread (%)		Monthly Rolling			Quarterly Rolling		
		VIX futures	Synthetic 1-month VT	10% OTM SPX puts	VIX futures	3-month VT	10% OTM SPX puts
Panel A. Full Sample							
N	BA_{Actual}	1,347	NA	1,342	1,322	1,323	1,323
	BA_{CS}	1,347	NA	NA	1,322	1,323	NA
	$BA_{VIXTerm}$	NA	1,342	NA	NA	NA	NA
M	BA_{Actual}	$109.70	NA	$59.09	$128.49	$2,070.97	$99.07
		(0.60%)		(75.72%)	(0.65%)	(8.35%)	(37.32%)
	BA_{CS}	337.41	NA	NA	262.94	1,596.83	NA
		(1.34)			(1.05)	(5.24)	
	$BA_{VIXTerm}$	NA	$3,898.52	NA	NA	NA	NA
			(14.62%)				
Mdn	BA_{Actual}	90.00	NA	30.00	100.00	750.00	55.00
		(0.48)		(53.06)	(0.56)	(7.25)	(18.75)
	BA_{CS}	157.76	NA	NA	127.05	425.00	NA
		(0.95)			(0.72)	(3.72)	
	$BA_{VIXTerm}$	NA	1,517.05	NA	NA	NA	NA
			(14.39)				
Max	BA_{Actual}	990.00	NA	1,470.00	1,650.00	25,000.00	1,500.00
		(2.46)		(200.00)	(11.10)	(43.28)	(200.00)
	BA_{CS}	4,922.70	NA	NA	4,284.70	43,875.00	NA
		(16.48)			(9.51)	(140.71)	
	$BA_{VIXTerm}$	NA	97,974.12	NA	NA	NA	NA
			(56.44)				
Min	BA_{Actual}	10.00	NA	5.00	10.00	50.00	5.00
		(0.02)		(1.74)	(0.02)	(0.35)	(1.60)
	BA_{CS}	0.12	NA	NA	0.09	0.00	NA
		(0.00)			(0.00)	(0.00)	
	$BA_{VIXTerm}$	NA	197.19	NA	NA	NA	NA
			(2.41)				
STD	BA_{Actual}	85.70	NA	117.20	107.03	3,053.77	137.70
		(0.42)		(63.66)	(0.50)	(5.08)	(47.03)
	BA_{CS}	506.63	NA	NA	393.34	3,841.03	NA
		(1.34)			(1.07)	(6.35)	
	$BA_{VIXTerm}$	NA	7,960.01	NA	NA	NA	NA
			(5.27)				

Skewness	BA_{Actual}	3.00 (0.99)	NA	5.84 (0.91)	5.03 (7.56)	2.66 (2.01)	3.82 (2.44)
	BA_{CS}	3.71 (2.89)	NA	NA	3.78 (2.31)	5.54 (9.20)	NA
	$BA_{VIXTerm}$	NA	5.79 (0.79)	NA	NA	NA	NA
Kurtosis	BA_{Actual}	19.69 (3.46)	NA	47.36 (2.50)	52.52 (144.57)	11.71 (8.51)	25.14 (8.36)
	BA_{CS}	21.82 (19.84)	NA	NA	23.08 (10.41)	41.75 (174.40)	NA
	$BA_{VIXTerm}$	NA	47.90 (6.25)	NA	NA	NA	NA

Panel B. Lehman Brothers Bankruptcy (September 2008 − December 2008)

N	BA_{Actual}	76	NA	76	76	76	76
	BA_{CS}	76	NA	NA	76	76	NA
	$BA_{VIXTerm}$	NA	76	NA	NA	NA	NA
M	BA_{Actual}	254.61 (0.52)	NA	397.08 (23.40)	246.18 (0.58)	8,914.67 (5.16)	439.19 (25.93)
	BA_{CS}	1,348.14 (2.84)	NA	NA	953.41 (2.19)	10,603.05 (6.44)	NA
	$BA_{VIXTerm}$	NA	26,887.52 (16.69)	NA	NA	NA	NA
Mdn	BA_{Actual}	230.00 (0.45)	NA	400.00 (16.28)	190.00 (0.45)	8,750.00 (4.97)	410.00 (15.03)
	BA_{CS}	1,025.15 (2.54)	NA	NA	625.00 (2.00)	7,475.00 (4.30)	NA
	$BA_{VIXTerm}$	NA	19,984.64 (15.50)	NA	NA	NA	NA
Max	BA_{Actual}	990.00 (1.75)	NA	1,470.00 (200.00)	1,350.00 (2.55)	25,000.00 (11.61)	1,500.00 (200.00)
	BA_{CS}	4,922.70 (8.39)	NA	NA	4,284.70 (6.47)	43,875.00 (37.29)	NA
	$BA_{VIXTerm}$	NA	97,974.12 (56.44)	NA	NA	NA	NA
Min	BA_{Actual}	10.00 (0.02)	NA	10.00 (4.38)	10.00 (0.02)	250.00 (0.73)	10.00 (5.67)
	BA_{CS}	10.00 (0.02)	NA	NA	13.29 (0.04)	0.00 (0.00)	NA
	$BA_{VIXTerm}$	NA	5,214.95 (2.76)	NA	NA	NA	NA
STD	BA_{Actual}	196.49 (0.38)	NA	304.15 (27.60)	218.56 (0.51)	4,989.16 (2.15)	297.89 (36.57)
	BA_{CS}	1,107.31 (2.23)	NA	NA	871.19 (1.71)	10,188.15 (6.24)	NA
	$BA_{VIXTerm}$	NA	19,371.58 (9.19)	NA	NA	NA	NA
Skewness	BA_{Actual}	1.10 (0.97)	NA	1.14 (4.35)	2.03 (1.61)	0.62 (0.53)	1.02 (3.63)
	BA_{CS}	0.96 (0.73)	NA	NA	1.19 (0.53)	1.24 (2.07)	NA
	$BA_{VIXTerm}$	NA	1.71 (1.30)	NA	NA	NA	NA
Kurtosis	BA_{Actual}	4.29 (3.53)	NA	4.45 (25.79)	9.88 (5.86)	3.93 (3.22)	4.76 (16.21)
	BA_{CS}	3.53 (2.68)	NA	NA	4.39 (2.20)	3.96 (9.72)	NA
	$BA_{VIXTerm}$	NA	5.69 (6.04)	NA	NA	NA	NA

Table 7.2: **Summary Statistics of Price Differences between Real-Market and Synthetic 3-Month Variance Futures (VT)** – Summary statistics for price differences between market VT and synthetic VT that is calculated from daily returns of the S&P 500 index, and the CBOE VIX Term Structure Bids, Asks, and Midpoints. The sample covers the period from June 14, 2004, to September 11, 2009. Defining $F_t^{synthetic\ VT}(T) = \left(1 - \frac{T-t}{\tau_1}\right) RUG_{T-\tau_1}^{Synthetic} + \left(\frac{T-t}{\tau_1}\right) VIX_{t,T,bid}^2$, these are given as the bid pricing error: $PE_{bid} = F_t^{Market\ VT}(T) - F_t^{synthetic\ VT}(T)$, where $VIX_{t,T,bid}$ is the bid quotation of CBOE VIX Term Structure with comparable days to expiration and $RUG_{T-\tau_1}^{Synthetic}$ is realized variance implicit in the daily returns of the S&P 500 index. Similarly, PE_{mid} and PE_{ask} are calculated from midpoints $VIX_{t,T}^{mid}$ and ask quotes $VIX_{t,T}^{ask}$, respectively. The unit of PE is the annualized variance point multiplied by 10000. For example, on March 4, 2005, the front-month VT contract had 10 business days remaining until settlement. The RUG reported by CFE that evening was 94.97 and the VT daily settlement price was 99.50. Using the above formula, we can calculate the implied forward variance (IUG) for the remaining ten days. IUG=123.06. Taking the square root of the IUG, one finds the futures price is implying an annualized S&P 500 return standard deviation or volatility of 11.09% over the next ten days. On March 4, 2005, the bid, midpoint and ask quotes of front-month CBOE VIX Term Structure are 10.96, 11.51 and 12.04, respectively, which give us an estimate of 120.122, 132.480 and 144.962 for IUG.

Synthetic Errors	PE_{bid}	PE_{mid}	PE_{ask}
Sample size	1323	1323	1323
M	24.7233	−3.8346	−32.3176
Mdn	8.5006	−1.4238	−12.8784
Maximum	542.3729	310.0932	105.2920
Minimum	−114.3666	−494.9200	−1125.9654
SE	62.4415	40.1845	71.5199
Q1	2.9785	−8.5093	−26.9828
Q3	26.7968	3.5121	−4.8220
Skewness	4.1088	−1.8077	−5.3837
Kurtosis	27.2165	29.2939	55.1695

used to calculate daily returns during the three-month period. The discrepancies between market VT and synthetic VT could also be primarily a function of relative liquidity in these two markets, given that VIX futures would keep trading because it is a lot more liquid, while we may observe "stale" quotes in VT.

Panel A of Figure 7.4 presents the cumulative P&L of a monthly rolling strategy of long synthetic 1-month variance futures. Prior to the Financial Crisis, we do not observe any "rough mirror image" resemblance between the red line and the blue line in the lower right-hand-corner graph, but that becomes the observation after the Financial Crisis.

7.2.2.2   Algorithm for 3-Month Rolls of 3-Month Variance Futures

The 3-month rolls of VT are rolled at the fifth business day before the expiration day. In other words, we roll on the second Friday of the contract month (i.e., five trading days ahead) to avoid any liquidity issues due to contract expiration. The following steps are used to construct the quarterly rolling of VT. On day t, we take a second nearby VT contract at the ask (where available) or synthetic ask price. Since the ask prices at the opening of the market are not available to our study, we use the opening prices plus half of the bid-ask spreads. The daily cumulative payoffs are calculated using daily settlement prices. The contracts are then closed at their bid prices (where available) or synthetic bid prices on the second Friday of the contract month. On the next day, we buy back the next second-nearby VT at the synthetic ask price, and so on.

Panel B of Figure 7.4 presents the cumulative gain and loss of a 3-month rolling strategy of long VT. Price data on the VT come from the transaction records provided by the CFE. Once again, prior to the Financial Crisis, we do not observe any "rough mirror image" resemblance between the red line and the blue line in the lower right-hand-corner graph, but that becomes the observation after the Financial Crisis.

7.2.3   OTM Put Options on SPX

The monthly series of out-of-the-money (OTM) SPX put options[11] are created by purchasing 5% (or 10%) OTM SPX puts monthly one month prior to their expiration. Given SPX options' low liquidity relative to that of the volatility derivatives market and the significant bid/ask spread in the options market, we will let any purchased options expire instead of trying to roll them forward, consistent with trading practice in the real world.

The monthly series of out-of-the-money (OTM) SPX put options are created by purchasing 5% (or 10%) OTM SPX puts one month prior to their expiration. In

---

[11]Some may argue that the SPY options should be used instead of the CBOE SPX options since the former is more liquid. However, the CBOE SPX options tend to be traded by institutions at larger sizes and therefore they are generally more consistent with the objective of this use case.

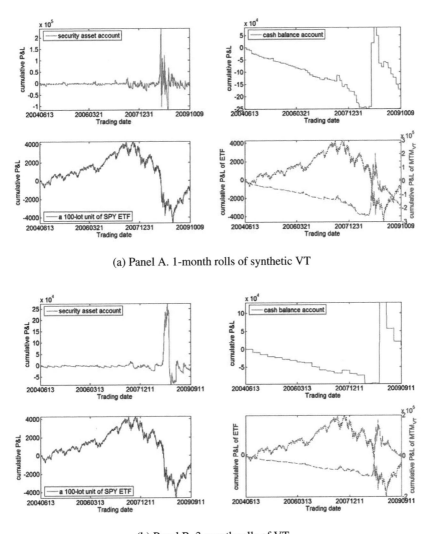

(a) Panel A. 1-month rolls of synthetic VT

(b) Panel B. 3-month rolls of VT

Figure 7.4: **Dollar P&Ls of the ETF, VT and cash balance account** – The 1-month roll strategy in Panel A covers the period from June 14, 2004, to October 9, 2009, while the 3-month roll strategy in Panel B is from June 14, 2004, to September 11, 2009. SPY ETFs are 1/10th of the value of the SPX and are typically traded in 100 "round-lots". Since the study aims to identify the number of contracts of VT required to hedge a 100-lot unit of SPY ETF, a multiplier for adjusting the unit size and unit dollar value, is applied to the hedged portfolio. The VT contract's multiplier is $50 per variance point. MTM_{VT} is the cumulative mark-to-market value of the asset and cash accounts of VT. The fourth subplot of each panel plots trading dates versus cumulative P&L of ETF with y-axis labeling on the left, and trading dates versus cumulative P&L of MTM_{VT} with y-axis labeling on the right.

real-life trading, longer-dated options are usually rolled up (by paying an additional premium) or rolled down (i.e. monetizing earned premium) with significant market moves. However, given the average maturity of the options in the series is only about 10 trading days, it is unlikely that they will be rolled them up or down in real life trading in view of the significant trading costs involved.

This use case accounts for the option premia in SPX put options primarily by using the "burn rate" (which can be thought of as a form of daily theta) implied by option premia.[12] Although an investor pays upfront cash for the premium, his mark-to-market value (MTM) at the end of the day is his negative cash position paid plus the value of his option. The act of purchasing the option in itself should not create any P&L shock. The interest charges are also ignored to simplify the analysis.[13] In general, the strategy is expected to maintain a negative cash balance until the option strategy generates enough profits to cover the outstanding debt. The P&L should be based on a sum of the cash borrowed to finance the positions and P&L from the option itself. One does not expect to see any negative value representing the entire option premium, unless the option expires at less than the original premium paid plus any interest cost, or unless the option position has lost most of its intrinsic value.[14]

Suppose a put option is purchased at regular intervals of length $\triangle t$. As described above, at time t we short an instantaneously maturing risk-free bond $B(t)$ to raise cash and then purchase a put option $Put(t, t + \triangle t)$ of maturity $\triangle t$, such that the net P&L at time t is zero. In other words, the combined position is a self-financed portfolio: The investor borrows cash in order to finance the purchase of the option, such that $B(t) = Put(t, t + \triangle t)$. Accordingly, interest based on a deterministic continuously compounded rate $R(t)$ should be paid when money is borrowed to

---

[12]Suppose that the investor has a securities account. He has to count both his asset and liability columns when computing his P&L. On day t he buys an option: the cash account is $-Put(t)$ while the asset account is $+Put(t)$. If he sells the option right away, the net account on day t is back at 0 P&L. On day $t + 1$, if the price of the underlying has not changed, the cash account remains at $-Put(t)$ and asset account at $Put(t + 1) = Put(t) - one \ day \ of \ theta$. Thus, *net P&L* on day $t + 1$ is equal to *one day of theta*. If the option expires worthless, his cumulative P&L become $-Put(t) - cumulative \ interest$ only at the expiration day. In other words, while he has already paid upfront cash for the option on day t, the full negative P&L for the option premium usually does not manifest itself until the expiration day.

[13]While small initially, interest rate charges can become quite significant over time, thus one may argue that there is a need to account for it as part of the cost of running a hedging strategy. However, both the negative carry in the volatility and variance futures and the premium in SPX options will run up identical financing costs if they have the same negative P&L, hedging effectiveness can be compared on an "apple-to-apple" basis without accounting for the interest rate charges.

[14] Some researchers treat the option premium as a negative P&L because "money is paid" upfront. Doing so results in a large P&L shock when the option is paid. Technically, that seems incorrect because one can buy the option in the morning and sell it in the afternoon. Thus, no P&L changes should be recorded for that day as long as the price of the option stays the same.

purchase the option. At time $t + \Delta t$, the mark-to-market value (MTM) of the self-financed portfolio is given as follows:

$$MTM(t + \Delta t) = Put(t, t + \Delta t) - B(t)e^{R(t)\Delta t}$$

where $B(t) = Put(t, t + \Delta t)$. We can repeat this net P&L calculation at time $t + l\Delta t$, where $l = 1, 2, 3, \dots$. The MTM value at time $(t + l\Delta t)$ of the $(l-1)$-th put strategy is given by

$$MTM(t + l\Delta t) = Put(t + (l-1)\Delta t, t + l\Delta t) -$$

$$Put(t + (l-1)\Delta t, t + (l-1)\Delta t)e^{R(t+(l-1)\Delta t) \times \Delta t}$$

The use case utilizes the formula above to estimate the P&L of a mechanical rolling strategy of buying one option and rolling it forward every month. The use case then runs statistics to estimate the appropriate hedging ratio each month by minimizing residuals (or other relevant alternative objective functions).

Since bids and asks right before expiration often do not reflect actual tradable values of the option, it is more reliable to use the exercise value of the option at the expiration date. Once a settlement price is published on a specific contract month, the movement of that put no longer reflects changes in the value of the underlying index; i.e., it is going into "settlement mode". Accordingly, we initiate a new contract on its expiration day to maintain the hedge. Typically, execution traders will be given at least one trading session to "build" a new position. To reflect real-world conditions, our use case initiates a new 5% (or 10%) OTM put a contract on the same trading day using closing prices. If the option expires in the money, one should include the exercise value into the cumulative P&L, i.e., one receives cash into the cash account if the option expires in the money. There is no value left in the option if it expires out of the money. Any interest receipts (charges) from the current period also become part of the positive (negative) P&L for the *next* period. Assuming that one put option expires on each Δt-interval, $Put(t + (l-1)\Delta t, t + l\Delta t) = (K(t + (l-1)\Delta t) - S(t + l\Delta t))^+$, where the final index settlement value is $S(t + l\Delta t)$ at expiration time $t + l\Delta t$ and the strike price is $K(t + (l-1)\Delta t)$.

The mark-to-market value for the put option on its first trading day $t + \Delta t + 1$ of the second rolling month will depend on whether interest charges (surpluses) from the first period will become part of the negative (positive) P&L for the second period.

Figure 7.5 presents the cumulative P&L of both the 1-month (Panel A) and 3-month (Panel B) rolling strategies using OTM SPX puts. Before the 2008 Financial Crisis, we observe a straight line representing the negative carry of any long-option

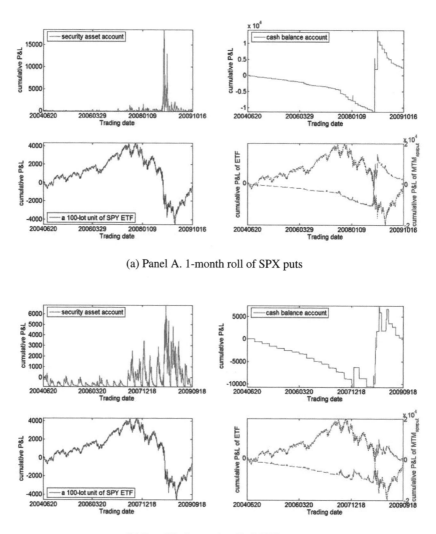

(a) Panel A. 1-month roll of SPX puts

(b) Panel B. 3-month roll of SPX puts

Figure 7.5: **Cumulative dollar P&Ls summing ETF, SPX puts and Cash Balance** – The 1-month roll strategy in Panel A covers the period from June 21, 2004, to October 16, 2009, while the 3-month roll strategy in Panel B is from June 21, 2004, to September 18, 2009. SPY ETFs are valued at one-tenth of the value of the SPX and are traded in 100 "round-lots". Since the study tries to figure out how many contracts of SPX puts are required to hedge a 100-lot unit of SPY ETF, a multiplier for adjusting unit size and unit dollar value is applied in the hedged portfolio. SPX options are traded $100 per point. MTM_{spxput} is the cumulative mark-to-market value of the asset and cash accounts of SPX puts. The fourth subplot of each panel plots trading dates versus cumulative P&L of ETF with y-axis labeling on the left, and trading dates versus cumulative P&L of MTM_{spxput} with y-axis labeling on the right.

strategy, with the line becomes steeper as we approach the Financial Crisis consistent with a steady increase in implied volatility toward the Financial Crisis. After the Financial Crisis, we observe the "rough mirror image" resemblance between the red line and the blue line in the lower right-hand-corner graph for SPX options. The upside for the 3-month roll is less impressive than that for the 1-month roll. This is not surprising since markets often recover after major shocks, translating into fewer opportunities to lock in profits with the 3-month roll.

7.3 Hedging Performance

7.3.1 1-Month VIX Futures

The use case conducts the empirical hedging analysis based on the seven different hedging methodologies as described in Section 4.2, by using VIX futures as a hedge to one unit of the SPX index. The rebalancing, done every month, takes place five business days prior to the expiration of the VIX futures to avoid well-known liquidity problems in the last week of trading of futures contracts. The use case focuses on a one-month out-of-sample hedging horizon, using data for the period December 2004 through March 2010. Hedge effectiveness is measured based on the magnitude of percentage drawdown reduction from before the hedge to after the hedge:

$$MaxDD\% \left(T; MTM^{before\ hedge} \right) - MaxDD\% \left(T; MTM^{after\ hedge} \right)$$

where $MTM^{before\ hedge} = \$10 \times SPX$; $MTM^{after\ hedge} = \$10 \times SPX + h \times \$1000 \times fvixfut_{cumP\&L}$; and $MaxDD\%(T; \cdot)$ is defined as the maximum peak to trough decline (before the next peak) for the period $[0, T]$, which is an empirical measure of the loss arising from potential extreme events preferred by the industry. We use the percentage Maximum Drawdown in this case, which is calculated as the percentage drop from the peak to the trough as measured from the peak:

$$MaxDD\% \left(T; \{MTM\}_{t=0}^{T} \right) = \max_{0 \leq t \leq T} \left[\frac{MTM_{0 \leq \tau \leq t}^{peak} - MTM(t)}{MTM_{0 \leq \tau \leq t}^{peak}} \right]$$

The graphical results are plotted in Figure 7.6. Descriptive statistics on both the unhedged and hedged profits and losses (P&Ls) are also reported in Panel A of Table 7.3, to follow:

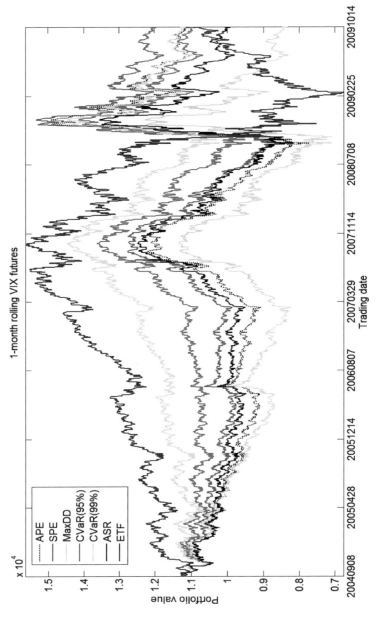

Figure 7.6: **VIX Futures 1-Month Rolling Contracts (8 Sep 2004 – 14 Oct 2009)** – The ETF line is the unhedged dollar MTM of one 100-lot basket of the S&P500. The APE line is the hedged MTM by minimizing the sum of absolute residuals. The SPE line is the hedged MTM by minimizing the sum of squared residuals. MaxDD is the hedged MTM by minimizing maximum drawdown. The CVaR(95%) and CVaR(99%) lines represent the hedged MTM by minimizing the Cornish-Fisher CVaR at 95% and 99% statistical confidence, respectively. Finally, the ASR line is the hedged MTM by maximizing the Alternative Sharpe Ratio of the hedged portfolio.

Table 7.3: **Descriptive Statistics on Hedging** – The first row gives the descriptive statistics on the unhedged SPX ETF. The remaining rows give the descriptive statistics on the hedged P&L under the seven different models used, ranked by the maximum drawdown reduction starting from the most effective hedging model. Panels A, B, C and D provide summary statistics on hedging with 1-month rolling VIX futures, 1-month rolling VT futures, 1-month rolling 5% OTM SPX puts and 1-month rolling 10% OTM SPX puts, respectively.

	N	Mean	Median	Max	Min	Stddev	Skew	E Kurt	%MaxDD	MaxDD %Red
Panel A. 1-Month Rolling VIX Futures										
Unhedged Daily P&L of SPX	1832	33.46	54.91	370.50	-518.12	175.15	-0.60	0.17	37.19	NA
Hedged P&L of CVaR (99%)	1832	90.14	69.85	397.94	-120.10	118.96	0.55	-0.37	33.31	3.88
Hedged P&L of Squared Residuals	1832	105.39	106.32	347.04	-184.19	108.10	0.06	-0.58	29.05	8.14
Hedged P&L of CVaR (95%)	1832	100.67	67.23	338.42	-135.87	117.01	0.25	-1.17	28.33	8.86
Hedged P&L of Absolute Residuals	1832	-6.03	-67.93	327.91	-421.79	172.36	0.04	-0.96	27.45	9.74
Hedged P&L of SR	1832	50.29	42.43	305.80	-264.12	108.40	-0.03	0.04	25.60	11.59
Hedged P&L of ASR	1832	55.76	44.00	303.52	-220.05	99.91	0.14	0.07	25.41	11.78
Hedged P&L of Max Drawdown	1832	-32.16	-19.66	168.02	-371.56	106.84	-0.71	0.22	14.06	23.13
Panel B. 1-Month Rolling VT Futures										
Unhedged Daily P&L of SPX	1832	33.46	54.91	370.50	-518.12	175.15	-0.60	0.17	37.19	NA
Hedged P&L of CVaR (95%)	1832	115.92	75.18	873.64	-143.36	159.83	1.55	4.01	73.13	-35.94
Hedged P&L of CVaR (99%)	1832	105.39	75.75	873.64	-122.26	152.81	1.85	5.61	73.13	-35.94
Hedged P&L of Squared Residuals	1832	108.40	86.31	733.45	-206.83	159.03	0.80	0.93	61.39	-24.20
Hedged P&L of Absolute Residuals	1832	63.68	62.45	488.34	-311.08	146.54	0.09	-0.16	40.88	-3.69
Hedged P&L of Max Drawdown	1832	75.78	58.84	354.95	-243.23	109.82	0.24	-0.13	29.71	7.48
Hedged P&L of ASR	1832	45.33	39.50	334.25	-193.98	72.49	0.19	0.30	27.98	9.21
Hedged P&L of SR	1832	73.06	54.37	320.48	-151.42	95.39	0.55	-0.36	26.83	10.36

Note the following technical points: First, all mark-to-market value (MTM) time series is starting at the *unhedged* value of one unit of the SPX index at the beginning of the empirical analysis, from December 2004 to March 2011, covering a period of extreme volatility due to the bankruptcy of Lehman Brothers. The in-sample data period allows for the use of roughly 2 months of data to estimate the first out-of-sample hedging ratio. Second, the summary statistics are computed based on raw daily P&Ls, without any time rescaling. Third, the maximum drawdown is computed based on the percentage drop from the peak to the trough as measured from the peak. Finally, in this specific analysis, we have computed the Cornish-Fisher CVaR at 95% and 99% confidence, but have noticed minimal differences between the two choices. One may conclude from the statistical results that:

1. Minimizing Cornish-Fisher CVaR is not effective in minimizing maximum drawdown. In addition, "second-order techniques" such as minimizing absolute residuals and squared residuals have not shown particularly effective performance as extreme downside hedges.
2. Although minimizing maximum drawdown is effective in reducing maximum drawdown, its overall performance in offering protection during a drawdown scenario without incurring unreasonable cost is less than impressive. This is not surprising considering the "look back" nature of maximum drawdown as a risk measure. It is generally believed that, under this method, one can only compute the correct hedging ratio after a significant drawdown has already happened. By then, the hedge is put on only when it is no longer needed while incurring heavy losses when the hedging instrument is "recoiling" its P&L.
3. Both the Sharpe Ratio and Alternative Sharpe Ratio perform reasonably as an objective function for extreme downside hedges.

7.3.2   3-Month Variance Futures

This subsection conducts the empirical hedging analysis based on the seven different hedging methodologies as described above, by using VT futures as a hedge to one unit of the SPX index. As described in Section 7.3.2, the contracts are rolled forward every quarter, but the hedging ratio is recomputed monthly. The graphical results are shown in Figure 7.8.

The standard descriptive statistics on both the unhedged and hedged profits and losses (P&Ls) are reported in Panel B of Table 7.3. Note the following technical points: First, all mark-to-market value (MTM) time series is starting at the *unhedged* value of one unit of the SPX index at the beginning of the empirical analysis, from December 2004 to March 2011, covering a period of extreme volatility due to

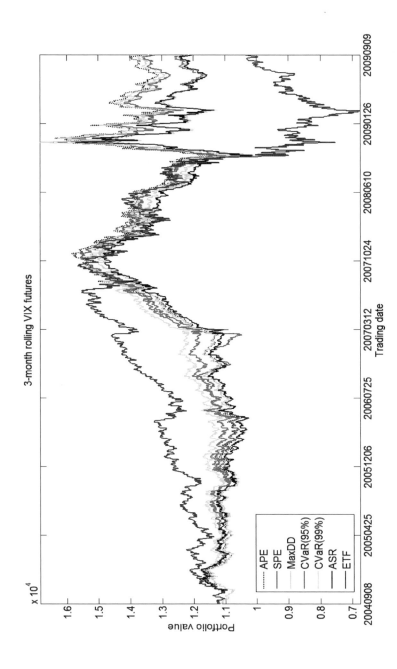

Figure 7.7: **VIX Futures 3-Month Rolling Contracts (September 8, 2004, to September 9, 2009)** – The ETF line is the unhedged dollar MTM of one 100-lot basket of the S&P500. The APE line is the hedged MTM by minimizing the sum of absolute residuals. The SPE line is the hedged MTM by minimizing the sum of squared residuals. MaxDD is the hedged MTM by minimizing maximum drawdown. The CVaR(95%) and CVaR(99%) lines represent the hedged MTM by minimizing the Cornish-Fisher CVaR at 95% and 99% statistical confidence, respectively. Finally, the ASR line is the hedged MTM by maximizing the Alternative Sharpe Ratio of the hedged portfolio.

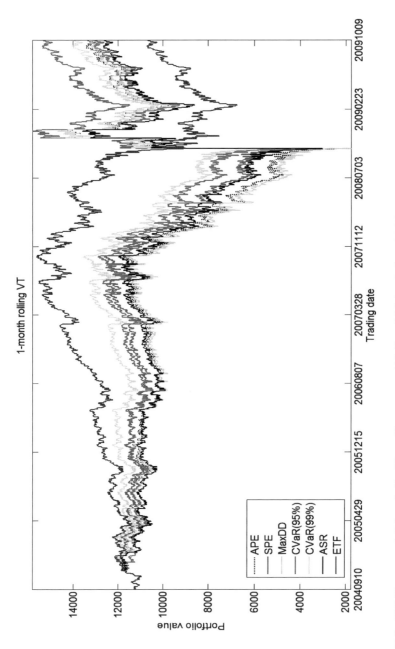

Figure 7.8: **VT Futures 1-Month Rolling Contracts (10 Sep 2004 – 9 Oct 2009)** – The ETF line is the unhedged dollar MTM of one 100-lot basket of the S&P500. The APE line is the hedged MTM by minimizing the sum of absolute residuals. The SPE line is the hedged MTM by minimizing the sum of squared residuals. MaxDD is the hedged MTM by minimizing maximum drawdown. The CVaR(95%) and CVaR(99%) lines represent the hedged MTM by minimizing the Cornish-Fisher expansion CVaR at 95% and 99% statistical confidence, respectively. Finally, the ASR line is the hedged MTM by maximizing the Alternative Sharpe Ratio of the hedged portfolio.

the bankruptcy of Lehman Brothers. The in-sample data period allows for the use of roughly 2 months of data to estimate the first out-of-sample hedging ratio. Second, summary statistics are computed based on raw daily P&Ls, without any time rescaling. Third, maximum drawdown is computed based on the percentage drop from the peak to the trough as measured from the peak. Finally, in this specific analysis, we have computed the Cornish-Fisher CVaR at 95% and 99%, but have noticed minimal differences between the two choices. One may conclude from the statistical results that:

1. Minimizing Cornish-Fisher CVaR is not effective in minimizing maximum drawdown. In addition, "second-order techniques" such as minimizing absolute residuals and squared residuals have not shown particularly effective performance as extreme downside hedges.
2. Minimizing maximum drawdown, maximizing Sharpe Ratio as well as maximizing the Alternative Sharpe Ratio are roughly similar in effectiveness in reducing maximum drawdown. However, in this case, minimizing maximum drawdown and maximizing Sharpe Ratio both give better performance in preserving upside.
3. In all cases, the trader ends up better off in the end by not hedging.

The practical issue with using the VT is that its implied negative carry costs can be very high. This implied negative carry is caused by the significant burn rate on the premia of options used to replicate the variance futures. Because VT is the square of the VIX, when the strategy benefits from the upside of VT, there can be a dramatic improvement to portfolio performance. In fact, the impressive surge followed by the expected "recoil" has resulted in a potential increase in maximum drawdown for some hedging models tested. It is quite likely that such an extreme swing, as well as the contract's low volatility, will deter real-life traders from using VT as a practical hedging solution.

7.3.3   1-Month OTM Put Options on SPX

This section conducts the out-of-sample hedging analysis based on the five different hedging methodologies as described above, by using 5% (and 10%) OTM SPX puts as a hedge to one 100-lot unit of the S&P500 ETF. The algorithm for creating the monthly rolls of synthetic 1-month SPX puts has been described in Section 7.3.3. The graphical results are plotted in Figures 7.9 and 7.10 for 5% OTM SPX puts, and in Figures 7.11 and 7.12 for 10% OTM SPX puts, to follow:

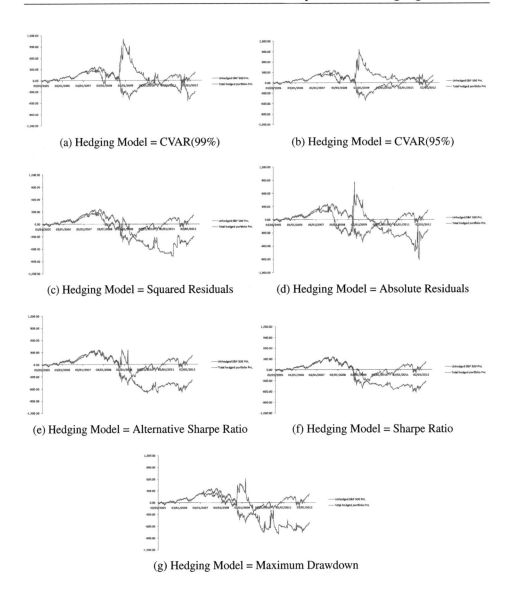

(a) Hedging Model = CVAR(99%)   (b) Hedging Model = CVAR(95%)

(c) Hedging Model = Squared Residuals   (d) Hedging Model = Absolute Residuals

(e) Hedging Model = Alternative Sharpe Ratio   (f) Hedging Model = Sharpe Ratio

(g) Hedging Model = Maximum Drawdown

Figure 7.9: **5% OTM SPX Put Options 1-Month Rolling Contracts (Dec 2004 – Mar 2011) by Different Hedging Models**

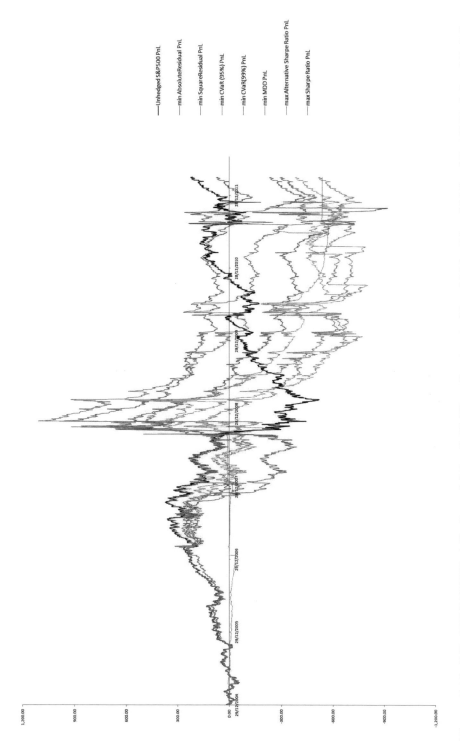

Figure 7.10: **5% OTM SPX Put Options 1-Month Rolling Contracts (Dec 2004 – Mar 2011) with All Hedging Models**

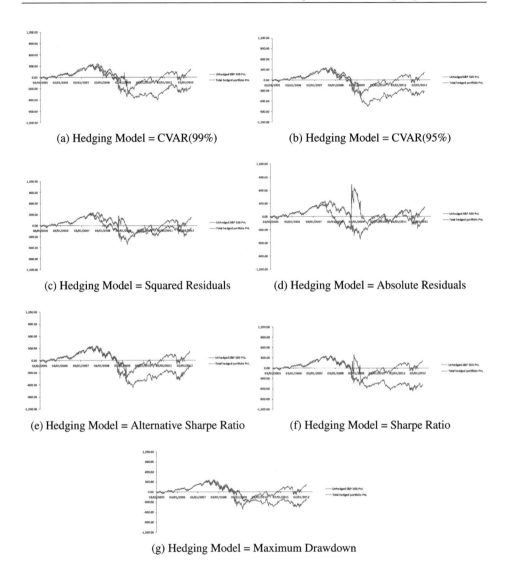

(a) Hedging Model = CVAR(99%)   (b) Hedging Model = CVAR(95%)

(c) Hedging Model = Squared Residuals   (d) Hedging Model = Absolute Residuals

(e) Hedging Model = Alternative Sharpe Ratio   (f) Hedging Model = Sharpe Ratio

(g) Hedging Model = Maximum Drawdown

Figure 7.11: **10% OTM SPX Put Options 1-Month Rolling Contracts (Dec 2004 – Mar 2011) by Different Hedging Models**

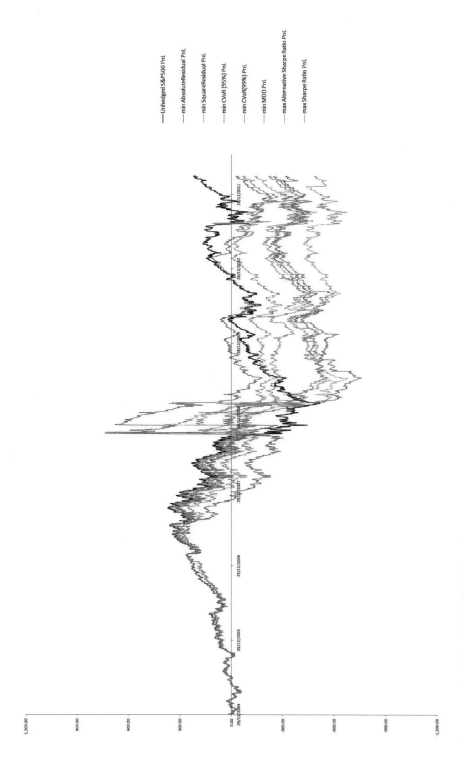

Figure 7.12: 10% OTM SPX Put Options 1-Month Rolling Contracts (Dec 2004 – Mar 2011) with All Hedging Models

The standard descriptive statistics on both the unhedged and hedged profits and losses (P&Ls) in Panels C and D of Table 7.3. Note the following technical points: First, all mark-to-market value (*MTM*) time series is starting at the *unhedged* value of one unit of the SPX index at the beginning of the empirical analysis, from December 2004 to March 2011, covering a period of extreme volatility due to the bankruptcy of Lehman Brothers. The in-sample data period allows for the use of roughly 2 months of data to estimate the first out-of-sample hedging ratio. Second, summary statistics are computed based on raw daily P&Ls, without any time rescaling. Third, maximum drawdown is computed based on the percentage drop from the peak to the trough as measured from the peak. Finally, in this specific analysis, we have computed the Cornish-Fisher CVaR at 95% and 99%, but have noticed minimal differences between the two choices. One may conclude from the statistical results that:

1. In general, all hedging schemes produce low hedging ratios in an upmarket and provide very reasonable protection during extreme events.
2. After an extreme event, all hedging schemes produce significantly higher hedging ratios, resulting in rather poor performance when the market recovers.
3. In all cases, the trader ends up better off by not hedging.

Monthly 10% OTM SPX puts go into the money roughly about once every decade. Very often, extreme downside hedges are costly propositions due to the constant need to pay premia without benefiting from any payoff, especially when market volatility shoots up (thereby increasing the costs of the options), but the net return to the portfolio manager (even after the option goes into money) is still far from sufficient to cover the cumulative option premia over time. Monthly 5% OTM SPX puts go into the money more often but they are also more expensive. Because of the steep premia of OTM puts, many portfolio managers either (i) underhedged with a smaller than suitable notional amount or (ii) use options further out of the money, potentially lowering the payoff when protection is needed the most. Based on our analysis, the observed burn rate is roughly 20% per year before the Financial Crisis, which likely deters to any real-life traders from using such an instrument as a practical hedging solution.

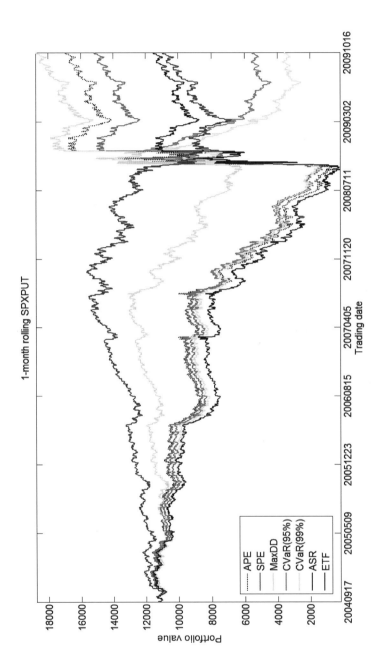

Figure 7.13: **SPX Put Options 1-Month Rolling Contracts (21 Jun 2004 – 16 Oct 2009)** – The ETF line is the unhedged dollar MTM of one 100-lot basket of the S&P500. The APE line is the hedged MTM by minimizing the sum of absolute residuals. The SPE line is the hedged MTM by minimizing the sum of squared residuals. MaxDD is the hedged MTM by minimizing maximum drawdown. The CVaR(95%) and CVaR(99%) lines represent the hedged MTM by minimizing the Cornish-Fisher CVaR expansion at 95% and 99% statistical confidence, respectively. Finally, the ASR line is the hedged MTM by maximizing the Alternative Sharpe Ratio of the hedged portfolio.

7.4   Overall Comparison of Choices of Objective Functions

This use case is a set of precisely constructed simulations of the complex algorithms used by the HedgeSPA Platform. The P&L graphs as shown in Figure 7.14 present empirical examples of combining the choices of instruments under different objective functions, to provide investors with a more visual way to choose an appropriate hedging/optimization strategy:

Our observations on a comparative basis are as follows:

1. As noted earlier, the negative carries from using VT futures and OTM SPX puts are way too high for them to be deployed as practical hedging solutions. The investor achieves a better outcome by not hedging. One can expect worse performance by using 10% OTM SPX puts than 5% OTM SPX puts, but in general, futures seem to have done better than options. This is quite surprising considering that in theory volatility and variance futures are created from a series of underlying SPX options. This observation is significant since there are not yet obvious theoretical justifications as to why using a synthesized product can be more efficient than using the relevant raw materials used to synthetically replicate the synthesized product. This does not appear to be caused by how the "smile" of the volatility curve is so steep that it becomes cost-ineffective to use way out-of-the-money put options when such an observation is consistent between 10% OTM SPX puts and 5% OTM SPX puts. Lee et. al. 2010 ([**Lee 2010**]) have shown by sophisticated simulation that the inability to carry out frictionless hedging due to liquidity conditions may result in significant deviation from theoretical option pricing. This is another piece of empirical evidence supporting such a result. The possible mechanism giving a plausible explanation for this observation will be an interesting topic for future research.

2. The overall winner in our empirical analysis is the VIX futures, which has provided both extreme downside protection and upside preservation under reasonable choices of hedging models. The pragmatic issue faced by real-world portfolio managers is whether the popularity of using VIX futures with the desirable tenor to hedge in reasonable size will fundamentally change the cost to hedge effectiveness ratios of using VIX futures as hedges. That is an empirical question that can only be satisfactorily answered by placing large trades directly in the VIX futures market.

3. In general, the clear winning strategy is to use liquid and efficiently priced hedging instruments with hedging objective functions that account for both upside and downside behaviors.

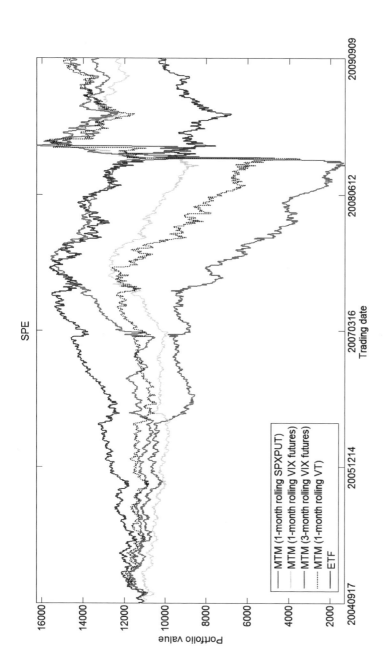

Figure 7.14: **Comparison of Different Hedging Instruments under the Squared Residuals Hedging Model** – The ETF line is the unhedged dollar MTM of one 100-lot basket of the S&P500. The 1-month rolling SPXPUT line is the hedged MTM by using 1-month rolling SPX puts. The 1-month rolling VIX futures line is the hedged MTM by using 1-month rolling VIX futures. The 3-month rolling VIX futures line is the hedged MTM by using 3-month rolling VIX futures. Finally, the 1-month rolling VT line is the hedged MTM by using 1-month rolling variance futures.

7.5 Step-by-Step Walk Through

The analysis above can be performed by using the hedging tool on the HedgeSPA core investment platform.

First, a user can select any combinations of desirable investment products to construct a hedging palette. That way, all the potential volatility derivatives discussed in this chapter can be put into the same hedging palette. The computer will choose the most effective one for the user. Then, the user can choose from the 6 hedging objective functions as discussed, so that the platform will recommend the appropriate positions in the hedging palette (such to user constraints including cash constraint), and the hedged portfolio will meet one of the following objectives:

1. Min VaR: minimizing Value-at-Risk
2. Min CVaR(95%): minimizing Conditional Value-at-Risk at 95% confidence level.
3. Max SR: maximizing portfolio Sharpe Ratio
4. Max ASR: maximizing the portfolio Alternative Sharpe Ratio (an advanced alternative to the Sharpe Ratio adjusted for both positive skewness and downside portfolio tail risk).
5. Min Variance: minimizing Portfolio Variance (or squared residuals)
6. Min MaxDD: minimizing the Maximum Drawdown of the Portfolio

To perform a total cost hedging with the investable cash, under **Selection Pane** → **Analytics** → **Decision/Execution** → **Hedging/Optimizaton**:

1. Specify your Investible Cash amount.

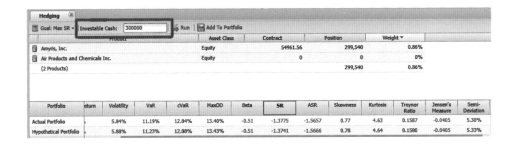

Figure 7.15: Investible Cash

2. Add one or more products to be used as hedging vehicles in the hedging analysis by dragging and dropping the product(s) into the Hedging Sub-panel.

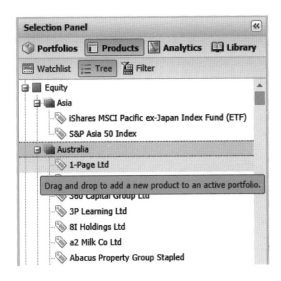

Figure 7.16: Dragging and Dropping Products into Hedging Sub-panel

3. Select the optimization criterion from the Goal drop-down list.

Performance Chart	Efficient Frontier	Hedging / Optimization									
Clear Panel	Goal: Min Variance ▼	Investable Cash:	822994.28	Constraints	Returns	Hedge	Optimize ▼	Add To Portfolio	Clean W		
	Min VaR		Asset Class	Contract to Buy/Sell		Position Change		Weight Change			
(0 Products)	Min CVaR					0		0.00%			
	Max SR										
Drag and dro	Max ASR	t tree/product search panel									
	⊘ Min Variance										
Portfolio	Min MaxDD	SR	ASR	Volatility	VaR	cVaR	MaxDD	Beta	Skewness	Kurtosis	Treyn Rati
Actual Portfolio	9.49%	0.5058	0.6001	14.80%	34.56%	38.88%	8.74%	0.33	-0.06	2.85	0.131
Hypothetical Portfolio	9.49%	0.5058	0.6001	14.80%	34.56%	38.88%	8.74%	0.33	-0.06	2.85	0.131

Figure 7.17: Specify Objective

4. Click "Run", and the results will be displayed, as follows:

- The optimized number of contracts, position, and weight of the selected products will be shown in the Proposed Position column.

Figure 7.18: Hedging Results

- The statistics of the actual and hypothetical portfolios will be shown at the bottom.

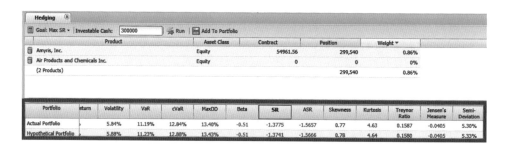

Figure 7.19: Hedging Statistics

5. Please notice that the **Hedging / Optimization** analytic tool comes with many useful, practical functions, including the ability to specify constraints:
- by product;
- by sector (relative to a chosen benchmark);
- by absolute sizes; and/or
- by the total number of positions allowed in the portfolio.

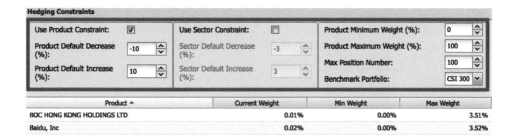

Figure 7.20: Hedging Constraints

6. The ability to specify product returns based on historical returns, expected returns (which can be uploaded as scores), or by scenarios (which is not shown here).

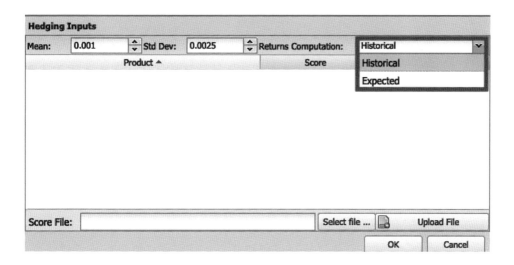

Figure 7.21: Choices of Returns

7. Other practical options include the ability to include the computations of a hedging/optimization analysis as *What-If* trades as part of the target portfolio, ability to clear those *What-If* trades, and the ability to confirm those *What-If* trades. In addition, there is an option to run the optimziation under the "Auto Optimize" option that allows optimization taking hours to complete on its own with the computational results automatically included as *What-If* trades in the target portfolio.

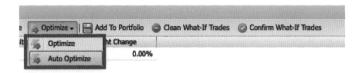

Figure 7.22: Auto-optimize to Include Recommendations as What-If Trades

Part II

SELECT ASSETS

INVESTMENT ANALYTICS IN THE DAWN OF ARTIFICIAL INTELLIGENCE

8. Alpha Selection Using Factors

8.1 Use Case

John is a professional investment manager of a large hedge fund. Right now his fund is not doing particularly well in meeting its return goal. Since his fund sponsors are seeking absolute returns, he plans to take a conservative approach towards asset selection despite a keen interest to outperform. However, he expects a bull market to come in one year and decides to take advantage of that opportunity to build up his reserve for rainy days.

His goal is to reach high absolute returns by smarter asset selection. He understands that he needs to invest in a basket of stocks to diversify the portfolio as well. By adding more and more stocks into a portfolio, the portfolio performs increasingly like a typical index. Due to the statistical law of large numbers, the active risk of the portfolio will turn lower and the portfolio cannot outperform. Hence, he needs to concentrate and focus his bets.

So how much should John concentrate to ensure that he still has a reasonable level of diversification while the portfolio can still focus its bets? Is there an objective criterion for the "right" number of stocks in a portfolio? Is concentration the only way to achieve out-performance?

8.2 Methodology

Suppose the investor wants to evaluate a group of stocks by country/industry, such as the 33 Morgan Stanley Technology (MSH) Index components as an arbitrary example, rank those stocks' predicted performance, and construct a long-short portfolio using the top-5 and bottom-5 stocks from this ranking. Simplistic technical analysis of historical price data alone is notoriously unreliable for predicting future returns. This observation makes an already complicated calculation even harder to handle.

Fundamental analysis helps us solve the problem in a more systematic way. By using advanced computational methods, we can handle such a process in three steps: first, we can collect the relevant data of the 33 stocks from its own company's financial statements and other information available on the public domains; second, the computer performs the model training and testing; finally, we can choose the top-5 and bottom-5 stocks.

Before undertaking any analysis, it is essential to clearly define the purpose of the analysis. An understanding of its purpose is particularly important in financial statement analysis because of the numerous available techniques and substantial data.

8.2.1 Balance Sheet 101

Any company balance sheet should show assets, liabilities, and shareholder equities. Assets are listed in the order of liquidity, and then followed by liabilities. Shareholder equities equal to assets minus liabilities. Alternatively, total assets equal liabilities plus shareholder' equities. This equation shows that assets were financed by either borrowing (under liability) or shareholder's fund (under shareholders' equity). Balance sheets typically list assets in one column, and liabilities and shareholder equities in the other, thus the description "balance", as shown in Table 8.1.

A cash business can measure its profits by summing its bank balance and any cash in hand. However, many goods and services are not paid for immediately, and businesses also build up inventories and acquire buildings and equipment in the course of doing business. Hence, businesses cannot convert the assets they hold into cash at the end of each period, because they have liabilities by owing money to suppliers and tax authorities. It will be impossible for a business to function as a going concern if their shareholders withdraw their original capital and profits at the end of each reporting period.

Table 8.1: Sample Balance Sheet

Sample Balance Sheet as of 31 Decemeber, 2015			
Assets		**Liabilities**	
Current assets		Current liabilities	
Cash	$2,200	Notes payable	$5,000
Temporary investments	10,000	Accounts payable	35,900
Accounts receivables	40,500	Wages payable	8,500
Inventory	31,000	Interest payable	2,900
Supplies	3,800	Taxes payables	6,100
Prepaid Insurance	1,500	Warranty liability	1,100
Total Current Assets	89,000	Unearned revenues	1,500
		Total current liabilities	61,000
Investments	36,000		
		Long term liabilities	
Property, plant & equipment		Notes payable	20,000
Land	5,500	Bonds payable	400,000
Land improvements	6,500	Total long term liabilities	420,000
Buildings	180,000		
Equipment	201,000	Total liabilities	481,000
Less (: accu depreciation)	-56,000		
Prop, plant & equip - net	337,000	**Stockholders' Equity**	
Intangible assets		Common stock	110,000
		Retained earnings	220,000
Goodwill	105,000	Accum other omprehensive income	9,000
Trade names	200,000	Less (:Treasury Stock)	-50,000
Total intangible assets	305,000		
		Total stockholders' equity	289,000
Other assets	3,000		
Total assets	$770,000	Total liabilities & stockholders' equities	$770,000

8.2.2 Fundamental Factors

Fundamental analysis involves looking at any financial reports, such as balance sheets. The balance sheet presents a company's current financial position by disclosing the resources that the company controls (assets) and its obligations to lenders and other creditors (liabilities) at a specific point in time. Shareholder equities equal to assets minus liabilities. This amount belongs to the company's shareholders. Shareholders' equity is the shareholders' residual interest in the company's assets after deducting its liabilities.

Using fundamental analysis implies getting down to the basics and focuses on creating a financial picture, identifying the intrinsic value of the business. It is the diametrical opposite of technical analysis, which focuses only on the trading and price history of stocks.

The indicators commonly used to fundamental analysis include:
1. Returns on assets and equity
2. Equity and preferred dividends
3. Sales, debt, and income
4. Liabilities and assets
5. Inventory and cost of goods sold
6. Cash flows, including sales cash flows, operating cash flows, and financial cash flows

a) Normalization and Standardization:
First, the data should be filtered for outliers, and any confirmed outliers should be removed from the data set. The data should also be normalized or standardized to make the variables roughly in the same proportion as each other, to minimize the occurrence of numerical issues. On our platform, there are many available factors for users to choose from. As one example, we may choose "Asset Turnover", "Current Ratio", "Debt-Equity Ratio" as independent variables.

We assume that the raw data is distributed as asymptotic normal distributions. To determine the Z-Score of each data point, the following equation is used:

$$X_{i,1\sigma} = \frac{X_i - X_s}{\sigma_{X,S}}$$

where:

X: Each data point i;
S: Average of all sample data points;
$\sigma_{X,S}$: Sample standard deviation of all sample data points; and
$X_{i,1\sigma}$: Data point i standardized to 1σ, also known as Z-Score.

b) Simple Linear Model:
A linear regression model on a data set of n statistical variables assumes a linear relationship between the dependent variable and the p-vector of regressors. This relationship is created by adding an unobserved error or random noise term to the fitted linear relationship between the dependent variables and regressors. The model can be described as:

$$y_i = \beta_0 + \beta_1 x_{1i} + \beta_2 x_{2i} + \ldots + \beta_k x_{ki} + \varepsilon_i, i = 1, 2, 3\ldots$$

or, in matrix form,

$$Y = X\beta^T + \varepsilon$$

where superscript T denotes the transpose matrix operation, and $X\beta^T$ is the inner product between vectors X and β. The model can be written in matrix form, as follows:

$$Y = [y_1, \quad y_2, \quad y_3, \quad \cdots \quad y_n],$$

$$X = [x_1, \quad x_2, \quad x_3, \quad \cdots \quad x_n] = \begin{bmatrix} x_{11} & x_{12} & x_{13} & \cdots & x_{1p} \\ x_{21} & x_{22} & x_{23} & \cdots & x_{2p} \\ \vdots & \vdots & \vdots & \ddots & \vdots \\ x_{n1} & x_{n2} & x_{n3} & \cdots & x_{np} \end{bmatrix},$$

$$\beta = [\beta_1, \quad \beta_2, \quad \beta_3, \quad \cdots \quad \beta_n],$$

where:

Y is called the endogenous variable;

X represent exogenous variables; and

β is a p-dimensional parameter vector.

Such a system usually cannot be solved closed-form. Our goal is to find those coefficients that "best" fit the equations by solving the folling least-square quadratic optimization problem, as follows:

$$\beta = argmin_S(\beta)$$

where the objective function S is given by

$$S(\beta) = \sum_{i=1}^{n} |y_i - \sum_{i=1}^{p} X_{ij}\beta| = ||Y - X\beta||$$

This minimization problem has a unique solution, if the n columns of the matrix are linearly independent, given by solving the normal equations

$$(X^T X)\beta = X^T Y.$$

The matrix $X^T X$ is called the Gramian matrix of X, and has certain desirable numerical properties such as being positive semi-definite. β is the coefficient vector of the least-squares hyperplane, expressed as:

$$\beta = (X^T X)^{-1} X^T Y$$

c) Neural Networks:

We can also replace linear regression with neural networks. The main difference between using linear regression and using neural networks are:

1. Non-linearity

   Neural networks can model non-linearity, while traditional linear regression can only accept a single model specification. By starting with more nodes and layers, the neural network is starting with a higher-order specification that can be filtered down to the linear model.

2. No Explicit Model Specification

   In theory, it is unnecessary for users to specify the exact "shape" of the neural network, such as the number of layers and nodes and the precise choice of input factors when insignificant factors can be filtered out during the "training" phase.

3. Multiple Horizon

   Another clear benefit of using a neural network that the neural network can be "trained" over multiple horizons (e.g., multiple quarters) and the error term from each horizon can be fed back to the network, as shown in Figure 8.1:

We crawl the internet and/or any other available data sources to find all relevant factors related to an asset universe. Earlier, we gave one example of an asset universe composed of stocks in the US healthcare sector. Typical factors may include company financials, regulatory filings, macroeconomic data, sentiment scores from news and social media, and more specialized information such as production and shipment data related to export-oriented sectors.[1]

Users are given the additional option to filter irrelevant factors as they see fit. One classic example is how inventory data are irrelevant to the internet software sector, because software vendors do not need to maintain inventories. Once the choice of factors is confirmed, the computer will try all possible combinations of factors, all possible combination of time frames, and all available methodologies in order to find the most predictive model based on the amount of historical data specified for the training. This method is analogous to how the `leaps()` function in **R** performs an exhaustive search for the best subsets of variables in x for predicting y in a linear regression. Instead of linear regression, the neural network can be thought of as a form of higher-order regression. We will discuss factor selection in detail in the next section. The approach is illustrated by the screenshot in Figure 8.2:

---

[1]The remaining discussion under *c) Neural Networks* is excerpted from Lee, Bernard, and Nicos Christofides, "Time-Constrained Predictive Modeling on Large and Continuously Updating Financial Datasets." JSM Proceedings, Statistical Learning and Data Science Section. American Statistical Association, Alexandria, VA, 2018, pp. 2831-2837.

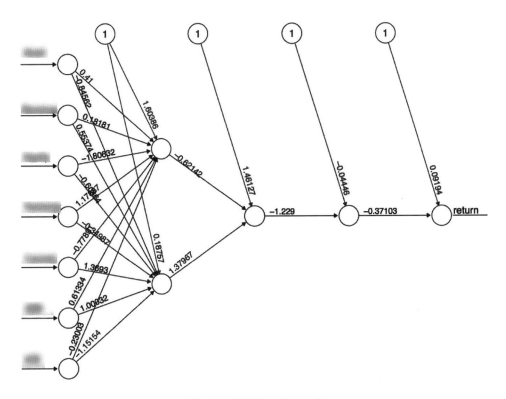

Error: 9.458065 Steps: 4

Figure 8.1: Typical Neural Network Configuration

In the case of leaps(), an exhaustive search can evolve into stepwise regression. Training and testing neural networks can be a time-consuming operation as compared to linear regression, so researchers are naturally interested in finding smart ways to cut down computational time. Next, we will discuss such parallel implementation methods.

The neural network training and testing algorithm has been isolated and parallelized at the National Supercomputing Center in Singapore with the following parameters:

```
Start of Training Period = 2
Testing Period = 4
Lag Period = 1
Number of Factors = 9
Number of Stocks = 60
Min Number of Factors = 2
Max Number of Factors = 5
```

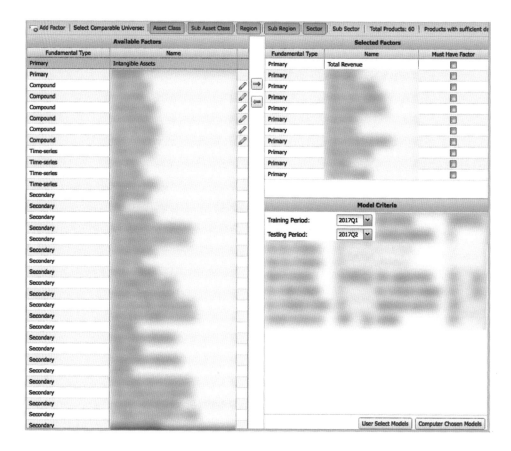

Figure 8.2: Factor Selection for Training and Testing

The `Start of Training Period` refers to the quarter when the neural network starts training and the `Testing Period` refers to the quarter for testing. The `Lag Period` represents the number of quarter(s) looking forward so as to predict the future returns of the assets. In our test case, quarters 2 and 3 are used for training, quarter 4 for testing, so as to predict asset returns in quarter 5. Most other input parameters are self-explanatory. The total number of subproblems to be solved will be:

$$Num\_Combo = C(Num\_Factors, Min\_Factors) + \cdots$$
$$+ C(Num\_Factors, Max\_Factors)$$

The parallelization is done by `OpenMP`.[2] Since migrating a production analytics platform to any specialized architecture such as a supercomputer is too complicated,

---

[2]See `https://www.openmp.org/`.

a separate I/O Manager is written in C++ to drive the computational code. The heavy computation is written in C and linked to the Fast Artificial Neural Network Library (FANN) `libfann`.[3] We did not link it to the vectorized `libcudann`[4] library because `libcudann` requires CUDA 3.2,[5] which is much older than the current version 9.x supported.

The specific loop around the parallelized call is implemented as a `for` loop for each training/testing subproblem:

```
#pragma omp parallel private(i_num_model)
{
    #pragma omp for
    for(i_num_model = num_model_start;
i_num_model < num_model_end; i_num_model++)
    {
        nn_factor_model_model_selection(i_num_model, r);
        //fann computation
    }
}
```

Three series of runs were performed based on 1, 2, 4, 5, 8, 12, 18 and 24 CPUs. We cut off the computation at 24 CPUs after no significant speed-up is observed. No parallelization was done for the first set of runs. The outermost set of curly brackets in the code above is accidentally omitted, which means that supercomputer can still parallelize the code. However, each processor is running the same set of code as if each of them is running the full computation on a single CPU. This turns out to be a good control set: the I/O time for consolidating the results with no computation speed-up will be correctly captured by this set. The second set of runs is based on Static Block Scheduling in which the tasks are handed out based on a static allocation algorithm. The final set of runs is based on dynamic ordered scheduling in which the tasks are handed out on a round-robin basis, but the start and completion must be ordered. Sometimes doing so may reduce I/O contention among processors. The completion times of these computational runs are shown in Figure 8.3.

Static Block Scheduling is the best performing algorithm, but it still shows a rather speed up beyond the first few processors. Dynamic Ordered Scheduling is worse than No Parallelization given the amount of I/O overhead involved.

This computational problem appears to be a classic embarrassingly parallel problem since we are feeding relatively small sub-problems (by industry standards)

---

[3]See https://github.com/libfann.
[4]See https://sourceforge.net/projects/libcudann/.
[5]See https://developer.nvidia.com/cuda-toolkit.

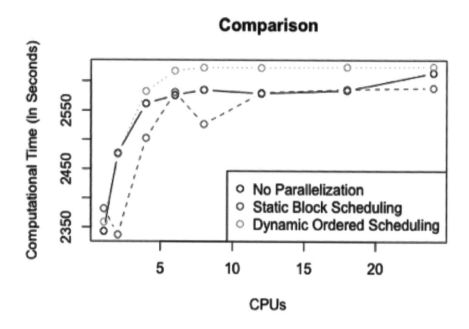

Figure 8.3: Speed-up Graph: Computational Time Versus CPUs

in a universe of US healthcare stocks to the neural network. However, financial data on an industrial scale is proven to create too much I/O contention and overhead to achieve reasonable speed up under a multi-CPU architecture. While a smart workaround with classic, low-level, master-to-slave message passing set up may be possible, such a technique is usually done on a one-off basis for scientific applications. Such an architecture is unlikely to be fail-safe if comparing one hundred different asset universes for a typical single-iteration institutional run may require one hundred calls. Further, our parallel code is written by parallel programmers with decades of related research and development experience. Without using a common parallel protocol such as OpenMP, it will be nearly impossible to keep up with the day-to-day maintenance of such parallel code for any practical industry application.

GPU-enhanced CUDA and/or other forms of hardware acceleration give speed-ups of 50 to 100 times to train and test neural networks, without incurring the cost of very large CPU-based clusters. Clearly, these results show that the best value added per development dollar spent is to focus on using a few powerful GPUs on a grid architecture, which is, in fact, available commercially today.

d) Sentiment Analysis:
Another common technique is the use of the sentiment analysis from news and social media related to a specific company to adjust its predicted performance.

The rationale for doing so is that predicted performance is usually based on factor information that is at least one or two-quarter old. We also compute sentiment scores based on specific keywords: e.g., the impact of news and social media from research in tobacco-related diseases on the stock prices of a tobacco company may be limited since investors of tobacco companies are likely to have discounted the impact of such news.

We can achieve our objective with a simple Bayesian linear regression to make a statistical inference based on posterior distribution derived from prior information available. For every predicted performance period, the cumulative events that have happened prior to that time contribute to the asset's predicted performance. Thus, dynamic sentiment scores will be divided into different time series $t = 1, \ldots, T$ the intervals of updates on predictions. For example, events happened between two predictions, one on 1 April 2015 and another on 1 June 2015 contributed to the predictions made on 1 July 2015. Therefore, we can use dynamic sentiment scores from 1 April 2015 to 1 July 2015 to analyze its impact on the asset price predictions made on 1 July 2015.

The Vector Autoregression Model for p periods within t-th time series is:

$$y_t = Ax_t + \varepsilon_t$$

where:

for $t = 1, \ldots, T$, (totaling T observations),
y_t is $M \times 1$ vector containing prediction on M time series variables,
ε_t is $M \times 1$ vector of errors,
A is $M \times (p+1)$ matrix of coefficients, and
x_t is $(p+1) \times 1$ vector containing p dynamic scores within the time series with a model intercept, with $x_{1,t} = 1$ for all t.

We can apply Bayesian inference to be as our next step. For any Bayesian model, there are three parts involved: Prior, Likelihood, and Posterior. The Bayesian approach treats the data, as given by the dynamic sentiment scores from a proprietary engine or a publicly-accessible API such as IBM Watson and the parameter vector of interest, A, as unknown. Inference about A is conditional on the data.

The likelihood is the information provided by the data regarding the parameters, which is,

$$\mathcal{L}(A, \sigma^2 | y, x) = \prod_{t=1}^{T} P(y_t | x_t, A, \sigma^2)$$

where $P(y_t | x_t, A, \sigma^2)$ is the conditional probability density function of y_t given the parameters and induced by the conditional distribution of ε_t.

Typically, priors on the parameters are $\pi(A)$, the Gaussian prior distribution, and $\pi(\sigma^2)$, the inverse-gamma prior distribution. According to Bayes' Theorem, the posterior distribution is given by:

$$\pi(A,\sigma^2|y,x) = \frac{\pi(A)\pi(\sigma^2)\mathscr{L}(A,\sigma^2|y,x)}{\int \pi(A)\pi(\sigma^2)\mathscr{L}(A,\sigma^2|y,x)dAd\sigma^2} \propto \pi(A)\pi(\sigma^2)\mathscr{L}(A,\sigma^2|y,x)$$

It contains all the information that we have on the parameter vector A after having updated our prior views by looking at the data. We can use the resultant posterior distribution to update the most recent prediction by taking the posterior mean.

Financial market time series is affected heavily by missing data and erroneous observations. These missing data and erroneous observations may be difficult to identify as outliers based on purely visual inspection of graphical displays. Thus, we look for a more sophisticated technique for detecting outliers in data sets.

The moving window filtering algorithm filter out financial market data outliers by adding clustering techniques to a moving window algorithm. The validity of a new observation is assessed based on its distance from a close neighborhood (or cluster) of valid past observations. We employ this chosen method for the detection of outliers.

Traditional variance analysis for outlier detection is not good enough because products in one portfolio may belong to different sub-universes (sub-asset class, country, etc) and it is impractical to group all assets together to detect outliers. We choose K-means clustering for outlier detection because the algorithm is able to divide the products into respective clusters automatically and is quick computationally. This algorithm is one of the simplest unsupervised learning algorithms.

First, the choice of k is determined by defining the elbow point. We will run the K-means clustering with $k = 1$, as follows. We plot out the mean distance to the centroid as a function of k, which is determined by the elbow point where the rate of decrease shifts dramatically. Next, we perform K-means clustering. Data points are grouped into different clusters to minimize the within-cluster sum of squares through the iteration process as shown below:

1. Initialize the center of the clusters	$\mu_i = $ some value $, i = 1, \ldots, k$
2. Attribute the closest cluster to each data point	$c_i = \{j : d(\mathbf{x_j}, \mu_i) \le d(\mathbf{x_j}, \mu_l), l \ne i, j = 1, \ldots, n\}$
3. Set the position of each cluster to the mean of all data points belonging to that cluster	$\mu_i = \frac{1}{|c_i|}\sum_{j\in c_i} \mathbf{x_j}, \forall i$
4. Repeat steps 2-3 until convergence	
Notation	$|\mathbf{c}| = $ number of elements in $\mathbf{c}$

(Source: http://www.onmyphd.com/?p=k-means.clustering)

After the data points have been put into different clusters, we calculate the "outlyingness" index for each value. Assuming normal distribution, for each cluster with dataset X, the outlyingness index is

$$O(xi, X) = |xi - med(X)|(med(X) * k)med(X)$$

$$= med(|xi - med(X)|)k$$

such that $\pm$MAD covers 50% between $\frac{1}{4}$ and $\frac{3}{4}$ of the standard normal cumulative density function, and

- if $O >= 1.96$, x is an outlier outside $0.025 - 0.975$ range.
- if $O >= 0.68$, x is an outlier outside $0.25 - 0.75$ range.
- if $O >= 1.29$, x is an outlier outside $0.1 - 0.9$ range.
- if $O >= 1.65$, x is an outlier outside $0.05 - 0.95$ range.

These ranges may be user-defined.

8.3 Factors

8.3.1 Compound Factors

The simple factors shown in the previous Section are directly extracted from the financial statements. Here are some brief explanations of the compound factors:

1. Fundamental Factors

   Asset Turnover: It can be calculated as revenues $\div$ assets. The asset turnover ratio measures a company's overall ability to generate revenues with a given level of assets. A ratio of 1.20 would show that the company is generating $1.20 of revenues for every $1 of average assets. A higher ratio indicates greater efficiency.
   Current Ratio: Namely, current assets $\div$ current liabilities. The current ratio expresses current assets to current liabilities as an indicator of a company's liquidity.
   Debt-Equity Ratio: The long-term debt-to-equity ratio is the ratio of long-term debt capital to equity capital. An increase in the long-term debt-to-equity ratio implies that a company's solvency has weakened.
   Gross Profit Margin: The gross profit margin measures the amount of gross profit that a company generated for each dollar of revenue, which can be computed as (revenues' cost of sales) $\div$ revenues. A higher level of gross profit margin suggests higher profitability and thus is generally more desirable.

2. Macro Factors

Consumer Price Index (CPI): Consumer price index (CPI) measures the changes in the price of a basket of consumer goods and services purchased by a typical household. Most countries use their own consumer price index (CPI) to track inflation in the domestic economy.[6]

GDP Growth Rate (%): GDP Growth Rate is the rate at which a nation's Gross Domestic Product (GDP) grows from one year to another. GDP is the market value of all officially recognized final goods and services produced within a country in a year.[7]

Current Account Balance: The difference between a nation's savings and its investment. The current account can be used as a health indicator of an economy, and is the sum of net income from abroad and net current transfers, and goods and services exports minus imports, or the balance of trade.

Composite Leading Indicator (CLI): The composite leading indicator aims to give early signals of turning points in business cycles. It aims to show the fluctuation of economic activity around its long-term level. CLIs is an indicator of short-term economic movements.[8]

Purchasing Power Parity (PPP): Purchasing power parity is a theory in economics that approximates the total adjustment that must be made on the currency exchange rate between countries that allow the exchange to be equal to the purchasing power in each country's currency.

Broad Money (M3): In economics, broad money is a measure of the money supply that includes more than just physical money such as currency and coins (also called narrow money). The measure generally includes demand deposits at commercial banks, and any monies held in easily accessible accounts.

Bank Non-Performing Loan to Total Gross Loans(%): The ratio of the value of nonperforming loans (NPLs) to the value of the loan portfolio (including NPLs, and before the deduction of specific loan loss provisions). The ratio of nonperforming loans to total gross loans is a proxy for asset quality. It can be an indicator of the quality of loan assets.[9]

---

[6]See https://www.investopedia.com/terms/c/consumerpriceindex.asp.

[7]See https://en.wikiquote.org/wiki/Gross_Domestic_Product.

[8]See http://www.oecd.org/sdd/compositeleadingindicatorsclifrequently askedquestionsfaqs.htm.

[9]See http://datahelp.imf.org/knowledgebase/articles/484369-in-financial-soundness-indicators-fsis-what-is.

8.3.2 Factor Set Definition

1. Minimum Number of Factors, Maximum Number of Factors, Must Have
   Factors

   Under **Factor Set Definition** tool, in "Selected Factors" window, there is a
   list of available factors to choose from. This window allows us to choose
   fundamental analysis factors from financial statements and other information
   such as macroeconomic factors. In the following example, we choose four
   factors including Total Revenue, Total Assets, Total Current Assets, Total
   Stockholder Equity as our "Must Have" Factors. Also, we set the Minimum
   Number of Factors to two and the Maximum Number of Factors to four in
   "Model Criteria" window shown in Figure 8.4. Doing this means any model
   tested must have a minimum of two factors out of the choices selected and
   a maximum of four factors. In Section 8.5 Implementation, there will be a
   step-by-step description of how to access and use the **Factor Set Definition**
   tool.

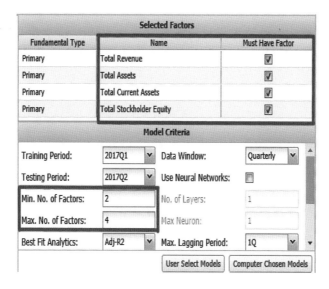

Figure 8.4: Selected Factors

2. Add Factor

   You may also choose factors you want to add by clicking "Add Factor" on the
   top left corner of the "Available Factors" window shown in Figure 8.5:

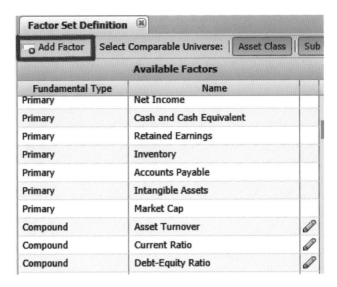

Figure 8.5: Factor Addition

Then, another window "Formula Editor" in Figure 8.6 will pop up, and you can define ratios based on a customized formula and name them accordingly, as follows:

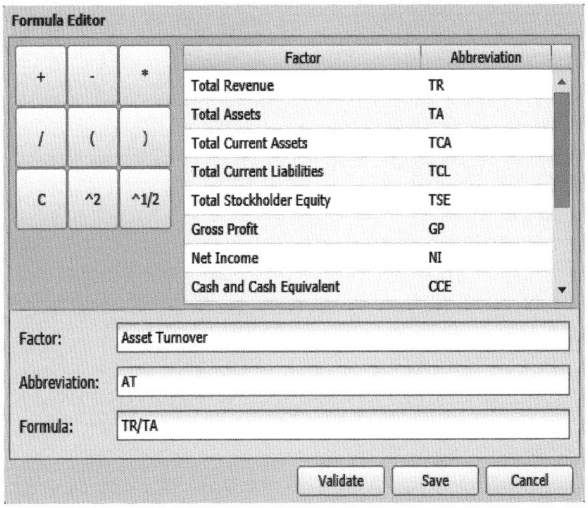

Figure 8.6: Formula Editor

8.4 Statistical Criteria

Before we click on "Computer Chosen Models", let's look at what and how many model criteria we can choose to help us get to the results. First, you can choose the number of factors you want to set in the model.

1. **Adjusted R^2**: Adjusted R-Squared is a modified version of R-Squared, and is an indication of the portion of the variance in the dependent variable that can be predicted by the independent variable. The formula is:

$$R^2_{adj} = 1 - \frac{(1-R^2)(n-1)}{n-k-1}$$

   where:

   n: The total number of data points.
   k: The total number of factors used in the computation.

2. **Rank Correlation**: This is the correlation of the ranks of the assets based on their *ex-ante* predictions and their actual *ex-post* performance. It is an assessment of the correlation between two different ways of assigning ranks to the members of an asset sub-universe. A correlation of 1 means that the ranked predictions perfectly correlate with the realized ranked performance of that sub-universe.

3. **BIC** *(only applicable to regression models)*: The Bayesian Information Criterion (BIC) is a criterion for model selection among a finite set of models; the lowest BIC is preferred. The BIC is formally defined as:

$$BIC = nln(SSE_p) - nlnn + lnn * p$$

   where:

   SSE_P: Sum squares of error with p parameters in the cross regression model,
   n: The number of data points in the sample, and
   p: The number of parameters in the cross regression.

4. **C-p Criterion**: Mallows's C-p assesses the fit of a regression model estimated using ordinary least squares. The measure is applied to model selection. The goal is to find the best model out of all possible ones created from a subset of these predictors. The lower the C-p value, the more predictive the model is. C-p criterion can be defined as:

$$C_p = \frac{1}{n}(RSS + 2d\sigma^2)$$

8.5   Implementation

On the HedgeSPA platform, the loading of data, calculation of factors, defining sub-universe, as well as model testing and calibration are fully automated, so that they are less tedious and more reliable. This whole process is easy to operate, which can be found under **Selection Panel** → **Analytics** → **Asset Selection** → **Factor Set Definition**. The following is an overview of how to do so.

1. First, construct a portfolio from the same or similar industry. Here, we construct a portfolio consisting of about 30 components from the high-tech industry in the US, using a relatively simple criterion such as their Sharpe Ratios.

2. Second, train and test Q4 predictions against actual Q4 returns by a series of cross-sectional regressions. Here, some selected factors such as Asset Turnover, Current Ratio.

3. Finally, rank the portfolio based on the factors set in step 2) by identifying the top five best performing components and bottom five worst performing components.

The following is a precise step-by-step worked example on the HedgeSPA core investment platform:

Step 1 First, on "Selection Panel", click "Products" and then "Filter". Here, the example we use is Apple (APPL):

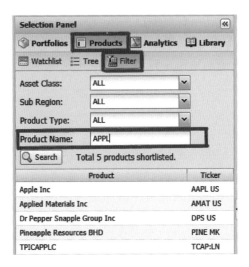

Figure 8.7: Choosing Apple Inc.

Step 2 Then, click on the "Analytics" button, and then choose "Factor Set Definition" under "Asset Selection":

Figure 8.8: Choosing Factor Set Definition

Step 3 In the "Selected Factors" window, you can choose the factors for your calculations. In this example, we choose "Total Revenue", "Total Assets", "Total Current Assets", and "Total Stockholder Equity" as factors. Then, click on the "Computer Chosen Models" button:

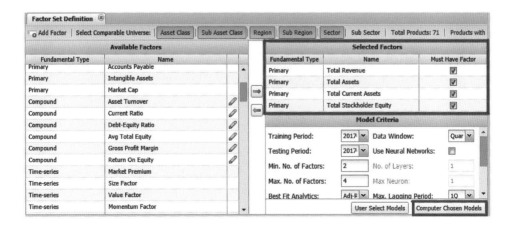

Figure 8.9: Choosing Factors

Step 4 The results from setting the factors above are shown below. The first six companies chosen are First Solar Inc, NVIDIA Corp, Electronic Arts Inc, Autodesk Inc, Activision Blizzard Inc, and Intuit Inc. For each model, we calculate the asset's "Predicted Alpha":

Product	Combined Rank ▲	Predicted Alpha				
		Linear Model 1	Linear Model 2	Linear Model 3	Linear Model 4	Linear Model 5
☑ First Solar Inc.	1	0.34823	0.35343	0.34612	0.35214	0.34930
☑ NVIDIA Corp	2	0.20257	0.20669	0.20052	0.20550	0.20359
☑ Electronic Arts Inc	3	0.05764	0.06226	0.05549	0.06102	0.05867
☑ Autodesk Inc	4	0.04263	0.04818	0.04029	0.04688	0.04367
☑ Activision Blizzard Inc	5	0.03131	0.03562	0.02946	0.03448	0.03227
☑ Intuit Inc	6	0.02207	0.02657	0.01973	0.02528	0.02316
☐ Oracle Corp	7	-0.00373	-0.00683	-0.00335	-0.00689	-0.00346
☐ Cognizant Technology Solutions Corp	8	-0.01010	-0.00732	-0.01194	-0.00844	-0.00909
☐ Red Hat Inc	9	-0.01639	-0.01097	-0.01869	-0.01226	-0.01534
☐ Corning Inc	10	-0.01651	-0.01261	-0.01806	-0.01385	-0.01539
☐ Xilinx Inc	11	-0.01830	-0.01286	-0.02053	-0.01415	-0.01725

Figure 8.10: Visualizing Alpha Rankings

8.5.1   Reviewing Fundamental Data

The **Product Fundamentals** tool allows users to do a quick review of the performance of the company representing the selected financial product, based on its financial statement, operation ratios, earning ratios, earning reports, valuation ratios, and segmentation. This tool could be found by clicking "Analytics" and then "Product Fundamentals", after you select a product.

Figure 8.11: "Analytics → Product Fundamentals"

The following is an example of a selected company's financial statement as shown on the "Product Fundamentals" tab:

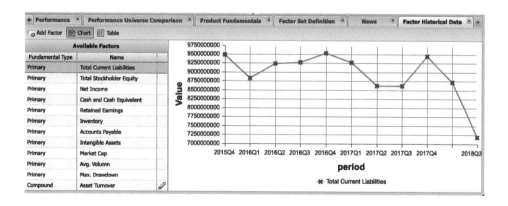

Income Statement	Currency	Value	Balance Sheet	Currency	Value	Cash Flow Statement	Currency		Period: 2018Q1
Total Revenue	HKD	250,898,000,000	Total Assets	HKD	25,147,474,000,000	Net Operating Cash Flow	HKD	504,	2014Q4
Gross Profit	HKD	82,712,000,000	Total Current Assets	HKD	24,545,889,000,0...	Capital Expenditures	HKD	-7,79	2015Q1
Net Income	HKD	60,317,000,000	Total Current Liabilities	HKD	18,303,870,000,0...	Sale of Fixed Assets & Businesses	HKD	2,07	2015Q2
Equity in Affiliates	HKD	602,000,000	Total Stockholder Equity	HKD	1,876,443,000,000	Purchase/Sale of Investments	HKD	-136	2015Q3
Consolidated Net Income	HKD	64,234,000,000	Cash and Cash Equivalent	HKD	2,836,293,000,000	Net Investing Cash Flow	HKD	-142	2015Q4
Minority Interest Expense	HKD	3,917,000,000	Retained Earnings	HKD	813,994,000,000	Cash Dividends Paid - Total	HKD	-1,89	2016Q1
Net Income After Extraordinaries	HKD	60,317,000,000	Intangible Assets	HKD	26,593,000,000	Issuance/Reduction of Debt Net	HKD	96,4	2016Q2
Net Income Available to Common	HKD	60,317,000,000	Net Property Plant & Equipment	HKD	251,037,000,000	Net Financing Cash Flow	HKD	80,99	2016Q3
EPS Basic	HKD	200,000	ST Debt & Current Portion LT Debt	HKD	335,367,000,000	Net Change in Cash	HKD	425,	2016Q4
Basic Shares Outstanding	HKD	294,356,000,000	Total Liabilities	HKD	23,171,996,000,0...	Net Interest Income after Provision	HKD		2017Q1
EPS Diluted	HKD	200,000	Accumulated Minority Interest	HKD	99,035,000,000	Non-Interest Income	HKD		2017Q2
Diluted Shares Outstanding	HKD	294,356,000,000				Non-Interest Expense	HKD	7	2017Q3
						Operating Income	HKD		2017Q4
						Investments - Total	HKD	6,546,843,000,000	2018Q1
						Net Loans	HKD	14,914,009,000,0...	
						Investment in Unconsolidated Subs.	HKD	21,308,000,000	
						Total Deposits	HKD	17,901,636,000,000	
						Total Debt	HKD	4,202,402,000,000	
						Provision for Risks & Charges	HKD	0	
						Deferred Tax Liabilities	HKD	-61,875,000,000	
						Preferred Stock Carrying Value	HKD	124,384,000,000	
						Common Equity Total	HKD	1,752,059,000,000	
						Exchange Rate Effect	HKD	-16,647,188,000,...	
						Free Cash Flow	HKD	496,221,359,000,...	

Figure 8.12: Product Fundamentals (Financial Statements)

In addition, the following is an example of the history of a specific factor as shown in the "Factor Historical Data" tab:

Figure 8.13: Product Fundamentals (Financial Statements)

8.5.2   Default Settings

Finally, we want to highlight one important feature. "Use Default Settings" allows each user to use user default settings for the universe comparison calculations, or revert to system default settings in the absence of user default settings. To create user deafult settings, click on "Save as Default Settings". This is shown on Figure 8.14 as follows:

Figure 8.14: Default Settings in Factor Set Definition

INVESTMENT ANALYTICS IN THE DAWN OF ARTIFICIAL INTELLIGENCE

9. Standard Derivative Instruments

9.1 Use Case

Here comes our good old friend John. He has mastered how to select assets for his portfolio on a longer-term basis from the previous chapter. He is interested in finding the best ways to switch asset around tactically.

John is considering switching out of Apple for Tesla. The long-term investment thesis is straightforward: Apple as a company is not as innovative as before, and it is increasingly turning into a general electronics player. Tesla's experiments on hybrid cars and driverless cars are proving successful. Nonetheless, both of them are tech players that move alongside the general trends of the tech markets: Obviously, there will be times when Apple is slightly overpriced relative to the tech sector while Tesla is underpriced relative to the same tech universe, or vice versa. A tiny difference in the time choice makes a large change in the profit.

To capture Tesla's upside given his less enthusiastic view on Apple, John is considering the use of two derivative instruments, namely selling a covered Apple call option to lower the cost to purchase a Tesla call option. This chapter will introduce the derivative pricing tools supported by the HedgeSPA platform.

9.2 Options Pricing Model

The **Options Pricing Model** is a stand-alone option pricing calculator. This tool computes option prices for both European and American options using the Black-Scholes model. This is achieved by clicking on "Analytics" and then "Options

Pricing Model" under "Valuation" as shown in Figure 9.1 once you have selected a product as the underlying.

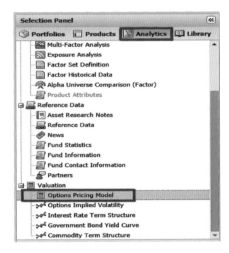

Figure 9.1: "Analytics → Options Pricing Model"

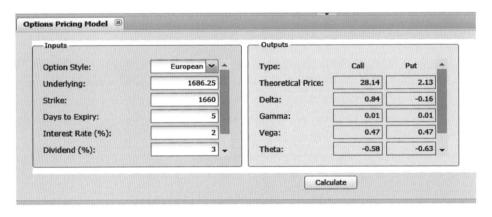

Figure 9.2: Options Pricing Model

9.2.1 Options Implied Volatility

The **Options Implied Volatility** tool as shown in Figure 9.4 plots the implied volatilities of the different options of an asset against the corresponding levels of strike prices. Such a curve is also called the "volatility smile", derived from actual and recent option prices quoted in the market. Hence, platform users may use this tool to calculate option prices that are not currently quoted. To access this tool, users should select a product as the underlying first. Users can click on "Analytics" and then "Options Implied Volatility" under "Valuation", as shown in Figure 9.3.

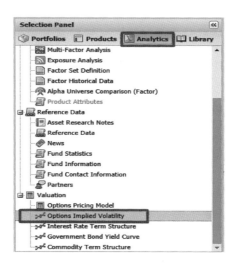

Figure 9.3: "Analytics → Options Implied Volatility"

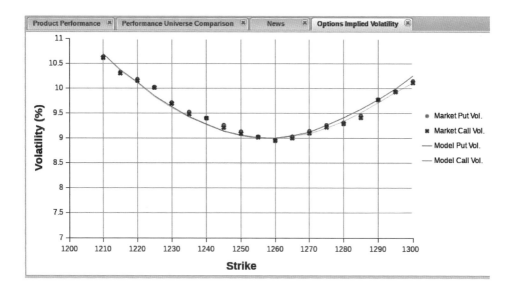

Figure 9.4: Options Implied Volatility Smile

9.3 Interest Rate Term Structure

The yield curve is a graph showing interest rates or bond yields across different maturities. The **Interest Rate Term Structure** tool plots the market's interest-rate yield curve against an interest-rate term structure model. Normally, the yield curve is a concave curve as short-term bonds (with shorter times to maturity) have lower yields compared to long-term bonds (with longer times to maturity). Such a yield curve is also known as the "normal" yield curve. When short-term bonds have higher yields than long-term bonds, such a yield curve is called "inverted". As the time to maturity increases, the market yield curve is expected to converge toward the term-structure model asymptotically when calibrated against actual transactions carried out in the market. To access the **Interest Rate Term Structure** tool, you need to select a product as the underlying first. Users can click on "Analytics" and then "Interest Rate Term Structure" under "Valuation", as shown in Figure 9.5.

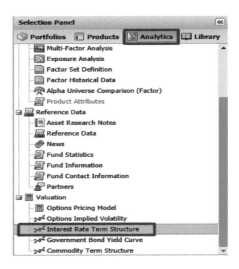

Figure 9.5: "Analytics → Interest Rate Term Structure"

The "sigma" as shown in Figure 9.6 is used to illustrate the volatility bands relative to the "average" yield curve.

9.4 Commodity Term Structure

The **Commodity Term Structure** tool works like the interest-rate term structure tool, except that it is intended to be applied to a selected market commodity curve, and plots the times to expiration against the prices of commodity futures. Users

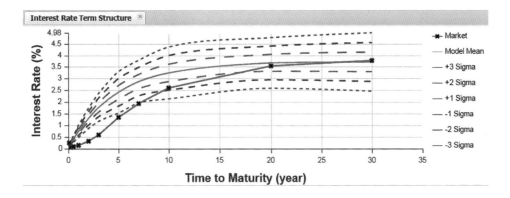

Figure 9.6: Interest Rate Term Structure

may also compare the respective commodity curves with a two-factor term structure
model provided by the HedgeSPA platform. The tool can be accessed by clicking
on "Analytics" first, and then "Commodity Term Structure" under "Valuation", as
shown in Figure 9.7 below:

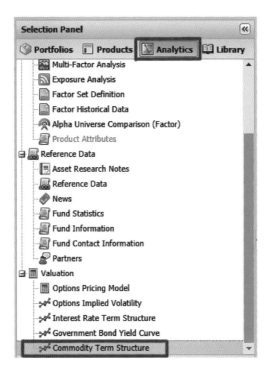

Figure 9.7: "Analytics → Commodity Term Structure"

Part III

DECIDE AND EXECUTE

INVESTMENT ANALYTICS IN THE DAWN OF ARTIFICIAL INTELLIGENCE

---

10. Rebalancing

10.1 Use Case

Rebalancing is about reallocating asset weights of a portfolio to maintain the expected asset allocation and its associated level of risk. For example, John may consider allocating 50% of his assets to the shares of Apple Inc. and the other 50% to iShares Barclays Aggregate Bond Fund (AGG). If the shares of Apple Inc. performed well during this period, its weight in the portfolio could have increased to 60%. In order to maintain the original asset allocation as communicated to his investors, John may decide to sell some of the shares of Apple Inc. and buy additional units of AGG.

There are many ways to go about performing the portfolio rebalancing process. This chapter will introduce a robust method of doing so on the HedgeSPA core investment platform.

10.2 Goals in a Typical Portfolio Rebalancing Process

Portfolio rebalancing is typically performed based on specific goals, scenarios, and parameters chosen by the user to run the best portfolio rebalancing plan, so as to achieve automated monthly or bi-weekly rebalancing with a clear view of both the portfolio's realized and implied returns.

The **Portfolio Rebalancing** tool in Figure 10.1 allows users to do optimization for selected products according to different criteria, including Max Sharpe Ratio and Max SCR Ratio/MCR (as defined by Solvency II style regulations). There are five categories of scenarios supported by the platform, including scenario sets, current scenarios, archived scenarios, historical scenarios, and user scenarios. The allowed parameters include relevant reference data such as initial buying weights and initial selling weights.

Figure 10.1: Portfolio Rebalancing Panel

To access the **Portfolio Rebalancing** tool, you need to click on "Analytics", and then double-click on "Portfolio Rebalancing" under "Decision/Execution", as shown below:

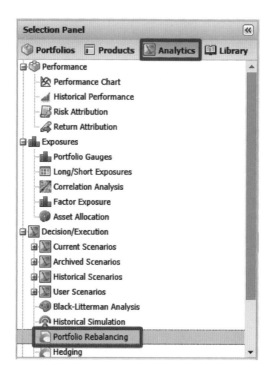

Figure 10.2: "Analytics → Portfolio Rebalancing"

To use this tool to generate rebalancing recommendations, users should select the products to be included in the rebalancing set first, and then drag and drop them into the **Portfolio Rebalancing** window. The following is the step-by-step instructions for using this tool.

Step 1 Drag and drop the products that you have selected. Then, click on "Goal: Max Sharpe Ratio" to choose your goal.

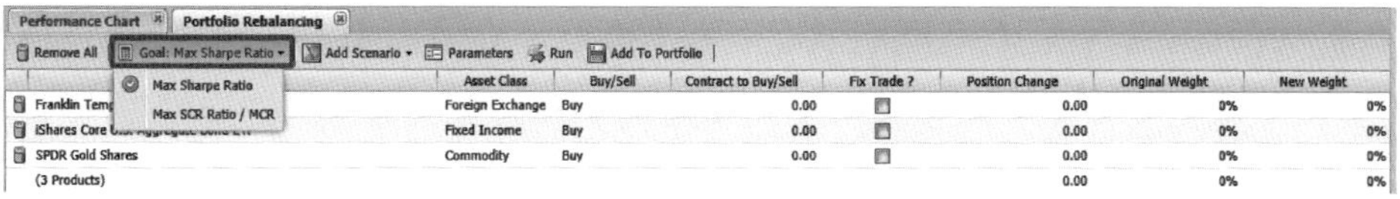

Figure 10.3: Specify Goal

Step 2 Add at least two scenarios with the total confidence level summing to 100%.

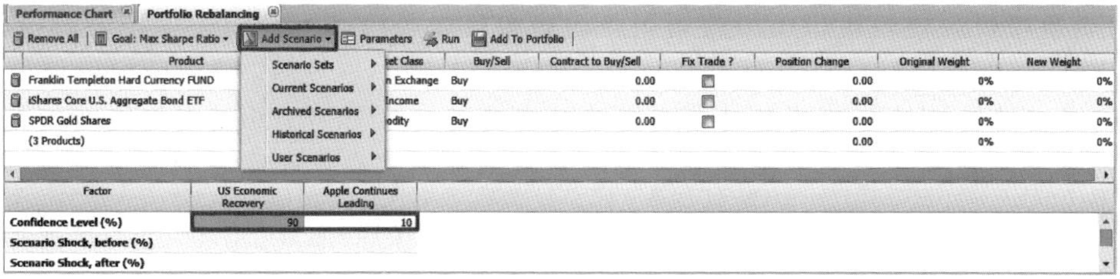

Figure 10.4: Choose Scenarios

Step 3 Click on the "Run" button to generate the results shown below.

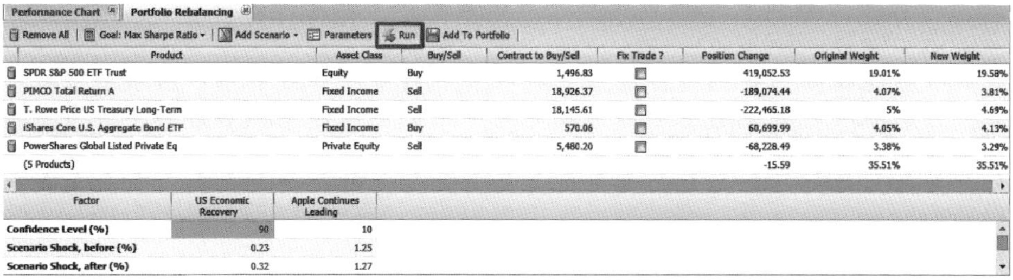

Figure 10.5: Review Results

The HedgeSPA platform computes the expected returns for the portfolios on the platform automatically. They are estimated asset-by-asset based on the econometric models constructed from the scenarios.

10.3   Methodology for Capital Adequacy

10.3.1   SCR Ratio and MCR Calculation

We calculate the baseline Solvency Capital Requirement (SCR) (or Minimum Capital Requirement (MCR)) and SCR coverage ratio based on formulas from the standard model as specified by Solvency II. The user can choose to apply his/her own internal models with regulatory approval. The first equation, or Equation 10.1, is:

$$SCR = BSCR + SCR_{op} + Adj$$

where:

$BSCR$: Basic Solvency Capital Requirement, defined by:
$BSCR = sqrt(\sum Corr_{r,s} \times SCR_r \times SCR_s)$;
$Corr_{r,s}$ = the entries of the matrix of correlation between different risks, $Corr$. The risk modules include market risk, life underwriting risk, non-life underwriting risk, health underwriting risk, counterparty default risk plus intangible asset risk;
SCR_r, SCR_s = Capital requirements for each SCR risk, according to the rows and columns of the correlation matrix $Corr$.
SCR_{op}: The capital requirement for operational risk;
Adj: Adjustment for the loss-absorbing capacity of technical provisions, security mechanisms and deferred taxes.

The next set of equations is given by:

$$MCR = 35\% \cdot SCR$$

$$SCR\_Coverage\_Ratio = Own\_Funds \div SCR$$

After these calculations: 1) Apply different scenarios (stress level as specified by Solvency II); 2) Obtain expected capital loss under each stress; and 3) Apply the correlation matrix to compute the capital requirement for each risk module.

Then, apply the correlation matrix again on all risk modules to compute $BSCR$ and SCR as shown in Equation 10.1.

10.3.2   Risk Modules

The risk modules as specified by the standard model in Solvency II include the following definitions as published by CEIOPS (Committee of European Insurance and Occupational Pensions Supervisors).[1] These risk module definitions are included in the text box below for ease of reference:

---

[1]Source: see https://eiopa.europa.eu/CEIOPS-Archive/Documents/Advices/CEIOPS-L2-Final-Advice-on-Standard-Formula-Health-underwriting-risk.pdf for details.

1. Non-life Underwriting Risk Module

   The non-life underwriting risk module reflects the risk arising from non-life insurance obligations, in relation to the perils covered and the processes used in the conduct of business. It should take into account the uncertainty in the existing insurance and reinsurance obligations as well as to the new business expected to be underwritten in the following 12 months. This can be calculated as a combination of the capital requirements for at least the following sub-modules:

   (a) the risk of loss, or of an adverse change in the value of insurance liabilities, resulting from fluctuations in the timing, frequency, and severity of insured events, and in the timing and amount of claim settlements (non-life premium and reserve risk);

   (b) the risk of loss, or of an adverse change in the value of insurance liabilities, resulting from significant uncertainty of pricing and provisioning assumptions related to extreme and/or exceptional events (i.e. non-life catastrophe risk).

2. Life Underwriting Risk Module

   The life underwriting risk module reflects the risk arising from life insurance obligations, in relation to the perils covered and the processes used in the conduct of business. It should be calculated as a combination of the capital requirements for at least the following sub-modules:

   (a) the risk of loss, or of an adverse change in the value of insurance liabilities, resulting from changes in the level, trend, or volatility of mortality rates, where an increase in the mortality rate leads to an increase in the value of insurance liabilities (mortality risk);

   (b) the risk of loss, or of an adverse change in the value of insurance liabilities, resulting from changes in the level, trend, or volatility of mortality rates, where a decrease in the mortality rate leads to an increase in the value of insurance liabilities (longevity risk);

   (c) the risk of loss, or of an adverse change in the value of insurance liabilities, resulting from changes in the level, trend or volatility of disability, sickness and morbidity rates (disability-morbidity risk);

   (d) the risk of loss, or of an adverse change in the value of insurance liabilities, resulting from changes in the level, trend, or volatility of the expenses incurred in servicing insurance or reinsurance contracts (life-expense risk);

(e) the risk of loss, or of an adverse change in the value of insurance liabilities, resulting from fluctuations in the level, trend, or volatility of the revision rates applied to annuities, due to changes in the legal environment or in the state of health of the individuals insured (revision risk);

(f) the risk of loss, or of an adverse change in the value of insurance liabilities, resulting from changes in the level or volatility of the rates of policy lapses, terminations, renewals and surrenders (lapse risk);

(g) the risk of loss, or of an adverse change in the value of insurance liabilities, resulting from the significant uncertainty of pricing and provisioning assumptions related to extreme or irregular events (life-catastrophe risk).

3. Health Underwriting Risk Module

The health underwriting risk module reflects the risk arising from the underwriting of health insurance obligations, whether it is pursued on a similar technical basis to that of life insurance or not, following from both the perils covered and the processes used in the conduct of business. It should cover at least the following risks:

(a) the risk of loss, or of an adverse change in the value of insurance liabilities, resulting from changes in the level, trend, or volatility of the expenses incurred in servicing insurance or reinsurance contracts;

(b) the risk of loss, or of an adverse change in the value of insurance liabilities, resulting from fluctuations in the timing, frequency, and severity of insured events, and in the timing and amount of claim settlements at the time of provisioning;

(c) the risk of loss, or of an adverse change in the value of insurance liabilities, resulting from the significant uncertainty of pricing and provisioning assumptions related to outbreaks of major epidemics, as well as the unusual accumulation of risks under such extreme circumstances.

4. Market Risk Module

The market risk module reflects the risk arising from the level or volatility of market prices of financial instruments which have an impact on the value of the assets and liabilities of the undertaking. It should properly reflect the structural mismatch between assets and liabilities, in particular with respect to the difference in duration between the assets and liabilities. It should be calculated as a combination of the capital requirements for at least the following sub-modules:

(a) the sensitivity of the values of assets, liabilities and financial instruments to changes in the term structure of interest rates, or in the volatility of interest rates (interest rate risk);

(b) the sensitivity of the values of assets, liabilities and financial instruments to changes in the level or in the volatility of market prices of equities (equity risk);

(c) the sensitivity of the values of assets, liabilities and financial instruments to changes in the level or in the volatility of market prices of real estate (property risk);

(d) the sensitivity of the values of assets, liabilities and financial instruments to changes in the level or in the volatility of credit spreads over the risk-free interest rate term structure (spread risk);

(e) the sensitivity of the values of assets, liabilities and financial instruments to changes in the level or in the volatility of currency exchange rates (currency risk);

(f) additional risks to an insurance or reinsurance undertaking stemming either from lack of diversification in the asset portfolio or from large exposure to default risk by a single issuer of securities or a group of related issuers (market concentration risk).

5. Counterparty Default Risk Module

The counterparty default risk module reflects possible losses due to unexpected default, or deterioration in the credit standing, of the counterparties and debtors of insurance and reinsurance undertakings over the following 12 months. The counterparty default risk module should cover risk-mitigating contracts, such as reinsurance arrangements, securitizations and derivatives, and receivables from intermediaries, as well as any other credit exposures which are not already covered in the spread risk sub-module. It can take into appropriate account of collateral or other security held by or for the account of the insurance or reinsurance undertaking and the risks associated therewith. For each counterparty, the counterparty default risk module can take into account the overall counterparty risk exposure of the insurance or reinsurance undertaking concerning that counterparty, irrespective of the legal form of its contractual obligations to that undertaking.

6. Intangible Asset Risk Module

   The Intangible asset risk module includes 80% of the amount of intangible assets, as recognized and valued.

7. Capital Requirement for Operational Risk

   The capital requirement for operational risk reflects operational risks to the extent that they are not already reflected in the risk modules referred to before. With respect to life insurance contracts where the investment risk is borne by the policyholders, the calculation of the capital requirement for operational risk takes into account the annual expenses incurred in respect of those insurance obligations. With respect to insurance and reinsurance operations other than those already referred to above, the calculation of the capital requirement for operational risk takes into account the volume of those operations, in terms of earned premiums and technical provisions which are held in respect of those insurance and reinsurance obligations. In this case, the capital requirement for operational risks does not exceed 30% of the Basic Solvency Capital Requirement relating to those insurance and reinsurance operations.

8. Adjustment for the Loss-absorbing Capacity of Technical Provisions and Deferred Taxes

   Adjustment for the loss-absorbing capacity of technical provisions and deferred taxes reflects potential compensation of unexpected losses through a simultaneous decrease in technical provisions or deferred taxes, or a combination of the two. That adjustment takes into account the risk-mitigating effect provided by future discretionary benefits of insurance contracts, to the extent that insurance and reinsurance undertakings can establish that a reduction in such benefits may be used to cover unexpected losses when they arise. The risk-mitigating effect provided by future discretionary benefits should be no higher than the sum of technical provisions and deferred taxes relating to those future discretionary benefits. For the purpose of this calculation, the value of future discretionary benefits under adverse circumstances can be compared to the value of such benefits from the underlying assumptions of the best-estimate calculations.

INVESTMENT ANALYTICS IN THE DAWN OF ARTIFICIAL INTELLIGENCE

11. Forward Scenarios and Historical Simulations

11.1 Use Case

The global economy is not doing well. Central banks in Japan and the EU are driving interest rates down to zero if not negative territories in order to stimulate their economies. The Chinese government is struggling to meet its growth targets and its estimated annual growth rate has been downgraded once again due to bad performance in exports, and a surging producer price index. The domestic economy also has many big changes to expect, under an American administration that is ready to risk her domestic economic growth to start trade wars.

Mary is a hedge fund manager. She is focused on how poor Chinese economic performance may impact global growth. She has two rough scenarios about the future trends of Chinese economic performance. One is an optimistic expectation that the Chinese economy will return to its past growth rate averaged at the high single digits. The other is a pessimistic projection that the Chinese economy has lost its momentum and is unlikely to return to what it used to be.

How should Mary codify each scenario quantitatively, identify key characteristics, and project her portfolio's performance under these two scenarios? How should these two scenarios impact her investment decision making? This chapter aims to help Mary better understand the key analytical insights in such market scenarios and what investment insights she can gain from a smart analysis of these scenarios.

Moreover, Mary also wants to look at some historical simulations and see how the adjusted portfolio would have performed under real historical data. This chapter will help her analyze under both forward-looking and historical scenarios.

11.2   Forward-Looking Scenarios

The **Scenario Analysis** tool allows users to explore the possible statistical impact of forward-looking market scenarios on their portfolios. To access **Scenario Analysis**, users should select a portfolio first. Then, users can click on "Analytics" and then choose scenarios from "Current Scenarios", "Archived Scenarios", "Historical Scenarios", or "User Scenarios", under "Decision/Execution", as shown below:

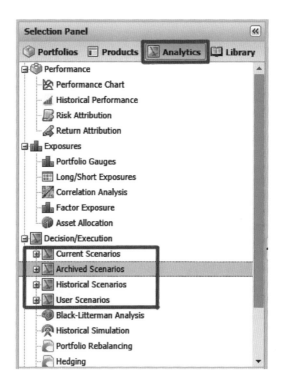

Figure 11.1: "Analytics → Scenarios"

Users can also use the tree structure as shown by Figure 11.2 below to select the suitable scenarios.

Figure 11.3 shows how this tool lets users select from a list of possible factors, specify their market views with a statistical price "shock" and then examine the potential statistical result on their portfolio using the platform's sophisticated multi-asset scenario models.

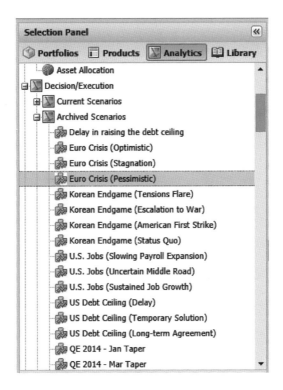

Figure 11.2: Scenarios Selection

Figure 11.3: Scenario Analysis under Euro Crisis (Pessimistic)

In each multi-asset scenario, users can select one factor in each asset category, including Equity, Bond, Foreign Exchange, and Commodity. Then, users choose one Equity and Bond factor each. Certain factors may also support sub-factors such as the S&P sector indices. These factors can be selected and changed using the drop-down selection box in Figure 11.4:

Figure 11.4: Index Selection

In Figure 11.3, for each selected factor, the current value of the chosen index will be displayed, followed by the new value after the factor shock, the change in numerical terms and the change in percentage terms. Users can then define the statistical "shock" to the chosen factor, or their "view" on its possible future change, in either percentage change or in absolute numerical terms using either the simple scrollbar or by directly entering the value in the change area. Further, the screen has an image with a description on the right. Users can click on "Full Description" in Figure 11.3 to read the complete description of the scenario. The platform's supplied scenarios are usually extracted from sell-side research published by the leading investment banks.

The results of **Scenario Analysis** as shown in Figure 11.5 will be displayed in the Scenarios columns at the right-hand side of the Portfolio view area in the top area of the Workspace. Each open scenario will be displayed in its own columns, with the statistical impact displayed on each asset in the portfolio and aggregate effect on the portfolio as a whole. Also, under each scenario, there are three columns named Position Change, Asset Change, and Scenario Price respectively. Position Change means the percentage of change in the weight of this position in the portfolio under the selected scenario. Asset Change means the percentage of change in the value of the invested asset under the selected scenario, and Scenario Price means the new price of the investment instrument under the selected scenario.

Description		Position in USD	Weight	Return	Euro Crisis (Optimistic)			Euro Crisis (Stagnation)			Euro Crisis (Pessimistic)		
Product	Asset Class	Actual	Actual	Historica...	Pos Chg	Asst Chg	Scen Prc	Pos Chg ▲	Asst Chg	Scen Prc	Pos Chg	Asst Chg	Scen Prc
Keppel Corporation Limited	Equity	214,232.87	1.44%	32.87%	0.01%	0.64%	7.29	0.02%	1.21%	7.33	0.10%	6.62%	7.72
Vanguard MSCI Pacific ETF	Equity	1,085,850.00	7.29%	10.63%	0.13%	1.78%	73.68	0.16%	2.13%	73.93	0.11%	1.49%	73.47
Genting Singapore PLC	Equity	541,500.22	3.63%	30.64%	0.10%	2.82%	1.25	0.17%	4.55%	1.28	-0.30%	-8.35%	1.12
Straits Times Index ETF	Equity	756,768.75	5.08%	19.05%	0.04%	0.75%	3.44	0.24%	4.64%	3.57	0.96%	18.82%	4.05
Ascendas Real Estate Investment Tr...	Equity	969,078.27	6.50%	7.39%	0.11%	1.70%	2.66	0.59%	9.05%	2.86	2.07%	31.82%	3.45
Keppel REIT Management Limited	Equity	579,967.45	3.89%	8.17%	0.10%	2.51%	1.15	0.60%	15.37%	1.29	1.98%	50.98%	1.69
SPDR Gold Shares	Commodity	2,426,800.00	16.28%	3.54%	0.17%	1.02%	122.58	0.68%	4.17%	126.40	3.32%	20.37%	146.06
Total		14,902,363.04	100.00%	405.05%	1.28%			-1.71%			-8.50%		

Figure 11.5: Results of Euro Crisis Scenario Analysis

11.3   Historical Simulation

Historical Simulation shows a histogram of a portfolio's historical performance under the specified start and end dates, based on the positions in the selected portfolio. The graph is plotted against the returns of the portfolio against the number of counts in each corresponding bucket of returns. This is the realized historical market data as applied to the portfolio's transaction history. To access the **Historical Simulation** tool, users should select a portfolio first, and click on "Analytics", then "Historical Simulation" under "User Scenarios", as in Figure 11.6 below:

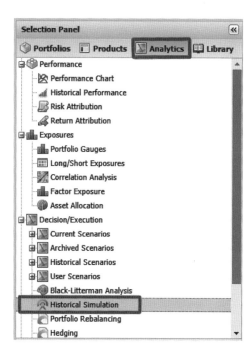

Figure 11.6: "Analytics → Historical Simulation"

The histogram in **Historical Simulation** in Figure 11.7 below will also be plotted against its best-fit normal distribution curve. The Values-at-Risk (VARs) at a 95% and 99% confidence levels are also displayed.

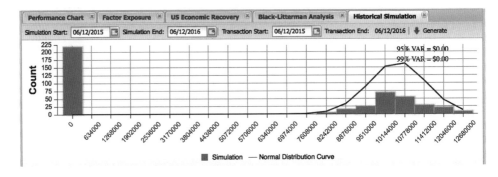

Figure 11.7: Historical Simulation

Note: since this function is based on the actual history of transactions, there must be at least one historical transaction performed on the portfolio in order to perform a historical simulation. This functionality will not work for users who prefer to submit "positions and tickers" to produce analytics.

INVESTMENT ANALYTICS IN THE DAWN OF ARTIFICIAL INTELLIGENCE

12. Combining Upside with Black Swan Scenarios

12.1 Use Case

Portfolio manager Jack manages an institutional fund of $150 million. The fund has no explicit liability profile to match and does not contain any investment with a near-term maturity date. Some of its holdings do not have daily liquidity, but historically only a minor percentage of its holdings may need to be withdrawn so as to support the cash needs of its sponsors. Hence, its investments cannot be wholly illiquid. The strategic allocation of the fund has been modeled by an investment consultant as an Asian High-Networth portfolio in Figure 12.1, as follows:

Description		Position in USD	Weight	Return	Chinese and Global Economies Diverge		
Product ▲	Asset Class	Actual	Actual	Historica...	Pos Chg	Asst Chg	Scen Prc
Ascendas Real Estate Investment Tr...	Equity	999,850.21	6.62%	7.44%	0.17%	2.50%	2.74
DBS Group Holdings Limited	Equity	536,436.49	3.55%	49.92%	0.72%	20.25%	34.45
Genting Singapore PLC	Equity	566,207.31	3.75%	28.86%	0.45%	11.95%	1.41
Keppel Corporation Limited	Equity	225,584.18	1.49%	34.08%	0.00%	-0.25%	7.51
Keppel REIT Management Limited	Equity	602,905.93	3.99%	11.81%	0.94%	23.63%	1.42
PIMCO 0-5 Year Hi Yld Corp Bond Id...	Fixed Inco...	1,000,700.00	6.63%	-0.20%	0.48%	7.22%	107.30
PowerShares Golden Dragon China	Equity	1,754,550.00	11.62%	27.53%	7.41%	63.73%	82.08
SPDR Barclays Aggregate Bond ETF	Equity	832,500.00	5.51%	4,380.32...	-0.16%	-2.98%	26.92
SPDR Gold Shares	Commodity	2,464,600.00	16.33%	2.64%	-6.35%	-38.90%	75.30
Straits Times Index ETF	Equity	788,645.90	5.22%	20.01%	0.53%	10.17%	3.87
Vanguard MSCI Pacific ETF	Equity	1,109,400.00	7.35%	10.64%	2.62%	35.66%	100.33
iPath S&P GSCI Crude Oil TR Index ...	Commodity	7,500.00	0.05%	-33.00%	0.01%	18.12%	0.18
iShares Core S&P500 ETF	Equity	4,207,650.00	27.87%	11.33%	9.89%	35.50%	380.09
Total		15,096,530.02	100.00%	254.47%	16.70%		

Figure 12.1: Asian High Networth Portfolio

Jack likes this allocation, which has enjoyed an exceptional last year, but simply allocating to the same asset buckets going forward is unlikely to achieve the same desirable results. Jack's goal is to generate a steady absolute return over the medium to the long term. His asset sponsors are well aware of that markets may swing up and down in the shorter term, and that artificially creating an absolute return vehicle may be very costly and hurt returns without achieving the sponsor's longer-term investment objectives.

Jack's challenge is to allocate to "good" sectors while maintaining some level of confidence that his portfolio will not be hurt by a massive drawdown later. His asset sponsors are prepared to accept such drawdowns assuming that the portfolio upside will be more than sufficient to pay for any potential downside. Hence, his asset sponsors demand to "trust but verify": They would like to see a sophisticated analysis that Jack's bets stand reasonable chances of paying off.

This chapter will show Jack how to achieve such a feat systematically.

12.1.1 Defining the Investment Problem

To achieve his complex investment goal, Jack faces several significant limitations associated with the characteristics of any multi-asset portfolio.

First, it is common knowledge among professional investors and proven by empirical research commissioned by Norges Bank Investment Management[1] that most institutional-sized portfolios derive their returns from beta instead of alpha due to their massive size. Intuitively, it is difficult for any large institution at a size comparable to a small financial market to outperform any one specific market: They will buy "up" the market on the way in and drive the market "down" on exit.

Second, any significant change to the portfolio will result in high transaction costs due to market impact, which will offset the benefits of trying to achieve meaningful returns. Further, hedging may not be a practical strategy for a large portfolio as such, because the massive size of any short positions required by an effective hedge may artificially induce a market crash.

Finally, there are always some investments in any portfolio that may be impossible to sell *en masse*, such as real estate investments.

After the financial crisis in 2008, the sponsors of Jack's fund modified his investment mandate to account for potential "Black Swan" scenarios in its routine portfolio rebalancing reviews, because it may be impossible to make any sudden,

---

[1]20 January 2014, *Review of the Active Management of the Norwegian Government Pension Fund Global*, https://www0.gsb.columbia.edu/faculty/aang/papers/AngBrandtDenison.pdf.

major changes to such a large portfolio or put on any hedge even with, say, 6 months of visibility that such a "Black Swan" event does happen. Yet, such a fund will not generate a healthy medium to long-term return if it is "permanently" positioned to avoid extreme events. Jack wants to find an optimal asset allocation that can take into account low-probability extreme events for a multi-asset portfolio.

12.1.2 Potential Scenarios on Watch

Back in 2014, China's domestic market was denied entry into internationally-watched MSCI's index benchmark for the third year in a row because the level of freedom in the buying and selling of China A shares was deemed insufficient for international investors to freely invest and divest in the view of MSCI. This rejection frustrated certain investors and was expected to serve as one way to motivate the Chinese government to take more aggressive actions towards financial market liberation. Therefore, Jack held the view that the speed at which the Chinese market would open up to foreign investors soon was going to accelerate, which he described as "Aggressive Chinese Market Liberation". Concurrently, the Middle East was not doing well due to the collapse of oil prices since the beginning of 2014. Jack believes that the Middle East would not recover soon, but might even slow down its growth, which he describes as "Middle East Deteriorates". Due to the increase in interest rate in the US, the dollar was getting stronger. However, Jack believed CNY would keep increasing its value once the Chinese government took action in the foreign exchange market, which he called "Chinese and Global Economies Diverge".

12.1.3 Traditional Approach

Traditionally, Jack would start with the classic approach of maximizing portfolio Sharpe Ratio. He first obtains the expected return of each asset under each scenario. From those expected returns, he calculates the optimal asset allocation under each scenario (See Figure 12.2). The key disadvantages of this approach are: a) there is no way to reflect the confidence level of each scenario; and b) transaction costs will be potentially prohibitive each time he changes his views. For instance, the Treynor-Black approach as described by [**Treynor 1973**] assumes that an analyst can make perfect forecasts on future alpha and allocate portfolio weights. Perfect foresight is at best an unrealistic assumption that only results in corner solutions and frequent and expensive switching of asset positions when forecasts change.

Description		Position in USD	Weight	Return	Aggressive Chinese Market Liberalization			Middle East Deteriorates			Chinese and Global Economies Diverge		
Product ▲	Asset Class	Actual	Actual	Historica...	Pos Chg	Asst Chg	Scen Prc	Pos Chg	Asst Chg	Scen Prc	Pos Chg	Asst Chg	Scen Prc
PowerShares Golden Dragon China	Equity	1,754,550.00	11.62%	27.53%	6.72%	57.79%	79.10	5.70%	49.05%	74.72	7.41%	63.73%	82.08
SPDR Barclays Aggregate Bond ETF	Equity	832,500.00	5.51%	4,380.32...	0.91%	16.59%	32.35	-0.16%	-2.96%	26.93	-0.16%	-2.98%	26.92
SPDR Gold Shares	Commodity	2,464,600.00	16.33%	2.64%	0.38%	2.30%	126.06	-1.25%	-7.64%	113.82	-6.35%	-38.90%	75.30
Straits Times Index ETF	Equity	788,645.90	5.22%	20.01%	3.71%	70.97%	6.00	-1.32%	-25.27%	2.62	0.53%	10.17%	3.87
Vanguard MSCI Pacific ETF	Equity	1,109,400.00	7.35%	10.64%	9.41%	128.09%	168.69	-1.75%	-23.76%	56.39	2.62%	35.66%	100.33
iPath S&P GSCI Crude Oil TR Index ...	Commodity	7,500.00	0.05%	-33.00%	0.03%	69.95%	0.25	0.02%	38.14%	0.21	0.01%	18.12%	0.18
iShares Core S&P500 ETF	Equity	4,207,650.00	27.87%	11.33%	23.13%	83.00%	513.33	-1.01%	-3.63%	270.32	9.89%	35.50%	380.09
Total		15,096,530.02	100.00%	254.47%	67.30%			-7.03%			16.70%		

Figure 12.2: Portfolio under Different Scenarios

Jack is also concerned about several practical considerations before choosing a specific implementation:

1. If the portfolio is structured on any specific scenario, it may result in a "corner solution" concentrated in a few assets, rather than a full range of diversified assets. Rebalancing from one corner solution to the next (after a change in investment view) will result in another major change in weights and therefore significant transaction costs; this approach may not be practical for large institutional portfolios because no one knows exactly which scenario may happen, and even their confidence may change.

2. The existing market views should be medium to long-term so as to be consistent with the portfolio's investment goal. Otherwise, the high transaction costs due to dramatic moves in positions even with slight changes in forward-looking scenarios will exceed any benefits from such portfolio rebalancing.

3. The rebalancing should be done with evidence of appropriate trade-offs between risks and return.

12.1.4   Stochastic Analysis Solution

To address the shortcomings of the single scenario approach as discussed above, Jack is going to try a multi-scenario analysis to obtain an optimal asset allocation that will improve under multiple views. The Stochastic Analysis tool allows Jack to input any number of views with the probability of each occurring assigned by Jack. Each view can describe the expected return of a portfolio under each scenario, Thus, such a model combines the three views that Jack holds (i.e., Figure 12.3 "Aggressive Chinese Market Liberation" View, Figure 12.4 "Middle East Deteriorates" View, and Figure 12.5 "Chinese and Global Economies Diverge" View), producing both the set of expected returns of assets and the optimal portfolio weights. Jack assigns his confidence level to each scenario (10%, 10%, and 80% respectively), which tilts the neutral weights of the portfolio in the direction following his beliefs. These views are shown as follows:

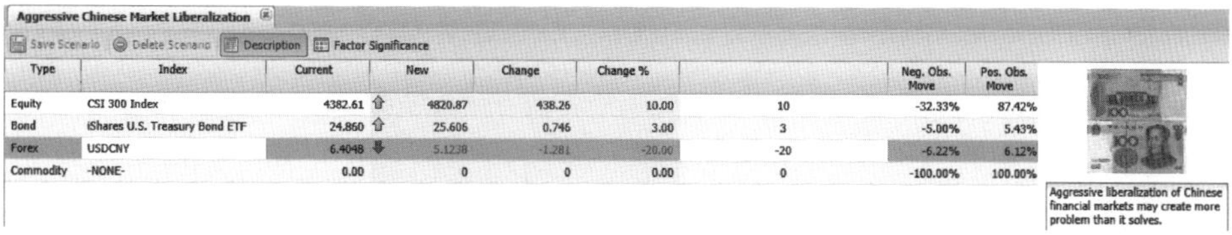

Aggressive Chinese Market Liberalization

Save Scenario Delete Scenario Description Factor Significance

Type	Index	Current	New	Change	Change %		Neg. Obs. Move	Pos. Obs. Move
Equity	CSI 300 Index	4382.61 ⇧	4820.87	438.26	10.00	10	-32.33%	87.42%
Bond	iShares U.S. Treasury Bond ETF	24.860 ⇧	25.606	0.746	3.00	3	-5.00%	5.43%
Forex	USDCNY	6.4048 ⇩	5.1238	-1.281	-20.00	-20	-6.22%	6.12%
Commodity	-NONE-	0.00	0	0	0.00	0	-100.00%	100.00%

Aggressive liberalization of Chinese financial markets may create more problem than it solves.

Figure 12.3: The "Aggressive Chinese Market Liberation" View

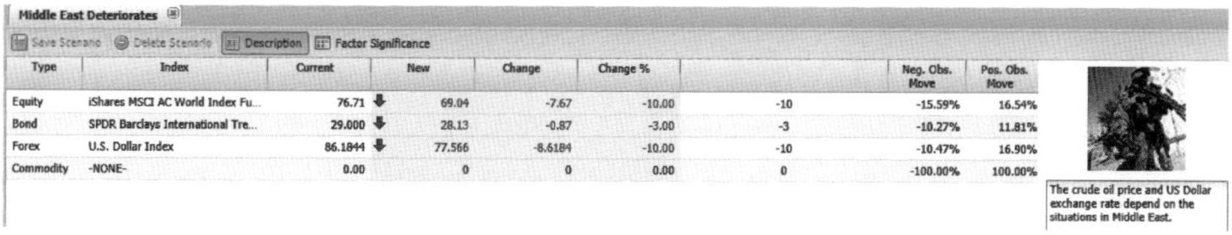

Middle East Deteriorates

Save Scenario Delete Scenario Description Factor Significance

Type	Index	Current	New	Change	Change %		Neg. Obs. Move	Pos. Obs. Move
Equity	iShares MSCI AC World Index Fu...	76.71 ⇩	69.04	-7.67	-10.00	-10	-15.59%	16.54%
Bond	SPDR Barclays International Tre...	29.000 ⇩	28.13	-0.87	-3.00	-3	-10.27%	11.81%
Forex	U.S. Dollar Index	86.1844 ⇩	77.566	-8.6184	-10.00	-10	-10.47%	16.90%
Commodity	-NONE-	0.00	0	0	0.00	0	-100.00%	100.00%

The crude oil price and US Dollar exchange rate depend on the situations in Middle East.

Figure 12.4: The "Middle East Deteriorates" View

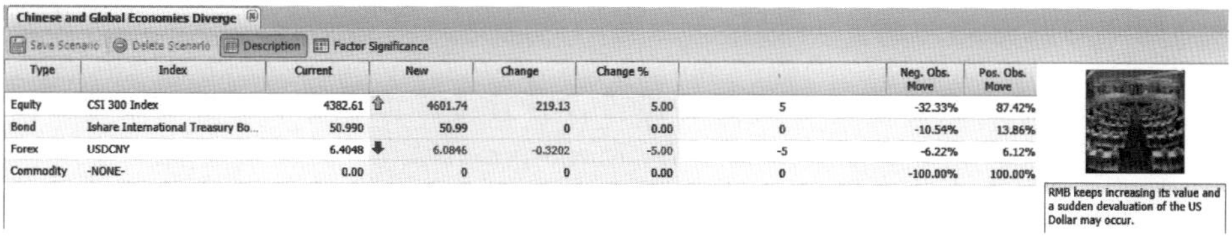

Chinese and Global Economies Diverge

Save Scenario Delete Scenario Description Factor Significance

Type	Index	Current	New	Change	Change %		Neg. Obs. Move	Pos. Obs. Move
Equity	CSI 300 Index	4382.61 ⇧	4601.74	219.13	5.00	5	-32.33%	87.42%
Bond	Ishare International Treasury Bo...	50.990	50.99	0	0.00	0	-10.54%	13.86%
Forex	USDCNY	6.4048 ⇩	6.0846	-0.3202	-5.00	-5	-6.22%	6.12%
Commodity	-NONE-	0.00	0	0	0.00	0	-100.00%	100.00%

RMB keeps increasing its value and a sudden devaluation of the US Dollar may occur.

Figure 12.5: The "Chinese and Global Economies Diverge" View

Besides overcoming all the challenges mentioned above in the traditional single-scenario approach, the stochastic analysis approach provides a solution that is intuitive, highly-diversified and less sensitive to small changes in a single input parameter. It also provides an accurate estimation of error maximization. To access the **Stochastic Analysis** tool, users can click "Analytics" and then look for "Decision/Execution". Users then click "Stochastic Analysis", which is immediately below "User Scenarios".

12.1.5 Outcome

Jack is happy to see that this alternative approach allows him to incorporate low-probability extreme events to construct a more stable portfolio. This recommendation gives Jack a more effective way to pursue his medium-to-long term investment

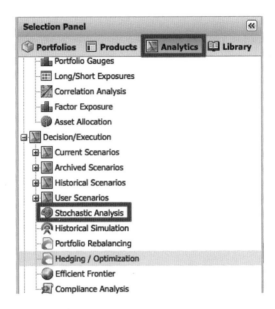

Figure 12.6: "Analytics → Stochastic Analysis"

thesis, with inexpensive "protection" against extreme downside outcomes that he does not need to pay option premia for, or comes with costs of carry that add up over time. Given that institutional portfolios tend to be very expensive to rebalance dramatically due to their massive size, now Jack has a scientific way to test his investment ideas under several scenarios simultaneously and get them right prior to implementation.

12.2 Methodology

12.2.1 Objective

The **Stochastic Analysis** tool allows investors to combine their views of different market scenarios with different confidence levels so as to achieve a better asset allocation. Through this analysis, a portfolio can achieve both a superior *ex-ante* upside and is in a better position to mitigate its downside risk. As one example, this tool can be used by investment professionals who want to specify a dominant view, but are also concerned about the potential impact of so-called "Black Swan" events in the market. Stochastic Analysis provides a practical way by which our investors can balance potential gains on the upside against protection from extreme downside scenarios.

12.2.2 Overview

Stochastic Analysis uses a Bayesian approach to combine the subjective views of an investor (the prior distribution) on asset returns with the market equilibrium vector of expected returns, so as to form a combined estimate (the posterior distribution) of expected returns. Basically, Stochastic Analysis can be thought of graphically as shown in Figure 12.7.

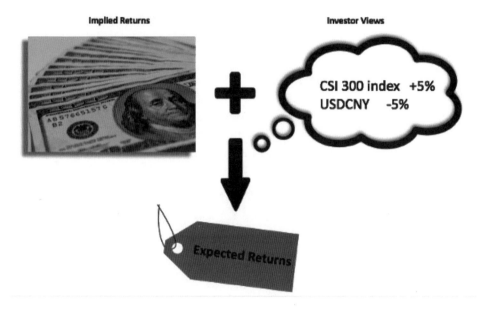

Figure 12.7: Combining Implied Returns and Investor Views

12.2.3 Formula

Notations:

Π Implied Return, which closed-form solution is provided by $\frac{\Sigma w_{mkt} \cdot (\mu^T w_{mkt})}{w_{mkt}^T \Sigma w_{mkt}}$ without position constraints, representing the return each asset must deliver so as to justify the amount of risk it contributes to the overall portfolio;

Σ Covariance matrix of asset returns;

μ Asset historical return;

τ A scalar for the investor to control the maximal change(s) of portfolio position(s), which lacks a simple intuitive explanation[2];

---

[2]See, for instance, *A Discussion of Tau*, http://www.blacklitterman.org/tau.html.

P Matrix representing an investor's view, with each column of matrix P representing an investor's view about the assets' weighted expected returns, and the normalized elements of the columns summing up to 1;

Q A column vector, in which each element is a total change of a portfolio's weighted expected returns under a particular view;

Ω Diagonal covariance matrix of errors terms expressing the uncertainty in each view;

I Identity matrix;

The Stochastic Analysis algorithm, as modified from the classic Black-Litterman model, is given by:

$$E(R) = \Pi + \tau \Sigma P^T [\Omega + \tau P \Sigma P^T]^{-1} (Q - P \Pi)$$

The key improvement over the classic Black-Litterman model is that the current portfolio weight (w_{mkt}) can be used as a sufficiently good estimator to the equilibrium market weight. There is no loss of generality from this feature because an investor who is interested in the classic Black-Litterman analysis can simply enter the equilibrium market weight as the current portfolio weight. The optimal asset weight is calculated by the equation:

$$w_{opt} = \frac{\Sigma^{-1} E(R)}{I^T \Sigma^{-1} E(R)}$$

12.2.4   Computational Process

A typical computation is done in the following 5 steps:

Step 1 Calculate the mark-to-market valuation, and the weights of the existing portfolio;

Step 2 Do a reversed optimization of the Sharpe Ratio to get the Implied Returns of the portfolio assets;

Step 3 Define the scenarios and the confidence or probability of each scenario;

Step 4 Estimate the scenario return of each asset to compute the P matrix and Q vector; and

Step 5 Compute the new optimal weights, by re-optimizing Sharpe Ratio, combining the implied equilibrium distribution and the view distribution.

Choosing the portfolio in Step 1 will lead to the results of Stochastic Analysis in the following schematic:

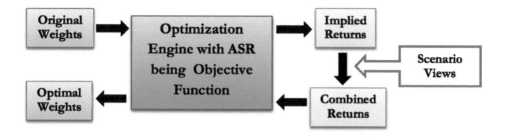

Figure 12.8: Stochastic Analysis Computational Process

The computation process on HedgeSPA platform corresponds to the following five steps of calculations (that can be verified against similar calculations performed in typical statistical packages such as R):

Step 1 Refresh portfolio weights
Compute w_{mkt} of the current portfolio using the latest mark-to-market values of assets.

Step 2 Compute implied returns Π
Given w_{mkt} of the current portfolio, use reversed optimization to find the vector of Implied Returns Π, such that those implied returns maximize $\frac{E(R_a-R_{rf})}{\sqrt{Var(R_a-R_{rf})}}$ based on existing portfolio weights, where R_a is the portfolio return and R_{rf} is the risk-free return. The close-form solution for the reversed optimization problem without position constraint is $\Pi = \frac{\Sigma w_{mkt}\cdot(\mu^T w_{mkt})}{w_{mkt}^T \Sigma w_{mkt}}$.

Step 3 Compute P matrix
Each column of the P matrix represents a view according to the asset-weighted expected returns. The elements in each column are scaled so that they sum up to 100%.

Step 4 Calculate the combined returns $E(R)$ from the implied returns and forward looking view $E(R) = \Pi + \tau\Sigma P^T[\Omega + \tau P\Sigma P^T]^{-1}(Q-P\Pi)$.

Step 5 Given $E(R)$ as computed above, find the optimal allocation of *new* asset weights to maximize $\frac{E(R_a-R_{rf})}{\sqrt{Var(R_a-R_{rf})}}$. We may solve the problem numerically to account for constraints and non-negative positions, but the result should be similar to the following closed-form solution: $w_{opt} = \frac{\Sigma^{-1}E(R)}{I^T\Sigma^{-1}E(R)}$.

It is not required to use the traditional Sharpe Ratio for this calculation. For instance, a possible alternative is to use the Alternative Sharpe Ratio introduced earlier, even though such a ratio is significantly more computationally intensive to perform both the reversed optimization and the subsequent forward optimization.

12.3 Worked Example

12.3.1 Overview

As mentioned earlier, the strategic allocation of Jack's fund can be modeled by an Asian High Net-worth portfolio, which produces a modest historical portfolio return of 1.39% in Figure 12.9 below. Jack's goal is to generate a steady absolute return over the medium to the long term. The asset sponsor is well aware of that markets may swing up and down in the shorter term, and that artificially creating an absolute return vehicle may be costly and hurt returns without achieving the sponsor's longer-term investment objectives.

Description		Position in USD	Weight	Return	Chinese and Global Economies Diverge		
Product ▲	Asset Class	Actual	Actual	Historica...	Pos Chg	Asst Chg	Scen Prc
Ascendas Real Estate Investment Tr...	Equity	999,850.21	6.62%	7.44%	0.17%	2.50%	2.74
DBS Group Holdings Limited	Equity	536,436.49	3.55%	49.92%	0.72%	20.25%	34.45
Genting Singapore PLC	Equity	566,207.31	3.75%	28.86%	0.45%	11.95%	1.41
Keppel Corporation Limited	Equity	225,584.18	1.49%	34.08%	0.00%	-0.25%	7.51
Keppel REIT Management Limited	Equity	602,905.93	3.99%	11.81%	0.94%	23.63%	1.42
PIMCO 0-5 Year Hi Yld Corp Bond Id...	Fixed Inco...	1,000,700.00	6.63%	-0.20%	0.48%	7.22%	107.30
PowerShares Golden Dragon China	Equity	1,754,550.00	11.62%	27.53%	7.41%	63.73%	82.08
SPDR Barclays Aggregate Bond ETF	Equity	832,500.00	5.51%	4,380.32...	-0.16%	-2.98%	26.92
SPDR Gold Shares	Commodity	2,464,600.00	16.33%	2.64%	-6.35%	-38.90%	75.30
Straits Times Index ETF	Equity	788,645.90	5.22%	20.01%	0.53%	10.17%	3.87
Vanguard MSCI Pacific ETF	Equity	1,109,400.00	7.35%	10.64%	2.62%	35.66%	100.33
iPath S&P GSCI Crude Oil TR Index ...	Commodity	7,500.00	0.05%	-33.00%	0.01%	18.12%	0.18
iShares Core S&P500 ETF	Equity	4,207,650.00	27.87%	11.33%	9.89%	35.50%	380.09
Total		15,096,530.02	100.00%	254.47%	16.70%		

Figure 12.9: The "Asian High Net-Worth" Portfolio

Jack comes up with three possible market outcomes, which he describes as "Chinese and Global Economics Diverge" (in Figure 12.3), "Aggressive Chinese Market Liberalization" (in Figure 12.4), and "Middle East Deterioration" (in Figure 12.5) scenarios with different shocks on his chosen market indices.

12.3.2 Definitions

1. Mathematical Models

   • Modeling Parameters
     a. This worked example uses 4 years of historical data from May 2012 to May 2016.

b. In Figure 12.9 above, the annual historical return for each asset is calculated using the forward 6-month rolling windows over those 4 years. For consistency, all the statistics are computed over the same horizon, but they may be annualized whenever appropriate.

c. The risk-free rate of return is set to be 0.1% during this period, and is assumed to be constant.

- Sharpe Ratio
  The Sharpe Ratio is given by $\frac{E[R_a-R_{rf}]}{\sqrt{Var[R_a-R_{rf}]}}$, where R_a is the asset return, R_{rf} is the risk-free asset return and risk of the portfolio is measured by the variance of excessive return. The Sharpe Ratio lets an investor know whether a higher return of a portfolio is achieved via better investment decisions (or alpha), or simply from taking excessive risk as measured by volatility (or beta). The greater a portfolio's Sharpe Ratio is, the better its risk-adjusted performance has been, although the Sharpe Ratio does come with some well-known shortcomings over its inability to properly account for portfolio tail risk.

- Portfolio Optimization and Reversed Optimization
  In this worked example, portfolio optimization is used to find the optimal asset weight allocation that maximizes/minimizes an objective function under specified constraints (e.g. non-negative weight is a common portfolio constraint), given the expected return of each asset under each scenario. Reversed portfolio optimization calculates the implied return of each asset in the portfolio so that the current weights are considered optimal under a specified choice of objective function.

2. Naïve Modeling

A typical "Naïve Modeling" strategy is to optimize the portfolio by maximizing portfolio Sharpe Ratio under each scenario. Such a model is implemented in two steps:

a. First Step: Calculate the expected returns under each view

The expected return for each asset under each view is calculated by individually running a regression on each asset's returns against the market factor returns under each view in Figure 12.2. The result is displayed in the "Asst Chg" column in Figure 12.10.

b. Second Step: Calculate the optimal weight allocation

Solve for $w = [w_1, w_2, \cdots w_{13}]^T$, in order to maximize the objective function $\dfrac{(E[R_a - R_{rf}])}{\sqrt{(Var[R_a - R_{rf}])}}$, subject to:

Constraint 1: $w_1 + w_2 \cdots w_{13} = 1$

Constraint 2: $w_i \geq 0$ for $i = 1, 2, \cdots, 13$

c. Final Step: Interpret the results from naïve modeling

Figure 12.10 shows the return shocks of the portfolio before optimization:

Description		Position in USD	Weight	Return		Chinese and Global Economies Diverge			Aggressive Chinese Market Liberalization			Middle East Deteriorates		
Product ▲	Asset Class	Actual	Actual	Historica...	Pos Chg	Asst Chg	Scen Prc	Pos Chg	Asst Chg	Scen Prc	Pos Chg	Asst Chg	Scen Prc
Ascendas Real Estate Investment Tr...	Equity	999,850.21	6.62%	7.44%	0.17%	2.58%	2.74	8.50%	128.37%	6.10	-2.74%	-41.38%	1.57
DBS Group Holdings Limited	Equity	536,436.49	3.55%	49.92%	0.72%	20.25%	34.45	1.87%	52.60%	43.72	-0.84%	-23.59%	21.89
Genting Singapore PLC	Equity	566,207.31	3.75%	28.86%	0.45%	11.95%	1.41	1.26%	33.63%	1.68	-0.40%	-10.68%	1.13
Keppel Corporation Limited	Equity	225,584.18	1.49%	34.08%	0.00%	-0.25%	7.51	0.43%	28.50%	9.68	-0.10%	-6.59%	7.03
Keppel REIT Management Limited	Equity	602,905.93	3.99%	11.81%	0.94%	23.63%	1.42	7.74%	193.85%	3.38	-2.76%	-69.23%	0.35
PIMCO 0-5 Year Hi Yld Corp Bond Id...	Fixed Inco...	1,000,700.00	6.63%	-0.20%	0.48%	7.22%	107.30	3.21%	48.38%	148.49	-0.42%	-6.29%	93.77
PowerShares Golden Dragon China	Equity	1,754,550.00	11.62%	27.53%	7.41%	63.73%	82.08	6.72%	57.79%	79.10	5.70%	49.05%	74.72
SPDR Barclays Aggregate Bond ETF	Equity	832,560.00	5.51%	4,380.32...	-0.16%	-2.98%	26.92	0.91%	16.59%	32.35	-0.16%	-2.96%	26.93
SPDR Gold Shares	Commodity	2,464,600.00	16.33%	2.64%	-6.35%	-38.90%	75.30	0.38%	2.30%	126.06	-1.25%	-7.64%	113.82
Straits Times Index ETF	Equity	788,645.90	5.22%	20.01%	0.53%	10.17%	3.87	3.71%	70.97%	6.00	-1.32%	-25.27%	2.62
Vanguard MSCI Pacific ETF	Equity	1,109,400.00	7.35%	10.64%	2.62%	35.86%	100.33	9.41%	128.09%	168.69	-1.75%	-23.76%	56.39
iPath S&P GSCI Crude Oil TR Index ...	Commodity	7,500.00	0.05%	-33.00%	0.01%	18.12%	0.18	0.03%	69.95%	0.25	0.02%	38.14%	0.21
iShares Core S&P500 ETF	Equity	4,207,650.00	27.87%	11.33%	9.89%	35.50%	380.09	23.13%	83.00%	513.33	-1.01%	-3.63%	270.32
Total		15,096,530.02	100.00%	254.47%	16.70%				67.30%			-7.03%	

Figure 12.10: Portfolio under the 3 Scenarios before Optimization

Table 12.1: Portfolio Return, Standard Deviation, and Sharp Ratio Optimized Individually Under the 3 Scenarios

Scenario	Original	Chinese and Global Econ. Diverge	Aggressive Chinese Liberalization	Middle East Deteriorates
Portfolio Return	0.3%	53.1%	95.1%	1.8%
Portfolio Stdev	6.2%	24.4%	65.7%	29.4%
Sharp Ratio	0.05	2.18	1.45	0.06

Table 12.1 shows that the portfolio optimized under each of the 3 scenarios ends up with more extreme portfolio returns and volatilities.

These charts and tables illustrate the type of "corner solutions" with very large changes in asset weights, which can rarely be executed by real-life portfolio managers in practice due to high transaction costs.

3. Mathematical Properties of the classic Black-Litterman Model

When the confidence level is 0% for every view, the optimal weight is given by w_{Mkt} and $E[R] =$ Implied Returns. When confidence level is 0% under the

Chinese and Global Economies Diverge view, the portfolio return is 1.39%, which corresponds to the original portfolio return in Figure 12.1. When there are no additional views added, the model gives the original asset weight allocation. The results are stated in Table 12.2, as follows:

Table 12.2: Portfolio Weights under 0% Confidence

No.	Assets	Weight	Return
1	Ascendas Real Estate Investment Trust	5.66%	10.24%
2	DBS Group Holdings Limited	1.87%	-36.15%
3	Genting Singapore PL	2.07%	-4.57%
4	Keppel Corporation Limited	1.03%	-32.59%
5	Keppel REIT Management Limited	3.53%	-14.93%
6	PIMCO 0-5 Year Hi Yld Corp Bond Idx ETF	6.23%	-4.49%
7	PowerShares Golden Dragon China	6.19%	-35.19%
8	SPDR Barclays Aggregate Bond ETF	11.55%	7.17%
9	SPDR Dow Jones Global Real Estate	15.91%	14.86%
10	SPDR Gold Shares	16.17%	22.84%
11	Straits Times Index ETF	4.04%	-18.09%
12	Vanguard MSCI Pacific ETF	5.33%	-14.38%
13	iShares Core S&P500 ETF	20.41%	-2.38%
	Portfolio Return	100%	1.39%

4. Additional Parameters and calculations about the views used in this worked example

(a) Inputs of Confidence Level and Tau:

Table 12.3: Input parameters of the Stochastic Analysis Model

Confidence Level	80%
Minimum Tau	0.01
Maximum Tau	0.1

(b) Correlation Matrix : Matrix gives the correlations between all pairs of asset returns.

Table 12.4: Correlation Matrix

Assets No.	No.1	No.2	No.3	No.4	No.5	No.6	No.7	No.8	No.9	No.10	No.11	No.12	No.13
No.1	0.038	0.031	0.035	0.027	0.020	0.010	0.014	0.002	0.000	0.009	0.007	0.025	0.015
No.2	0.031	0.096	0.065	0.071	0.052	0.017	0.056	0.004	-0.012	0.022	0.001	0.061	0.035
No.3	0.035	0.065	0.098	0.075	0.039	0.016	0.054	0.004	-0.005	0.024	-0.001	0.053	0.032
No.4	0.027	0.071	0.075	0.189	0.045	0.015	0.099	0.009	-0.029	0.060	-0.016	0.056	0.073
No.5	0.020	0.052	0.039	0.045	0.044	0.011	0.030	0.003	-0.011	0.015	0.005	0.037	0.022
No.6	0.010	0.017	0.016	0.015	0.011	0.006	0.009	0.001	0.000	0.004	0.003	0.013	0.007
No.7	0.014	0.056	0.054	0.099	0.030	0.009	0.115	0.004	-0.024	0.032	-0.007	0.040	0.042
No.8	0.002	0.004	0.004	0.009	0.003	0.001	0.004	0.001	-0.002	0.003	-0.001	0.003	0.004
No.9	0.000	-0.012	-0.005	-0.029	-0.011	0.000	-0.024	-0.002	0.033	-0.008	0.009	-0.008	-0.015
No.10	0.009	0.022	0.024	0.060	0.015	0.004	0.032	0.003	-0.008	0.024	-0.005	0.017	0.024
No.11	0.007	0.001	-0.001	-0.016	0.005	0.003	-0.007	-0.001	0.009	-0.005	0.045	0.003	-0.008
No.12	0.025	0.061	0.053	0.056	0.037	0.013	0.040	0.003	-0.008	0.017	0.003	0.046	0.026
No.13	0.015	0.035	0.032	0.073	0.022	0.007	0.042	0.004	-0.015	0.024	-0.008	0.026	0.034

(c) P Matrix, Q Matrix and Ω Matrix

An intuitive interpretation of the the P Matrix, Q Matrix and Ω Matrix is paraphrased as follows:[3]

> Moving from views to the inputs used in the classic Black-Litterman model can be confusing. First, the model does not specify views on all assets. In the thirteen asset example, the number of views k is 3; thus, the View Vector Q is a 3×1 column vector. The uncertainty of the views is expressed by a normally-distributed error term vector ε with a mean of 0 and covariance matrix Σ. Hence, a view is given by $Q + \varepsilon$.
>
> Conceptually, the classic Black-Litterman model is a weighted average of the Implied Return vector Π and the View Vector Q, in which the relative weightings are computed from the scalar τ and the uncertainty of the views Ω. Unfortunately, the scalars and the uncertainties in the views are abstract without simple intuitive explanations. If an investor expresses great the confidence in the expressed views, the new return vector will be closer to the expressed views. Alternatively, if the investor is not confident in the expressed views, the new return vector should be closer to the Implied Return vector Π.

---

[3]Source: see https://faculty.fuqua.duke.edu/~charvey/Teaching/BA453_2006/Idzorek_onBL.pdf for a complete explanation.

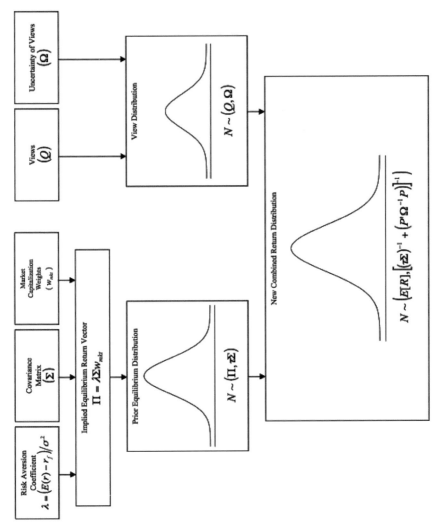

Figure 12.11: Graphical Representation of Classic Black-Litterman Process

Asian HNW ⊠						
🛒 Buy | 🛒 Sell | 💿 Fields: Black-Litterman ▾ | ⏱ Calc. Horizon: 1 Year ▾ | ✒ Use Active Return | 🗄 Include Cash | 🗓 Use Weekly						

Description	Weight	Return	Black-Litterman Analysis			
Product ▲	Actual	Simple	New Weight	Weight Chg	New Return	Ret Chg
Ascendas Real Estate Investment Tr...	6.62%	2.97%	6.92%	0.29%	0.36%	-7.09%
DBS Group Holdings Limited	3.55%	45.81%	3.50%	-0.05%	0.15%	-49.76%
Genting Singapore PLC	3.75%	14.09%	3.73%	-0.02%	0.02%	-28.83%
Keppel Corporation Limited	1.49%	23.87%	1.52%	0.02%	0.76%	-33.32%
Keppel REIT Management Limited	3.99%	5.97%	4.10%	0.10%	0.15%	-11.66%
PIMCO 0-5 Year Hi Yld Corp Bond Id...	6.63%	-0.01%	6.64%	0.01%	0.05%	0.25%
PowerShares Golden Dragon China	11.62%	31.82%	10.71%	-0.91%	0.15%	-27.37%
SPDR Barclays Aggregate Bond ETF	5.51%	-1.87%	5.61%	0.10%	659.60%	-3,720.72%
SPDR Gold Shares	16.33%	2.28%	17.58%	1.25%	-0.02%	-2.66%
Straits Times Index ETF	5.22%	12.46%	5.28%	0.05%	0.30%	-19.71%
Vanguard MSCI Pacific ETF	7.35%	12.25%	7.25%	-0.09%	0.22%	-10.41%
iPath S&P GSCI Crude Oil TR Index ...	0.05%	-96.95%	0.05%	0.00%	0.50%	33.50%
iShares Core S&P500 ETF	27.87%	13.98%	27.12%	-0.75%	0.09%	-11.24%
Total	100.00%	12.31%	100.00%	0.00%	37.13%	-217.34%

Figure 12.12: Sample Results from Stochastic Analysis

P: The P Matrix describes an investor's views. Each column of matrix P represents an investor's view about the assets' weighted expected returns, whose elements sum up to 1.

Table 12.5: P Matrix

View1	View 2	View3
0.0132	0.1080	0.1985
0.0492	0.0199	0.0317
0.0237	0.0107	0.0187
0.0000	0.0044	0.0057
0.0785	0.1033	0.2067
0.0426	0.0460	0.0342
0.3784	0.0549	-0.2701
-0.0511	0.0434	0.0033
0.1466	0.1969	0.3987
-0.5885	0.0061	0.1351
0.0388	0.0435	0.0871
0.1798	0.1041	0.1050
0.6887	0.2588	0.0456

Q: A column vector, in which an element represents a total change of a portfolio's weighted expected returns under a particular view.

Table 12.6: Q Matrix

View1	View 2	View3
10.57%	65.72%	-12.29%

Diagonalized (Ω) Matrix : Diagonal covariance matrix of error terms describing the uncertainty in each view.

Table 12.7: Diagonalized Ω Matrix

View1	View 2	View3
0.0023	0.0000	0.0000
0.0000	0.0006	0.0000
0.0000	0.0000	0.0009

Description	Weight	Return	Black-Litterman Analysis		
Product ▲	Actual	Simple	New Weight	Weight Chg	New Return	Ret Chg
Ascendas Real Estate Investment Tr...	6.62%	2.97%	6.92%	0.29%	0.36%	-7.09%
DBS Group Holdings Limited	3.55%	45.81%	3.50%	-0.05%	0.15%	-49.76%
Genting Singapore PLC	3.75%	14.09%	3.73%	-0.02%	0.02%	-28.83%
Keppel Corporation Limited	1.49%	23.87%	1.52%	0.02%	0.76%	-33.32%
Keppel REIT Management Limited	3.99%	5.97%	4.10%	0.10%	0.15%	-11.66%
PIMCO 0-5 Year Hi Yld Corp Bond Id...	6.63%	-0.01%	6.64%	0.01%	0.05%	0.25%
PowerShares Golden Dragon China	11.62%	31.82%	10.71%	-0.91%	0.15%	-27.37%
SPDR Barclays Aggregate Bond ETF	5.51%	-1.87%	5.61%	0.10%	659.60%	-3,720.72%
SPDR Gold Shares	16.33%	2.28%	17.58%	1.25%	-0.02%	-2.66%
Straits Times Index ETF	5.22%	12.46%	5.28%	0.05%	0.30%	-19.71%
Vanguard MSCI Pacific ETF	7.35%	12.25%	7.25%	-0.09%	0.22%	-10.41%
iPath S&P GSCI Crude Oil TR Index ...	0.05%	-96.95%	0.05%	0.00%	0.50%	33.50%
iShares Core S&P500 ETF	27.87%	13.98%	27.12%	-0.75%	0.09%	-11.24%
Total	100.00%	12.31%	100.00%	0.00%	37.13%	-217.34%

Note: Asian HNW — Buy | Sell | Fields: Black-Litterman ▾ | Calc. Horizon: 1 Year ▾ | Use Active Return | Include Cash | Use Weekly

Figure 12.13: Results from the HedgeSPA Platform

(d) Finally, we will compare the calculation results between a stochastic analysis done semi-manually using a spreadsheet (likely to result in more significant numerical errors by the nature of any spreadsheet calculations) and computational results from the HedgeSPA platform using professional computational libraries are written in C++, in order to illustrate the rough size of the numerical errors observed.

On the HedgeSPA platform, the stochastic analysis model is given by the following table. They are comparable, but there are noticeable numerical errors:

$$E(R) = \Pi + \tau \Sigma P^T [\Omega + \tau P \Sigma P^T]^{-1}(Q - P\Pi)$$

Assuming we are doing a comparison against a spreadsheet: First, we should calculate $\tau \Sigma P^T$, and then we need to compute $[\Omega + \tau P \Sigma P^T]^{-1}$, and finally $\tau \Sigma P^T [\Omega + \tau P \Sigma P^T]^{-1}$, as follows:

Table 12.8: Computations of $\tau \Sigma P^T$

0.0199	0.0155	0.0154
0.0527	0.0289	0.0132
0.0467	0.0273	0.0136
0.0668	0.0357	-0.0025
0.0309	0.0183	0.0106
0.0106	0.0069	0.0054
0.0638	0.0240	-0.0179
0.0033	0.0019	0.0001
-0.0124	-0.0008	0.0149
0.0196	0.0120	0.0002
-0.0007	0.0028	0.0108
0.0382	0.0217	0.0109
0.0319	0.0165	-0.0005

Table 12.9: Computations of $[\Omega + \tau P \Sigma P^T]^{-1}$

270.1850	-234.5155	45.6034
-234.5155	1019.1116	-186.3331
45.6034	-186.3331	560.4212

Table 12.10: Computations of $\tau \Sigma P^T [\Omega + \tau P \Sigma P^T]^{-1}$

0.1219	0.4153	0.3317
0.4039	0.7292	0.2219
0.3411	0.7174	0.2342
0.4776	1.0605	-0.2499
0.2268	0.4718	0.1974
0.0741	0.1787	0.1105
0.5400	0.6401	-0.5807
0.0235	0.0547	-0.0080
-0.1232	-0.0360	0.3982
0.1250	0.3777	-0.0603
-0.0178	0.0495	0.2762
0.2856	0.5582	0.1910
0.2359	0.4721	-0.0959

Table 12.11: Computations of Posterior Returns $E(R)$

Assets	Posterior returns
Ascendas Real Estate Investment Trust	0.7%
DBS Group Holdings Limited	1%
Genting Singapore PLC	1%
Keppel Corporation Limited	2%
Keppel REIT Management Limited	0.8%
PIMCO 0-5 Year Hi Yld Corp Bond Idx ETF	0.2%
PowerShares Golden Dragon China	2%
SPDR Barclays Aggregate Bond ETF	0.0%
SPDR Dow Jones Global Real Estate	1%
SPDR Gold Shares	0.1%
Straits Times Index ETF	1%
Vanguard MSCI Pacific ETF	1.2%
iShares Core S&P500 ETF	1%

Table 12.12: Spreadsheet versus HedgeSPA Platform Results

Posterior Weights from Spreadsheet	HedgeSPA Platform results
6%	6%
2%	2%
2%	2%
2%	1%
4%	4%
6%	6%
6%	6%
11%	11%
15%	16%
16%	15%
4%	4%
5%	5%
20%	21%
100%	100%

12.4 Conclusion

Investors may face many known limitations and challenges when they try to generate a steady absolute return during the medium-to-long term. The Stochastic Analysis process is a solid choice to address these challenges, because the process can overcome the disadvantages of the traditional single-scenario approach, and provides an accurate estimation of a maximizing portfolio solution under multiple scenarios. Hence, the Stochastic Analysis tool on the HedgeSPA core investment platform can help investors to achieve a stable and profitable medium-to-long term investment.

Part IV

DELIVER REPORTS

INVESTMENT ANALYTICS IN THE DAWN OF ARTIFICIAL INTELLIGENCE

13. Customary Back Office Reporting

13.1 Use Case

Manually generating certain reports may be tedious but the requirement to do so is almost inevitable for most asset managers. Although many asset managers would rather spend their time managing their clients' portfolios to achieve better performance, they need to manage their clients' expectations. Investor relations professionals at key asset managers need to generate, format, save, and email and/or printed reports whenever clients request them. This chapter talks about the contents typically expected by the end-investors of our asset manager users and the intuitive interpretation of such contents.

For example, our portfolio manager Jack has a few upcoming appointments with major clients for portfolio reviews, during which he will suggest new ideas to the clients. His junior analysts have created certain manual reports for him; however, he always finds minor mistakes. It bothers Jack to give his clients less-than-professional reports, so he continues to spend a significant amount of time cleaning up the outputs from junior analysts while seeking a more automated way to generate similar reports.

13.2 Investment Reports

On the HedgeSPA Platform, you can find these reports by clicking on "Analytics" and then "Reports". These reports are organized by a tree structure as shown in Figure 13.1:

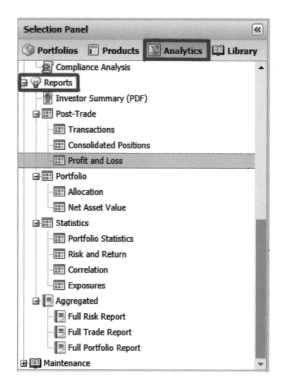

Figure 13.1: "Analytics → Reports"

13.2.1   Investor Summary

Investor Summary as shown in Figure 13.2 produces a single-page PDF report which highlights some of the key risk-return information for the selected portfolio with graphical representation. This is a report that can be readily customized by a professional investment manager for regular (usually after every trading day) and automated reporting to asset sponsors.

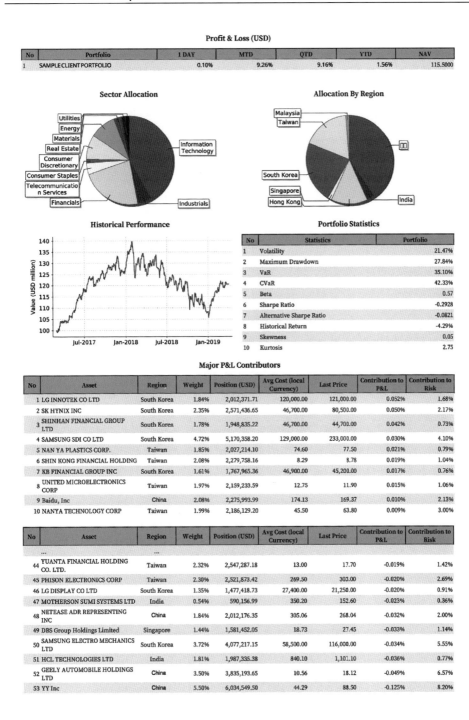

Profit & Loss (USD)

No	Portfolio	1 DAY	MTD	QTD	YTD	NAV
1	SAMPLE CLIENT PORTFOLIO	0.10%	9.26%	9.16%	1.56%	115.5000

Sector Allocation

Allocation By Region

Historical Performance

Portfolio Statistics

No	Statistics	Portfolio
1	Volatility	21.47%
2	Maximum Drawdown	27.84%
3	VaR	35.10%
4	CVaR	42.33%
5	Beta	0.57
6	Sharpe Ratio	-0.2928
7	Alternative Sharpe Ratio	-0.0821
8	Historical Return	-4.29%
9	Skewness	0.05
10	Kurtosis	2.75

Major P&L Contributors

No	Asset	Region	Weight	Position (USD)	Avg Cost (local Currency)	Last Price	Contribution to P&L	Contribution to Risk
1	LG INNOTEK CO LTD	South Korea	1.84%	2,012,371.71	120,000.00	121,000.00	0.052%	1.68%
2	SK HYNIX INC	South Korea	2.35%	2,571,436.65	46,700.00	80,500.00	0.050%	2.17%
3	SHINHAN FINANCIAL GROUP LTD	South Korea	1.78%	1,948,835.22	46,700.00	44,700.00	0.042%	0.73%
4	SAMSUNG SDI CO LTD	South Korea	4.72%	5,170,358.20	129,000.00	233,000.00	0.030%	4.10%
5	NAN YA PLASTICS CORP.	Taiwan	1.85%	2,027,214.10	74.60	77.50	0.021%	0.79%
6	SHIN KONG FINANCIAL HOLDING	Taiwan	2.08%	2,279,758.16	8.29	8.78	0.019%	1.04%
7	KB FINANCIAL GROUP INC	South Korea	1.61%	1,767,965.36	46,900.00	45,200.00	0.017%	0.76%
8	UNITED MICROELECTRONICS CORP	Taiwan	1.97%	2,159,233.59	12.75	11.90	0.015%	1.06%
9	Baidu, Inc	China	2.08%	2,275,993.99	174.13	169.37	0.010%	2.13%
10	NANYA TECHNOLOGY CORP	Taiwan	1.99%	2,186,129.20	45.50	63.80	0.009%	3.00%

No	Asset	Region	Weight	Position (USD)	Avg Cost (local Currency)	Last Price	Contribution to P&L	Contribution to Risk
...	...							
44	YUANTA FINANCIAL HOLDING CO. LTD.	Taiwan	2.32%	2,547,287.18	13.00	17.70	-0.019%	1.42%
45	PHISON ELECTRONICS CORP	Taiwan	2.30%	2,521,873.42	269.50	303.00	-0.020%	2.69%
46	LG DISPLAY CO LTD	South Korea	1.35%	1,477,418.73	27,400.00	21,250.00	-0.020%	0.91%
47	MOTHERSON SUMI SYSTEMS LTD	India	0.54%	590,156.99	350.20	152.60	-0.023%	0.36%
48	NETEASE ADR REPRESENTING INC	China	1.84%	2,012,176.35	305.06	268.04	-0.032%	2.00%
49	DBS Group Holdings Limited	Singapore	1.44%	1,581,452.05	18.73	27.45	-0.033%	1.14%
50	SAMSUNG ELECTRO MECHANICS LTD	South Korea	3.72%	4,077,217.15	58,500.00	116,000.00	-0.034%	5.55%
51	HCL TECHNOLOGIES LTD	India	1.81%	1,987,335.38	840.10	1,101.10	-0.036%	0.77%
52	GEELY AUTOMOBILE HOLDINGS LTD	China	3.50%	3,835,193.65	10.56	18.12	-0.049%	6.57%
53	YY Inc	China	5.50%	6,034,549.50	44.29	88.50	-0.125%	8.20%

Figure 13.2: Investor Summary in PDF Format

13.2.2 Transactions

The reports in this subsection show detailed information on all account activities during the statement period, including the history of the fund's subscription and redemption activities. They keep track of every investment activity. The reports use industry-standard definitions including the following:[1]

1. Purchases: Any money coming into your account. Contributions, employer contributions, or rollovers, for example.
2. Withdrawals: Any money you've taken out of your account, such as a loan.

   Other common types of transactions in an investment account include:
1. Contributions: The money deposited into your account. You might have this automatically withdrawn from your paycheck. This may also include any matching from an employer who contributes a certain amount to your account.
2. Dividends: Sometimes companies distribute a portion of their earnings to stockholders, and it's called a dividend.
3. Gains and losses: This is your investment return, but it shows how much a specific investment has increased or decreased in value. Often, it's shown as a percentage. If you have already bought and sold the investment, this is called a "realized" gain or loss.
4. Exchange In and Exchange Out: Your investment plan may be managed by a company that picks specific funds for you. If so, they may decide to exchange one fund for another, and this exchange will be noted on your statement.

The **Transactions** tool produces a report as shown below. It gives a complete list of all portfolio transactions that occurred during the reporting date, which is typically the most recent trading day, or a range of reporting dates specified by the user.

No	Date	Product	CUSIP	Currency	Type	Qty	Price	Commission	Position Size
1	2016-05-03	American Funds Growth Fund of Amer A	399874106	USD	BUY	1000	42.12	0.00	42,120.00
2	2016-05-07	Fortress Investment Group LLC	34958B106	USD	SELL	1000	4.49	0.00	-4,490.00
3	2016-05-14	Goldman Sachs Commodity Strategy A	38143H381	USD	BUY	1000	10.98	0.00	10,980.00
4	2016-06-27	American Funds Growth Fund of Amer A	399874106	USD	BUY	1000	35.10	0.00	35,100.00
5	2016-06-29	PIMCO Total Return A	72200Q851	USD	BUY	1000	10.42	0.00	10,420.00

---

[1]Source: see https://twocents.lifehacker.com/how-to-read-your-investment-statements-and-actually-un-1682433880 for details.

13.2.3   Consolidated Positions

The **Consolidated Positions** reports identify consolidated positions, which details the positions in the portfolio at the reporting date, including individual assets and their values, yield, ratings, and tickers. In addition, the report displays based currency, exchange rate, unrealized profits and losses which help reinvestments. This information helps identify over-concentration in a specific country/sector that has been doing well.

Figure 13.3 shows one example of the Consolidated Positions Report:

Consolidated Positions Report

No	Product	Asset Class	Contract	Currency	Exch Rate	Weight	Avg Price (local Currency)	Position in USD
1	Cash in USD	Cash	39,023,432.9	USD	1	45.39%	1	39,023,432.9
2	SPDR S&P 500 ETF Trust	Equity	50,000	USD	1	16.12%	146.1	13,856,500
3	Goldman Sachs Commodity Strategy A	Commodity	500,000	USD	1	7.14%	5.8	6,135,000
4	SPDR Gold Shares	Commodity	9,000	USD	1	1.27%	163.2	1,092,060
5	PowerShares Global Listed Private Eq	Private Equity	200,000	USD	1	2.89%	10.2	2,486,000
6	PIMCO Total Return A	Fixed Income	300,000	USD	1	3.47%	11.2	2,982,000
7	iShares Core U.S. Aggregate Bond ETF	Fixed Income	28,000	USD	1	3.45%	111	2,964,640
8	T. Rowe Price US Treasury Long-Term	Fixed Income	300,000	USD	1	4.24%	13.3	3,645,000
9	Franklin Templeton Hard Currency FUND	Foreign Exchange	200,000	USD	1	1.72%	9.7	1,482,000

Figure 13.3: Consolidated Positions Report

13.2.4   Portfolio Summary

Portfolio Summary is usually divided into a few parts: the long stock portfolio, the short stock portfolio, and the portfolios for options, bonds, funds, and cash. Here, we use the stock portfolio for illustration purposes.

The long stock portfolio contains the names of shares that you hold. Typically, each position is shown with the share's ticker symbol, description of the company, and the number of shares held by the investor. Furthermore, some of the industry-standard definitions of column headings under each position in this report are given below:[2]

---

1. Purchase Price displays the original cost per share of your purchase.
2. Current Price displays the current market value per share. This value will change with time.
3. Total Value reports the current total dollar value of your holdings. Say you have bought 100 shares of Apple Inc. The Total Value will be equal to 100 times its Current Price per share of Apple Inc.
4. Today's Change gives the dollar amount and % Change representing your gains or losses for each position as a result of today's market activity.
5. Total Gain/Loss gives the dollar amount and % Change representing your total gains or losses since the positions were first entered into.
6. Short stock portfolios are treated differently primarily because of the need to keep track of stock borrowing, cash collaterals and cross-product margining.

13.2.5 Profit and Loss

The following formula is used to calculate Total P& L:

$$P\&L_{Total} = P\&L_{Realized} + P\&L_{Unrealized}$$

Realized and unrealized P&L can be calculated based on different fill-matching algorithms including FIFO (First In First Out), LIFO (Last In First Out), and Average Cost. The Average Cost methodology is defined mathematically, and the LIFO and FIFO methodologies are defined by their algorithms. LIFO and FIFO have their well-known problems with fairness issues, but are easily traceable when mistakes are made. They are generally more popular among wealth managers and private banks when portfolios are relatively small. The Average Cost methodology generally avoids fairness issues. However, even when computers are widely used by the financial industry today, a minor mistake can be a nightmare to trace and correct. This method is more commonly applied by major institutions on portfolios with inception dates within the last two decades. The following is a sample

---

[2]Source: see https://www.investopedia.com/university/simulator/portfolio-summary.asp for details.

Profit & Loss Report available on the HedgeSPA Platform, as follows:

Profit & Loss Report

No	Product	Asset Class	Currency	Contracts	Avg-Cost (local currency)	Position in USD	Yest Close	P&L in USD
1	Cash in USD	Cash	USD	39,023,432.9	1	39,023,432.9	1	0
2	Franklin Templeton Hard Currency FUND	Foreign Exchange	USD	200,000	9.7	1,482,000	7.4	-454,000
3	Goldman Sachs Commodity Strategy A	Commodity	USD	500,000	5.8	6,135,000	12.3	3,240,000
4	iShares Core U.S. Aggregate Bond ETF	Fixed Income	USD	28,000	111	2,964,640	105.9	-141,960
5	PIMCO Total Return A	Fixed Income	USD	300,000	11.2	2,982,000	9.9	-384,000
6	PowerShares Global Listed Private Eq	Private Equity	USD	200,000	10.2	2,486,000	12.4	438,000
7	SPDR Gold Shares	Commodity	USD	9,000	163.2	1,092,060	121.3	-376,470
8	SPDR S&P 500 ETF Trust	Equity	USD	50,000	146.1	13,856,500	277.1	6,553,500
9	T. Rowe Price US Treasury Long-Term	Fixed Income	USD	300,000	13.3	3,645,000	12.2	-351,000

Figure 13.4: Profit & Loss Report

13.2.6 Allocation

Asset allocation is the decision of how much to invest in each investment category or asset class. A particular asset allocation may have a significant effect on the actual risk and return results for a portfolio of securities. In HedgeSPA's **Allocation** report, the asset allocation section lists the portfolio allocation by each asset class, region, and sector.

1. Asset Class: A broad category of investments, such as cash, foreign exchange, commodity, fixed income, private equity, and equity.
2. Weight: Portfolio weight of a specific asset class.
3. PCTR: Percentage Contribution to Tail Risk, or the asset class' percentage contribution to overall portfolio tail risk.
4. Historical Return: The historical return delivered by the asset or asset class.
5. Implied Return: The return an asset or asset class must create in order to pay for its risk contributions to the overall portfolio.

Asset Allocation Report

No	Group	Weight	PCTR	HistRet	ImplRet
1	Cash	45.49%	84.58%	-1.41%	0.74%
2	Foreign Exchange	1.76%	2.58%	-1.34%	0.58%
3	Commodity	8.12%	12.02%	3.54%	1.19%
4	Fixed Income	11.27%	22.69%	-15.65%	2.39%
5	Private Equity	2.88%	-1.77%	0.13%	-0.24%
6	Equity	16.14%	-20.10%	6.46%	-0.49%

Regional Allocation Report

No	Group	Weight	PCTR	HistRet	ImplRet
1	N/A	45.49%	84.58%	-1.41%	0.74%
2	Developed Markets	38.93%	13.54%	-0.31%	2.82%
3	Global	1.23%	1.87%	-6.56%	0.60%

Sector Allocation Report

No	Group	Weight	PCTR	HistRet	ImplRet
1	N/A	85.65%	100.00%	-8.28%	4.16%

Figure 13.5: Allocation Report

13.2.7 Net Asset Value

13.2.7.1 NAV Calculation

Net asset value (NAV) is the value of an entity's assets minus the value of its liabilities, often in relation to open-end or mutual funds, since the shares of such funds are registered with the relevant regulatory authorities and are both invested and redeemed at their net asset value. Official valuation usually takes significant time to compute by administrators to minimize potential errors. For day-to-day use, most portfolio managers only require a basic indicative NAV report. Net asset value can either state the total equity in an investment vehicle, or the net asset value per share after dividing the total equity by the total number of investor shares. However, it is not always the case of a simple division due to different fees charges based on purchase time and different fee arrangements used by different share classes, as follows:

$$Net\,Asset\,Value(NAV) = \frac{Dollar\,Market\,Value\,of\,Fund\,Assets - Fund\,Liabilities}{Number\,of\,Investor\,Shares\,Outstanding}$$

One industry-standard method of calculating net asset value has been included below for the ease of reference:[3]

---

[3]Source: see https://www.wikihow.com/Calculate-the-Net-Asset-Value for details.

Step 1 Choose the valuation date.

The net asset value (NAV) of a mutual fund, hedge fund, or ETF changes every day when the stock market is open, as the value of the fund's investments fluctuates. For a net asset value calculation to be valuable, you must use fund data for the calculation on a date that is relevant to your needs. Choose a specific date and ensure all the values used to calculate your fund net asset value comes from this date. Even for a portfolio with assets spanning multiple time zones, the industry practice is to use the same date unless an alternative valuation methodology is explicitly documented.

Step 2 Calculate the total value of the fund's securities at the end of the valuation date.

The fund's securities are its ownership of stocks, bonds, and any other securities. As these securities' values are posted daily, you can learn the value of your fund's investment in each security at the end of the valuation date. This total should include the value of any cash in the portfolio on the valuation date, as well as any short term or long term assets being held by the fund.

Step 3 Subtract outstanding fund liabilities.

In addition to investments, the fund is likely to have some outstanding liabilities. These are the amounts that the fund has borrowed in order to make additional investments, in the hopes that the fund's returns on these investments will be better than the interest that it pays on its outstanding loans. Subtract the fair market value of these debts from the total value of the securities that you have calculated. The fund's prospectus will list each of its assets and liabilities. Download the prospectus online or contact the fund's investor relation professionals for the information. Many newspapers carry daily stock listings showing the closing prices of publicly traded stocks.

Step 4 Divide by the number of outstanding shares in the fund.

The result of this calculation is the net asset value or the value of one share's portion of the assets owned by the fund. If you own multiple shares in the fund, you can multiply the NAV by the number of shares you own to learn the market value of your investment. The NAV generally determines the purchase or sale price of a mutual fund share, so you should expect to be able to sell back your shares for relatively close to the NAV. For mutual funds or unit trusts, NAV per share is calculated every day. It is based on the closing prices of the securities in the fund.

Current NAV is the amount that reflects the following items, with estimates used where necessary or appropriate:

Valuation/Timing Guidance

1. Portfolio securities market quotations that are readily available: Current market value.
2. Portfolio securities market quotations that are NOT readily available: Fair value as determined in good faith by the board of directors of the registered investment entity.
3. Changes in the holdings of portfolio securities: Must be reflected no later than in the first calculation of the first business day following the trade date.
4. Changes in the number of outstanding shares of the registered company: Must be reflected no later than in the first calculation on the first business day following such change. It should include changes resulting from distributions, redemptions or repurchases.
5. Expenses: Must be included to the date of calculation. Expenses may include any investment advisory fees.
6. Dividends receivable: Included to the date of calculation either at ex-dividend dates or record dates, as appropriate.
7. Interest income and other income: Must be included to the date of calculation.

13.2.7.2 Net Asset Value Report

Net Asset Value is a report that provides a breakdown of the change in the fund's indicative net asset values as shown in Figure 13.6.

Net Asset Value Report

	Qtr-On-Qtr Change as of 2018-07-01 (USD)	Qtr-To-Date Change as of 2018-07-13 (USD)
Investment Income		
Interest Income	0.00	0.00
Dividend Income	0.00	0.00
Net fair value gains/(losses) on financial assets and at fair value through profit or loss	5067619.91	0.00
Total Investment Income	5067619.91	0.0
Expenses		
Administration fees	0.0	0.0
Custodian and sub-custodian fees	0.0	0.0
Directors' fees	0.0	0.0
General expenses	0.0	0.0
Management fees	0.0	0.0
Total Operating Cost	0.00	0.0
Financial Costs		
Bank interest expenses	0.0	0.0
Total Finance Cost	0.00	0.0
Grand Total	0.00	0.0

Figure 13.6: Net Asset Value Report

The investment objective of any portfolio is to maximize current income as well as future capital appreciation. This report shows the incomes and dividends earned by the investments on a quarter-on-quarter and for quarter-to-date basis, both of which are critical to investment planning and evaluating investment performance.

The income statement presents the financial results over a specified period, typically one quarter or one year. The income statement presents the revenue generated during the period, both the expenses incurred and the profit earned.

The basic equation underlying the income statement is given as follows:

$$Revenue - Expenses = Income$$

Typically, the income statement will provide the Revenues followed by Interest Income, Dividend Income and Net Fair Value Gains/(Losses) on financial assets and at fair value with profits (or losses). The most important sources of investment income are dividends (company paying out a portion of its profits) and capital gains (increase in share price). Dividends and capital gains must be separated because their tax treatments are often different.

Commissions due to stock turnover, management, and insurance are then deducted to reach operating income. Generally speaking, you can attribute them as fund expenses and adviser fees. Of course, there may be trading costs and taxes as well. Other expenses may include custodian fees and bank interest expenses (for margin interest).

13.2.8 Portfolio Statistics

There are many statistical measures available for looking at a mutual fund, ETF, stock or a combination of these in the total portfolio. In an investment report, we offer these statistics so that the clients can understand the portfolio's performance at a deeper statistical level. These statistics include:

1. Volatility is the standard deviation of a portfolio's return, measured on a rolling 1-year window basis.

2. Maximum Drawdown measures the maximum peak to trough drawdown in the value of a portfolio, before a new peak is reached.

3. Value-at-Risk is the expected maximum loss in portfolio value over a specified period, at a given level of statistical confidence.

4. The Conditional Value at Risk (also known as Expected Shortfall) is the expected loss over a specified time horizon given that the loss is greater than or equal to the Value at Risk (VaR).

5. Beta is a measure of the market risk of a portfolio as compared to the overall market. Lower beta indicates lower systematic market risk, and vice versa.

6. Sharpe Ratio is the excess returns over a risk-free rate generated per unit of risk as measured by standard deviation. It tells you whether your portfolio's returns are due to smart investing (alpha) or excessive market risk (beta).

7. The Alternative Sharpe Ratio (ASR) is similar to Sharpe Ratio but incorporates the appropriate higher moment information including skewness and excess kurtosis, and is a robust departure from the assumption of normality in portfolio returns.

8. Historical Return shows the average historical annual return of the asset.

9. Skewness measures the asymmetry from the normal distribution and the skewness of the portfolio and assets.

10. Kurtosis measures the "peakedness" of the probability distribution.

Portfolio Statistics Report

Statistics	Portfolio
Volatility (%)	3.9
Maximum Drawdown	6.2
VaR	7.5
CVaR	9
Beta	-0.6
Sharpe Ratio	-0.3
Alternative Sharpe Ratio	-0.3
Historical Return	0.7
Skewness	0.9
kurtosis	5.6

Consolidated Positions Report

No	Product	Asset Class	Contract	Currency	Exchange Rate	Weight	Avg Price (local Currency)	Position in USD
1	Cash In USD	Cash	39,023,432.9	USD	1	45.43%	1	39,023,432.9
2	SPDR S&P 500 ETF Trust	Equity	50,000	USD	1	16.26%	146.1	13,964,500
3	Goldman Sachs Commodity Strategy A	Commodity	500,000	USD	1	6.88%	5.8	5,910,000
4	SPDR Gold Shares	Commodity	9,000	USD	1	1.24%	163.2	1,063,170
5	PowerShares Global Listed Private Eq	Private Equity	200,000	USD	1	2.85%	10.2	2,448,000
6	PIMCO Total Return A	Fixed Income	300,000	USD	1	3.49%	11.2	2,997,000
7	iShares Core U.S. Aggregate Bond ETF	Fixed Income	28,000	USD	1	3.47%	111	2,979,480
8	T. Rowe Price US Treasury Long-Term	Fixed Income	300,000	USD	1	4.31%	13.3	3,705,000
9	Franklin Templeton Hard Currency FUND	Foreign Exchange	200,000	USD	1	1.76%	9.7	1,508,000

Figure 13.7: Portfolio Statistics Report

13.2.9 Risk and Return

Risk and Return produces a report which provides a detailed position-level view of the risk-return characteristics of individual positions, as shown in Figure 13.10.

Portfolio Risk Analysis includes Volatility, PCTR, Value at Risk, Conditional Value at Risk (cVaR), MVaR, MCVaR, Maximum Drawdown (MaxDD).

Marginal Contribution (%) of an individual asset to portfolio Value-at-Risk (MVaR) measures the weighted marginal contribution of an asset to the portfolio VaR as measured by the Cornish-Fisher expansion. Marginal Contribution (%) of the individual asset to portfolio Expected Shortfall (MCVaR) measures the weighted marginal contributions of each asset to the portfolio's expected shortfall measured by discrete approximation. They can also be found in "Fields: Risk Analysis", which is under the specific portfolio shown in Figure 13.8.

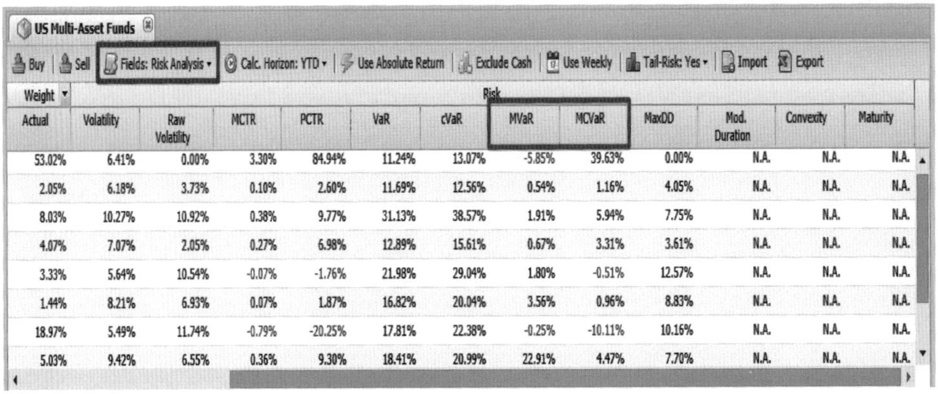

Weight	Risk											
Actual	Volatility	Raw Volatility	MCTR	PCTR	VaR	cVaR	MVaR	MCVaR	MaxDD	Mod. Duration	Convexity	Maturity
53.02%	6.41%	0.00%	3.30%	84.94%	11.24%	13.07%	-5.85%	39.63%	0.00%	N.A.	N.A.	N.A.
2.05%	6.18%	3.73%	0.10%	2.60%	11.69%	12.56%	0.54%	1.16%	4.05%	N.A.	N.A.	N.A.
8.03%	10.27%	10.92%	0.38%	9.77%	31.13%	38.57%	1.91%	5.94%	7.75%	N.A.	N.A.	N.A.
4.07%	7.07%	2.05%	0.27%	6.98%	12.89%	15.61%	0.67%	3.31%	3.61%	N.A.	N.A.	N.A.
3.33%	5.64%	10.54%	-0.07%	-1.76%	21.98%	29.04%	1.80%	-0.51%	12.57%	N.A.	N.A.	N.A.
1.44%	8.21%	6.93%	0.07%	1.87%	16.82%	20.04%	3.56%	0.96%	8.83%	N.A.	N.A.	N.A.
18.97%	5.49%	11.74%	-0.79%	-20.25%	17.81%	22.38%	-0.25%	-10.11%	10.16%	N.A.	N.A.	N.A.
5.03%	9.42%	6.55%	0.36%	9.30%	18.41%	20.99%	22.91%	4.47%	7.70%	N.A.	N.A.	N.A.

Figure 13.8: “Specific Portfolio → Fields: Risk Analysis”

Portfolio Return Analysis includes Historical Return, MCTRet, Implied Return, 6-Month Beta, and Ranking.

Marginal Contribution to Target Portfolio Return (MCTRet) measures the marginal contribution of an individual asset to the total target portfolio return. The ranking is assessing the assets by the difference between the asset's historical return and its current implied return from highest to lowest. They can also be found in “Fields: Return Analysis”, which is under the specific portfolio as well.

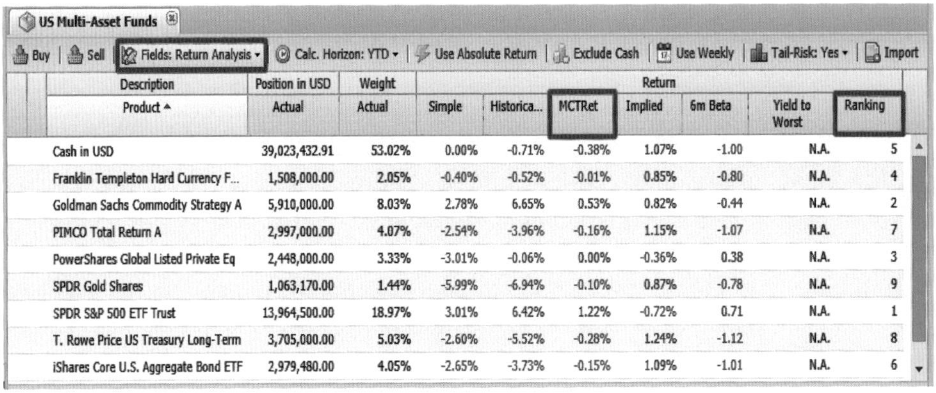

Description	Position in USD	Weight	Return						
Product	Actual	Actual	Simple	Historica...	MCTRet	Implied	6m Beta	Yield to Worst	Ranking
Cash in USD	39,023,432.91	53.02%	0.00%	-0.71%	-0.38%	1.07%	-1.00	N.A.	5
Franklin Templeton Hard Currency F...	1,508,000.00	2.05%	-0.40%	-0.52%	-0.01%	0.85%	-0.80	N.A.	4
Goldman Sachs Commodity Strategy A	5,910,000.00	8.03%	2.78%	6.65%	0.53%	0.82%	-0.44	N.A.	2
PIMCO Total Return A	2,997,000.00	4.07%	-2.54%	-3.96%	-0.16%	1.15%	-1.07	N.A.	7
PowerShares Global Listed Private Eq	2,448,000.00	3.33%	-3.01%	-0.06%	0.00%	-0.36%	0.38	N.A.	3
SPDR Gold Shares	1,063,170.00	1.44%	-5.99%	-6.94%	-0.10%	0.87%	-0.78	N.A.	9
SPDR S&P 500 ETF Trust	13,964,500.00	18.97%	3.01%	6.42%	1.22%	-0.72%	0.71	N.A.	1
T. Rowe Price US Treasury Long-Term	3,705,000.00	5.03%	-2.60%	-5.52%	-0.28%	1.24%	-1.12	N.A.	8
iShares Core U.S. Aggregate Bond ETF	2,979,480.00	4.05%	-2.65%	-3.73%	-0.15%	1.09%	-1.01	N.A.	6

Figure 13.9: “Specific Portfolio → Fields: Return Analysis”

Portfolio Risk Report

No	Product	Volatility	PCTR	VaR	cVaR	MVaR	MCVaR	MaxDD
1	Cash in USD	6.41%	84.94%	11.24%	13.07%	-5.85%	39.63%	0.00%
2	Franklin Templeton Hard Currency FUND	6.18%	2.60%	11.69%	12.56%	0.54%	1.16%	4.05%
3	Goldman Sachs Commodity Strategy A	10.27%	9.77%	31.13%	38.57%	1.91%	5.94%	7.75%
4	iShares Core U.S. Aggregate Bond ETF	6.74%	6.56%	12.60%	15.27%	2.59%	3.12%	3.80%
5	PIMCO Total Return A	7.07%	6.98%	12.89%	15.61%	0.67%	3.31%	3.61%
6	PowerShares Global Listed Private Eq	5.64%	-1.76%	21.98%	29.04%	1.80%	-0.51%	12.57%
7	SPDR Gold Shares	8.21%	1.87%	16.82%	20.04%	3.56%	0.96%	8.83%
8	SPDR S&P 500 ETF Trust	5.49%	-20.25%	17.81%	22.38%	-0.25%	-10.11%	10.16%
9	T. Rowe Price US Treasury Long-Term	9.42%	9.30%	18.41%	20.99%	22.91%	4.47%	7.70%

Portfolio Return Report

No	Product	Hist	MCTRet	Implied	6m Beta	Ranking
1	Cash in USD	-0.71%	-0.38%	1.07%	-1	5
2	Franklin Templeton Hard Currency FUND	-0.52%	-0.01%	0.85%	-0.8	4
3	Goldman Sachs Commodity Strategy A	6.65%	0.53%	0.82%	-0.4	2
4	iShares Core U.S. Aggregate Bond ETF	-3.73%	-0.15%	1.09%	-1	6
5	PIMCO Total Return A	-3.96%	-0.16%	1.15%	-1.1	7
6	PowerShares Global Listed Private Eq	-0.06%	-0.00%	-0.36%	0.4	3
7	SPDR Gold Shares	-6.94%	-0.10%	0.87%	-0.8	9
8	SPDR S&P 500 ETF Trust	6.42%	1.22%	-0.72%	0.7	1
9	T. Rowe Price US Treasury Long-Term	-5.52%	-0.28%	1.24%	-1.1	8

Figure 13.10: Risk and Return Report

13.2.10   Correlation

Correlation analysis measures the relationship between any two assets within a portfolio to help the investor to determine if those two assets are positively or negatively correlated. The **Correlation Report** displays an easy-to-read matrix of correlation coefficients among all individual assets within the selected portfolio, along with its portfolio benchmark.

Correlation Report

No	Asset	Asce	DBS	Gent	iSha	Kepp	Kepp	PIMC	Powe	SPDR	Stra	Vang	iSha
1	Ascendas Real Estate Investment Trust	1.0000	0.5212	0.4361	0.3023	0.3718	0.4284	0.3417	0.4153	0.1923	0.5694	0.5460	0.6075
2	DBS Group Holdings Limited	0.5212	1.0000	0.5858	0.4629	0.6751	0.3335	0.4384	0.4581	0.1040	0.8943	0.6727	0.8377
3	Genting Singapore PLC	0.4361	0.5858	1.0000	0.3950	0.4749	0.2941	0.3410	0.4449	-0.0781	0.6411	0.4891	0.4804
4	iShares Core S&P500 ETF	0.3023	0.4629	0.3950	1.0000	0.3840	0.1621	0.7563	0.7136	-0.0606	0.5150	0.7581	0.6157
5	Keppel Corporation Limited	0.3718	0.6751	0.4749	0.3840	1.0000	0.3789	0.4144	0.3377	0.0140	0.7622	0.6006	0.6747
6	Keppel REIT Management Limited	0.4284	0.3335	0.2941	0.1621	0.3789	1.0000	0.0791	0.1079	-0.1786	0.3932	0.2550	0.3122
7	PIMCO 0-5 Year Hi Yld Corp Bond Idx ETF	0.3417	0.4384	0.3410	0.7563	0.4144	0.0791	1.0000	0.6932	0.1159	0.4822	0.7015	0.6216
8	PowerShares Golden Dragon China	0.4153	0.4581	0.4449	0.7136	0.3377	0.1079	0.6932	1.0000	0.2442	0.5088	0.7269	0.6484
9	SPDR Gold Shares	0.1923	0.1040	-0.0781	-0.0606	0.0140	-0.1786	0.1159	0.2442	1.0000	-0.0172	0.1952	0.2750
10	Straits Times Index ETF	0.5694	0.8943	0.6411	0.5150	0.7622	0.3932	0.4822	0.5088	-0.0172	1.0000	0.6791	0.8265
11	Vanguard MSCI Pacific ETF	0.5460	0.6727	0.4891	0.7581	0.6006	0.2550	0.7015	0.7269	0.1952	0.6791	1.0000	0.8533
12	iShares MSCI Singapore Index Fund (ETF)	0.6075	0.8377	0.4804	0.6157	0.6747	0.3122	0.6216	0.6484	0.2750	0.8265	0.8533	1.0000

Figure 13.11: Correlation Report

13.2.11   Exposures

Factor Exposure shows the portfolio's exposures to a set of market factors. Through this analysis, users can quickly determine how's each asset is correlated with every factor or the portfolio's overall performance. The report shows the results of the **Factor exposure** analytics tool.

Single Factor Exposure Report

No	Product	Factor	Beta	SPY	Total
1	Franklin Templeton Hard Currency FUND	United States	0.12	0.01	0.01
2	Goldman Sachs Commodity Strategy A	United States	0.28	0.05	0.05
3	iShares Core U.S. Aggregate Bond ETF	United States	-0.02	-0.00	-0.00
4	PIMCO Total Return A	United States	-0.05	-0.00	-0.00
5	PowerShares Global Listed Private Eq	United States	0.76	0.05	0.05
6	SPDR Gold Shares	United States	0.06	0.00	0.00
7	SPDR S&P 500 ETF Trust	United States	1.00	0.40	0.40
8	T. Rowe Price US Treasury Long-Term	United States	-0.12	-0.01	-0.01

Figure 13.12: Exposures Report

13.2.12   Aggregated Reports

Aggregated reports include **Full Risk Report**, **Full Trade Report**, and **Full Portfolio Report**. They combine the reports mentioned above to generate reports on related information with a single press of the button, which helps to save users' time.

13.2.12.1   Full Risk Report

Full Risk Report provides a full report which combines the Portfolio Statistics, Consolidated Positions, Risk and Return, and Allocation reports.

13.2.12.2   Full Trade Report

The following is a graphical representation of the trading lifecycle, which is a sequence of processes that go through the front, middle and back offices at an asset manager:

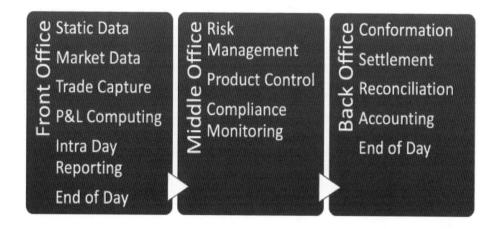

Figure 13.13: Front, Middle and Back-office Processes at a Typical Asset Manager

An industry-standard summary of the different stages of a trade's lifecycle are include below for the ease of reference:[4]

Figure 13.14: Stages of a Trade's Lifecycle

1. Trade Capture

   Trade capture for all transaction types is usually performed on a screen-based system and can be through manual input or fed from another live transaction system. When evaluating a transaction, front-office employees evaluate a trade's potential, its associated market risk, and its counterparty risk to assess the "fit" of the transaction with other exposure.

---

[4]Source: see http://ba4investmentbanks.blogspot.com/2009/11/generic-trading-lifecycle.html for details.

Middle-office staff, or the risk managers, evaluate the effects of the aggregate trades booked within the firm's portfolios, and the total positions held. VaR, Monte Carlo simulations and other statistical tools are used to perform these evaluations. Reports are generated intra-day and at the end of the day for the trading activities.

2. Verification and Confirmation

Once the trade has passed initial validation, a more comprehensive verification can begin. In the trade capture system, the essential elements of the trade are matched (or verified) when the deal is done. Trades that have the settlement date the same as the trade date, like certain spot foreign exchange deals, require telephone confirmations as an extra security check.

The relevant category of SWIFT messages is exchanged with counterparties in the trade to confirm the details of the trade. There are different categories of SWIFT messages for the different trade types: e.g., FX, money market or derivatives.

The essential generic information included in a confirmation for all deals consists of the following: reference number, type of transaction, name, location of counterparty, price dealt, the amount(s), currency(ies) involved, and details of the transaction, including actions, value dates and settlement instructions.

3. Settlement and Netting

Once the confirmation process has been completed, a trade is ready for settlement. Depending on the transaction, this can take many forms. It can range from the settlement of an FX trade on the value date, or cash settlement of difference for many derivatives, through to delivery against payments for bonds or securities. The back-office operations staff process the trade. The principal concern is that the settlement of the trade is completed.

Most assets have several events during their trading lifecycle. For example, a loan may be paid down at the start date, have interim payments, reprice interest if on a floating-rate basis and finally be repaid with interest at maturity. Bank treasury systems have been developed to produce the required SWIFT message to meet the event on the required date using the MT200 series via their gateway into the SWIFT

system. This message will be generated to, say, a correspondent agent bank or national payment carrier.

A final check of payments is carried out before releasing their payments file to ensure everything is correct. If a netting agreement is in place, then netting is performed before payments are made.

4. Reconciliation

Cash reconciliation falls into two categories: internal (positions) and external (Nostro accounts representing agents' correspondents' accounts). Nostro is a banking term to describe an account that a bank holds with a foreign bank, and it is usually denominated in a foreign currency.

Reconciliations are based on exception reporting. Typically, an incoming SWIFT file will be matched to an outstanding deal file, using a proprietary software package or an in-house developed tool. Matched, probable match or unmatched reports are produced, based on key fields such as value date, value, counterparty, etc.

5. Accounting

Accounting is usually considered to be the last phase of the trading lifecycle and some of the activities involved in the accounting process are as shown below:

- Accounting entries are usually generated based on a code profile held for product type on a time-event basis.
- Transactions in base or counter currencies are tracked and revalued. This is for the purpose of determining profit and loss.
- Forward books of outstanding items in the portfolio will normally be revalued on a mark-to-market basis.

13.2.12.3   Consolidated Reports

Certain consolidated report templates are available on the HedgeSPA platform for the user's convenience. The **Full Risk Report** combines Portfolio Statistics, Consolidated Positions, Portfolio Risk and Portfolio Return, Asset Allocation, Regional Allocation and Sector Allocation reports. The **Full Trade Report** provides a full report which combines the Consolidated Positions, Transactions, and Profit & Loss reports. An example is given in Figure 13.15, as follows:

Consolidated Positions Report

No	Asset	Asset Class	Contract	Currency	Exchange Rate	Weight	Avg Price (local Currency)	Position in USD
1	Ascendas Real Estate Investment Trust	Equity	500,000	SGD	1.4	7.45%	2.4	1,040,974.5
2	Keppel REIT Management Limited	Equity	700,000	SGD	1.4	4.55%	1.3	635,658.9
3	SPDR Gold Shares	Commodity	20,000	USD	1	17.94%	163.2	2,507,400.1
4	Vanguard MSCI Pacific ETF	Equity	15,000	USD	1	7.14%	54.6	998,250
5	Straits Times Index ETF	Equity	300,000	SGD	1.4	5.18%	3.3	724,252.5
6	Keppel Corporation Limited	Equity	40,000	SGD	1.4	1.34%	10.8	186,637.1
7	Genting Singapore PLC	Equity	600,000	SGD	1.4	3.36%	1.4	469,546
8	DBS Group Holdings Limited	Equity	25,000	SGD	1.4	3.33%	14.8	464,747.1
9	PowerShares Golden Dragon China	Equity	35,000	USD	1	9.85%	19.6	1,375,850
10	PIMCO 0-5 Year Hi Yld Corp Bond Idx ETF	Fixed Income	10,000	USD	1	7.12%	103.6	995,600
11	iShares Core S&P500 ETF	Equity	15,000	USD	1	30.19%	146.6	4,218,900.2
12	Cash in USD	Cash	355,500	USD	1	2.54%	1	355,500

Transactions Report

-- No Transactions --

Profit & Loss Report

No	Asset	Asset Class	Currency	Contract	Avg Price (local Currency)	Position in USD	Close	P&L in USD

Figure 13.15: Full Trade Report

Finally, the **Full Portfolio Report** combines Portfolio Statistics, Consolidated Positions, Portfolio Risk, Portfolio Return, Asset Allocation, Regional Allocation, Sector Allocation, Transaction, and Profit & Loss reports. An example is given in Figure 13.16, as follows:

Portfolio Statistics Report

No	Statistics	Portfolio
1	Volatility	11.23%
2	Maximum Drawdown	16.92%
3	VaR	19.31%
4	CVaR	24.09%
5	Beta	0.83
6	Sharpe Ratio	-0.4522
7	Alternative Sharpe Ratio	-0.2263
8	Historical Return	-3.08%
9	Skewness	-0.26
10	Kurtosis	2.92

Consolidated Positions Report

No	Asset	Asset Class	Contract	Currency	Exchange Rate	Weight	Avg Price (local Currency)	Position in USD
1	Cash in USD	Cash	0	USD	1	0.00%	1	0
2	Bank of Communications Co., Ltd.	Equity	1,708,087	HKD	7.8	1.36%	0.8	1,458,006.3
3	Bank of China Limited	Equity	3,137,999	HKD	7.8	1.40%	0.4	1,495,199
4	CITIC Securities Co Ltd	Equity	660,525	HKD	7.8	1.60%	2	1,716,698.5
5	Wuliangye Yibin Co	Equity	186,824	CNY	6.9	1.78%	8	1,903,118.7
6	YONYOU NETWORK TEC	Equity	350,074	CNY	6.9	1.49%	3.7	1,595,734
7	ZHEJIANG HUAYOU CO	Equity	303,183	CNY	6.9	1.55%	4.3	1,655,304.4

Figure 13.16: Full Portfolio Report

INVESTMENT ANALYTICS IN THE DAWN OF ARTIFICIAL INTELLIGENCE

14. Additional Reporting

14.1 Use Case

Portfolio manager Jack needs to evaluate the performance of his investment. Naturally, the most obvious way is to compare the performance this year with the performance last year. But how does he make that comparison so that the result of his analysis is meaningful? Also, how can his analysis be done in a way to help his asset sponsors slice and dice his investment performance against his peers? What about reporting all the accounting details like fees, investor subscriptions and redemptions? Finally, what about tracking the details of each transactions to ensure that all portfolio positions are correctly accounted for?

14.2 Maintenance and Accounting Reports

This chapter talks about the typical accounting reports for portfolio performance analysis, as well as related maintenance details:

1. Custom Benchmark
2. Product-Benchmark Mapping
3. Accounting Details
4. Reinvestment Schedule
5. Subscription Redemption Details
6. Transactions

14.2.1 Custom Benchmark

A benchmark is the "yardstick" against which the performance of a security, mutual fund or investment manager can be measured. The performance of most "long-only" investment is compared to a benchmark. There is a large collection of indexes that are used as benchmarks, including the S&P 500, the Dow Jones Industrial Average, the Russell 2000 Index and even a basket of competitor funds. International investors like to use the MSCI Indices. One of the most widely used benchmarks for fixed income is the Barclays Capital U.S. Aggregate Bond Index (with AGG as its ETF ticker).

Custom Benchmark analytics tool is shown in Figure 14.2 enables users to create, edit and manage custom composite (and typically multi-asset) benchmarks. These benchmarks will assume daily rebalancing to the weights according to industry convention. To access this tool, please click on "Analytics" and then double-click "Maintenance". According to Figure 14.1, under "Maintenance", you can find and choose "Custom Benchmark" to do portfolio analysis.

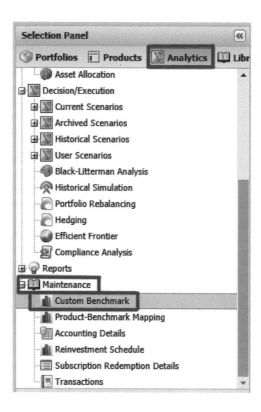

Figure 14.1: Analytics → Maintenance → Custom Benchmark

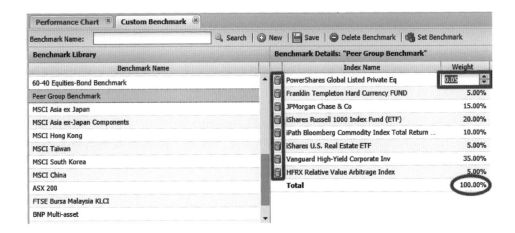

Figure 14.2: Custom Benchmark

When you use the **Custom Benchmark** tool, you can delete indexes by clicking small trash bin signs and change their weights by typing number directly or clicking arrows. Please remember that the sum of the weights should be equal to 100% when a custom benchmark is designed for a "typical" portfolio. For any asset-liability portfolio, the benchmark does not need to be 100% since the benchmark is used to represent the liability. For example, the asset side of the portfolio can be 100%, but the liability side can be 95%, and then we have a 5% surplus in the portfolio.

14.2.1.1 Choosing Benchmarks

The benchmark should reflect the investor's risk tolerance, return goal and investment strategy. For example, the TOPIX may be an appropriate benchmark for a portfolio investing in Japanese equities, but it is clearly not appropriate for any portfolio investing in global equities markets, bonds, and alternative investments. Thus, comparing a portfolio to an incorrect benchmark could result in poor analysis. All portfolio managers want to choose a benchmark that will make their portfolios look fantastic. Certain portfolios, such as real estate or hedge funds, have no natural benchmarks. Further, a portfolio should be measured against its benchmark over a sufficiently long period.

A benchmark should also mirror the investment style of the portfolio. Mutual funds, international investors, and other investors use different indexes as benchmarks for their investment portfolios because the type of investments made is of a different nature.

14.2.1.2 Creating Benchmarks

Any given financial index has limited utility. For example, the S&P 500 can tell us a lot about how blue-chip U.S. equities are performing or how an actively managed large-cap stock fund is faring relative to the market at large, but it gives little insight into the performance of a globally diversified portfolio of stocks, bonds, and other asset classes, and less still into how this portfolio is progressing toward meeting a specific investor's goals.

It is not uncommon to create a customized benchmark for our clients, which is better aligned with their goals and willingness and ability to assume the associated risk.

14.2.1.2.1 Weighted Average Benchmark

A common way is to combine multiple industry-standard indexes, each representing distinct asset classes, into a mix that mimics the portfolio. Such a blended benchmark is inherently more representative of an investor's true experience than any single index. The following describes how to create a "balanced" benchmark. You multiply the benchmark index for each asset class to the target percentage weight of that asset class in the client portfolio. For example, a "balanced" portfolio for a Singapore investor may consist of 30% Singapore fixed income, 30% Singapore equities, 20% U.S. equities, and 20% global developed equities. The respective returns for the benchmark indices were 3.5%, 7.8%, 5.6%, and 4.4%. Then:
Weighted Average Benchmark = (30% × 3.5%) + (30% × 7.8%) + (20% × 5.6%) + (20% × 4.4%) =5.39%. Hence, your custom benchmark return is 5.39%.

14.2.1.3 Using Benchmarks to Evaluate Performance
14.2.1.3.1 Risk-Adjusted Return

Each portfolio has a particular expected return and risk profile. The concept of risk-adjusted return is used to adjust the returns of portfolios with different risk levels so that they can be compared effectively against a benchmark with a known return and risk profile. Risk-adjusted return is the return of the investment if its risk level was the same as the benchmark, here we use the market return as the proxy:

$$R_A = R_{rf} + \frac{\sigma_m}{\sigma_A}(R_A - R_{rf})$$

If an asset has a lower risk level than the market, the return of the asset above the risk-free rate is given a boost. On the other hand, if the asset has a higher than market risk level, the return above the risk-free rate is reduced.

14.2.1.3.2 Tracking Error

The difference in the portfolio and benchmark returns is called the tracking error. It indicates whether a portfolio is volatility or "tight" relative to its benchmark.

Benchmarks not only measure the returns of portfolios but also measure their "active risk". "Active risk" is simply the volatility of the daily "active returns", or the portfolio return minus benchmark returns.

There are different applications for tracking errors. For example, the goal of passive managers is to replicate their benchmarks, despite less than perfectly. Tracking errors measure the degree of success in that replication. The goals of active managers are to make their portfolio returns beat benchmark returns. Tracking errors help measure the degrees of the portfolio manager's success in doing so.

14.2.2   Product Benchmark Mapping

Unlike the custom benchmark which allows users to determine the individual benchmarks' weights, product benchmark mapping enables users to define detail benchmark for each asset in a portfolio. Users are allowed to attach their assets to any desirable benchmark (bucket) based on their own asset bucketing preference. These are the standard definitions of several industry-preferred benchmarks:[1]

Index	Origin	Description
Dow Jones Industrial Average (DJIA)	U.S.	Price-weighted average of 30 publicly traded U.S. "blue-chip" stocks
FTSE 100	UK	Market capitalization-weighted index of the 100 largest UK companies traded on the London Stock Exchange
Hang Seng Index	Hong Kong	Free float-adjusted market capitalization index, consisting of the 50 largest companies, on the Hong Kong Stock Exchange
MSCI World Index	Global Equities	Free float-adjusted market capitalization index, consisting of 23 developed market country indexes
NASDAQ Composite	U.S.	Market capitalization-weighted index of approximately 3,000 common equities listed on the NASDAQ stock exchange
Nikkei 225	Japan	Price-weighted, yen-denominated equity index, consisting of the top 225 blue-chip companies listed on the Tokyo Stock Exchange
S&P 500	U.S.	Market capitalisation-weighted index that tracks the performance of 500 U.S. large-cap stocks

Given the many benchmarks to choose from, deciding which index or combination of indexes to use can be difficult. It is simply not effective to use the Nikkei 225

---

[1]These are standard definitions published by the index providers or collected from third-party sources such as `https://en.wikipedia.org/wiki/PetroChina`.

index to evaluate IBM or the S&P 500 index to evaluate Toyota. Although some portfolio managers want to choose a weak benchmark to make his/her portfolio performance looks better, you should also consider the clients' needs, because they have their own ideas to evaluate you and the portfolio. Some reasonably global portfolios with decade-long track records are known to leave the S&P 500 index as their stock benchmark due to legacy reasons and calculate fees as such, much to the irritation of their investors. One industry website suggests some typical questions to consider from the end-investor's perspective:[2]

1. Client's performance goals and risk tolerance – An investor with low-risk tolerance will most likely select an index with a shorter duration or higher credit quality. An investor looking for a high return may select an index with a track record of high long-term returns, which might also exhibit performance volatility and carry the chance of negative absolute returns over shorter investment horizons.

2. Client's need for liquidity – An investor looking to invest operating cash that will be used to meet short-term liabilities or obligations will need a highly liquid portfolio, and would most likely select an index with a very short duration. This type of investor would want to stay away from riskier benchmarks that contain less liquid securities and exhibit greater interest rate sensitivity. Cash investors may also select custom benchmarks designed to match their liquidity profiles.

3. The range of securities to invest in – A benchmark should be a "good fit" for the portfolio given the range of securities. A broad investment universe can potentially help increase return and reduce volatility. If the benchmark is "too narrow," however, it may be difficult to make noticeable contributions to the portfolio's overall performance through active management.

HedgeSPA provides the **Product-Benchmark Mapping** analytics tool shown as Figure 14.3, which enables users to define detail benchmark for each product in a portfolio. It is different from the **Custom Benchmark** tool, which allows a user to determine the individual benchmarks' weights. In **Product-Benchmark Mapping**, users are allowed to attach their products to any desirable Benchmark (bucket) based on their own asset bucketing preference. Here is an example of choosing the iShares Core U.S. Aggregate Bond ETF (AGG) by clicking on the drop-down menu button.

---

[2]Source: see `https://europe.pimco.com/en-eu/resources/education/ understanding-benchmarks` for details.

Performance Chart ⊠	Product-Benchmark Mapping ⊠
Product	Benchmark
Franklin Templeton Hard Currency FUND	iShares MSCI AC World Index Fund
iShares Core U.S. Aggregate Bond ETF	iShares Core U.S. Aggregate Bond ETF
T. Rowe Price US Treasury Long-Term	iShares Core U.S. Aggregate Bond ETF ▾
Goldman Sachs Commodity Strategy A	iShares MSCI AC World Index Fund
SPDR Gold Shares	iShares Core U.S. Aggregate Bond ETF
SPDR S&P 500 ETF Trust	iShares MSCI AC World Index Fund
Cash in USD	iShares MSCI AC World Index Fund
PIMCO Total Return A	iShares Core U.S. Aggregate Bond ETF
PowerShares Global Listed Private Eq	iShares MSCI AC World Index Fund

Figure 14.3: Product-Benchmark Mapping

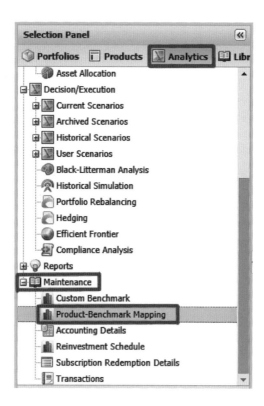

Figure 14.4: "Analytics → Maintenance → Product-Benchmark Mapping"

To access the **Product-Benchmark Mapping** tool, please click "Analytics" first and then double-click on "Maintenance". After that, the user can click "Product-Benchmark Mapping".

14.2.3 Accounting Details

Accounting Details shown as Figure 14.6 enables users to view entries for accounting reporting purposes. To ensure the integrity of the report, accounting entries must be reversed out and only for restricted users with administrative access rights. See below on how to get access to this tool.

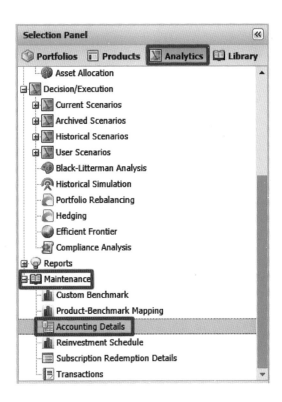

Figure 14.5: "Analytics → Maintenance → Accounting Details"

Entry Type	Value
Administration fees	2,171.92
Custodian and sub-custodian fees	1,085.96
Directors' fees	1,809.94
General expenses	542.98
Management fees	3,619.87
Performance fees	72,397.43
Bank interest expenses	1,809.94
Administration fees	2,123.96
Custodian and sub-custodian fees	1,061.98
Directors' fees	1,769.97
General expenses	530.99
Management fees	3,539.93
Performance fees	70,798.70
Bank interest expenses	1,769.97
Administration fees	2,165.36

Figure 14.6: Accounting Details

HedgeSPA is not a general ledger system. However, we allow users to enter general accounting entries in order to obtain reasonable NAV reports. These accounting entries can be adjusted as and when the official accounting entries become available, which usually takes time. The goal is to allow portfolio managers to continue to manage their portfolios with good faith estimates on important fund metrics such as NAV and subscriptions.

14.2.4   Subscription Redemption Details

Subscriptions and redemptions generate entries in the fund register as well as creating cash flows, payments, and receipts. Cash flows will be included in the cash forecast, which shows the total receipts of cash and total payments including those generated by subscriptions and redemptions as well as from other sources such as asset transactions.

The purchase and sale of the shares and units in a fund are settled via the transfer agency. The processes are shown in the following figure:

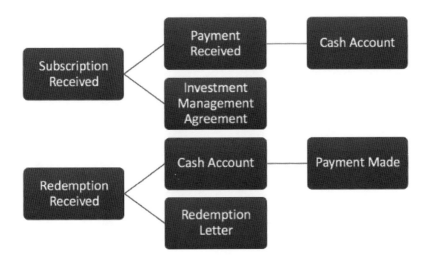

Figure 14.7: Typical Processes for Subscriptions and Redemptions

Before any subscription or redemption is processed and assuming it has been submitted in the prescribed format, customary due diligence under relevant laws and regulations will be undertaken. This will involve verifying the identity of the investor, which can be a private individual, a financial institution or a corporate entity, the source, or destination of the monies, and the status of the applicant in relation to the type of fund that they want to be associated with. The latter is part of the process of verifying if a potential investor is qualified for the more lightly regulated non-retail or alternative investment funds.

The **Subscription Redemption Details** tool generates a report which shows the history of the fund's subscription and redemption activities. To access it, please click on "Analytics" and then "Maintenance". After that, you will find "Subscription Redemption Details" and double-click on it.

To use the **Subscription Redemption Details** tool, you should click the "Add" button, and then a new row will be added into the panel. After that, you can click on the empty space of the "Type" column, and a drop-down menu will appear. In this menu, "SUBSCRIBE" means buying, and "REDEEM" means selling. "REINVEST" means using additional income, including capital gains or interest, to reinvest assets. Similarly, you can fill up the rest of the information by clicking on the empty space of the beneath column. You need to fill in how many shares or funds you want to subscript or redeem in the "Unit" Column at what "NAV Price".

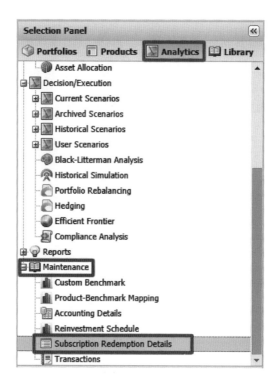

Figure 14.8: "Analytics → Maintenance → Subscription Redemption Details"

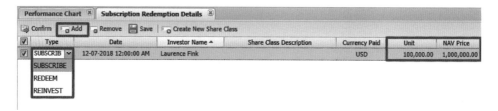

Figure 14.9: Subscription Redemption Details

14.2.5 Transactions

14.2.5.1 General Ledger Accounts

Transactions generate entries in the records of the fund. These records will be used to produce information about the fund over a period by analyzing the entries in each ledger.

The individual ledger accounts are held as part of the general ledger (GL), and the GL enables a full analysis of all the transactions within the fund. The number of ledgers within the GL depends on the fund and its activities, but there are certain ledger accounts that are common across all funds. These accounts include the following entries:

- Bank accounts – deposit accounts, client segregated account
- Prime broker and/or brokers – cash account, margin account, interest receivable and payable, dividends, commissions
- Other counterparties – negotiated products, OTC derivatives, cash flows receivable and/or payable
- Investments – investments at cost, unrealized gains, and losses
- Accounts receivables – subscriptions and other amounts receivable
- Prepayments – prepaid registration and license fees, directors fees, etc.
- Accounts payables – fees such as management, administration, performance, audit, legal, other organizational fees, redemptions, and other payable items
- Equity – retained earnings, equity
- Income – dividend, interest, realized gains and losses and other income
- Expenses – costs including fees and sundry expenses.

14.2.5.2 Portfolio Records

There are many key areas of portfolio administration and fund records that will need to be managed by the operations, accounting or transfer agency team, including the following:

- Records of assets held – There should be a clean record of all the assets currently held by the portfolio.
- Changes to assets held – This may include buys and sells and should be reconciled with transactions and cash accounts.
- Income and benefits accruing from the assets – Some assets may generate income or other benefits such as new shares, and these must be identified, reconciled and posted to the accounting records of the fund for incorporation into the value of the fund.
- Records of fees and expenses – These records should show the fees and expenses charged to the fund (not the investment manager), including such items as audit fees.

- Valuations of the total assets of the fund – Periodically the total assets and liabilities of the fund will be calculated to produce the net asset value (NAV) of the fund.
- Records of the purchase and sales of units or shares in the fund by investors – A fund will need to maintain the details of the investors who have put capital into the fund and who are on the register as shareholders or unitholders, and the total number of shares or units they own. The fund register contains the details and is updated as and when there are changes to the ownership of the shares or units.
- Records of distribution of capital, income, or dividend to investors – There should be a clear record if a fund makes a distribution of capital, income, or dividend to its investors.
- Records of any performance related to fees due to the manager – In some funds, a performance fee is payable to the investment manager provided certain requirements are met. In some circumstances, a process of equalization will be applied to ensure that the manager and individual investors are being treated fairly in relation to the performance fee. A record of the fee calculation, equalization, and amount paid are kept in the fund accounting records.
- The tax situation pertaining to the fund – There may be tax situations that apply to the fund. If so, the record of the tax accrual and payments, including any withholding tax recovered under tax treaties, will be included in the fund's accounting records.

The importance of the proper maintenance of the records of the fund should be obvious: this is often a compliance requirement by regulations. Equally important, the proper recording of the fund's register of investors and their holdings is vital for both the calculation of the NAV and the distribution of any income.

14.2.5.3 Transactions

The **Transactions** log tool displays all the trading transactions that have been made associated with the open portfolio, including cash transactions. The **Transactions** tool cab be found at the bottom of the "Analytics" window after double-clicking "Maintenance", as in Figure 14.10.

After the user creates a position in the Portfolio Grid, they can come to the transactions screen to either "Confirm Transactions" or "Cancel Transactions". Note that once a position has been confirmed, the transaction can only be edited or removed by restricted users with administrative access rights.

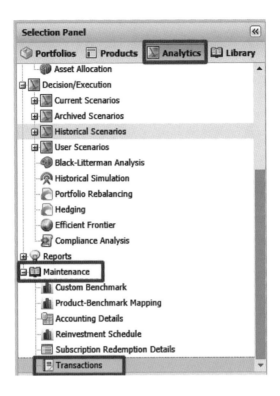

Figure 14.10: "Analytics → Maintenance → Transactions"

	Product	Type	Unit	Price	Total	Commission	Status	Date
	Franklin Templeton Hard Cu...	BUY	100.000000	7.810000	781.0000000	0.000000	Cancelled	2016-01-04 00:00:00.0
	Franklin Templeton Hard Cu...	SELL	100.000000	7.810000	781.0000000	0.000000	Cancelled	2016-01-04 00:00:00.0
	Alphabet Inc	BUY	1000.000000	701.789978	701789.9780000	0.000000	Cancelled	2016-01-21 00:00:00.0
	Alphabet Inc	BUY	1000.000000	737.599976	737599.9760000	0.000000	Cancelled	2016-03-22 00:00:00.0
	Alphabet Inc	BUY	1000.000000	737.599976	737599.9760000	0.000000	Cancelled	2016-03-22 00:00:00.0
	Alphabet Inc	BUY	1000.000000	737.599976	737599.9760000	0.000000	Cancelled	2016-03-22 00:00:00.0
	Alphabet Inc	BUY	1000.000000	718.770020	718770.0200000	0.000000	Cancelled	2016-04-25 00:00:00.0
	Franklin Templeton Hard Cu...	BUY	1000.000000	7.740000	7740.0000000	0.000000	Cancelled	2016-04-27 00:00:00.0
	Alphabet Inc	BUY	1000.000000	723.150024	723150.0240000	0.000000	Cancelled	2016-04-27 00:00:00.0
	Alphabet Inc	BUY	1000.000000	734.150024	734150.0240000	0.000000	Cancelled	2016-06-10 00:00:00.0

Figure 14.11: Transactions

INVESTMENT ANALYTICS IN THE DAWN OF ARTIFICIAL INTELLIGENCE

---

15. Compliance Analysis

15.1 Use Case

Typical asset sponsors want reports to ensure that various statistics of their portfolios are consistent with the "limits" specified by the Investment Management Agreements. However, asset managers do not want to be surprised only when any limits are breached. They want to have a way to monitor those limits and take the appropriate actions ahead of any imminent breach.

For example, portfolio manager Jack has major clients who want to specify a list of statistical limits in his portfolio. While he is aware that his clients will terminate the mandate because of poor performance, he does not want any breaches on other statistical limits to be used as future excuses for fee negotiation. He appreciates the need for limits, but he also feels that some limits are not helpful in guiding portfolios to good performance. In every reporting cycle, his junior analysts have to spend a large amount of time going through these limits, and under his current process, he is only notified of problems after a breach. He is seeking a more automated way to monitor limits such as the list below:

1. Excessive beta against the benchmark
2. Excessive leverage
3. Overconcentration in any particular stock, sector, or country
4. Average number of days to liquidate the portfolio
5. Maximum portfolio drawdown
6. Maximum percentage of undeployed cash

15.2 Monitoring Compliance Rules

The **Compliance Analysis** tool can be used to check whether a selected list of assets can be added to a selected list of portfolios while still maintaining compliance with the portfolio risk profiles or other statistical investment guidelines. The **Compliance Analysis** tool could be accessed by clicking "Analytics" and double-clicking "Compliance Analysis" under "Decision/Execution" shown in Figure 15.1.

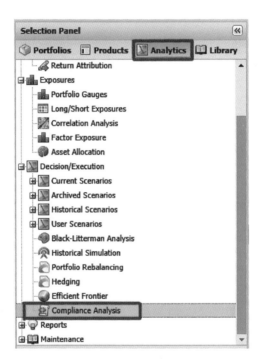

Figure 15.1: Analytics → Compliance Analysis

Compliance Analysis is a top-level multi-portfolio tool and as such is opened in the top portion of the platform Workspace, on the same level as individual portfolios.

When **Compliance Analysis** is first opened, you can add portfolios and products by simply dragging and dropping from the Selection Panel on the left-hand side onto the appropriate panel, including "Portfolios" window and "Products" window, in the Compliance Analysis tool. After adding portfolios, the user will need to specify the possible 'Investable Cash' with which they want to test investment product Compliance.

Compliance Analysis							
Run Analysis Clear All							

Portfolios				**Products**			
Portfolio	Risk Profile	Investable Cash ▾		Product	Asset Class	Region	Currency
Asian HNW	CONSERVATIVE	$50,000.00		SingTel	Equity	Singapore / ASEAN	SGD
Asian Sovereign Wealth	CONSERVATIVE	$500,000.00		Aberdeen Asia Bond Instituti...	Fixed Income	Developed Markets	SGD
Long Short Equities - Asia	CONSERVATIVE	$1,000,000.00		PowerShares DB Agriculture ...	Commodity	Developed Markets	USD
US Multi-Asset Funds	CONSERVATIVE	$0.00		Lord Abbett Emerging Marke...	Foreign Exchange	Developed Markets	USD

Figure 15.2: Compliance Analysis

Finally, as shown in Figure 15.3, the "Scenario" button located in the middle of the screen allows the user to select whether this analysis will be run under "None" (the current conditions) or one of many possible forward-looking statistical market scenarios, such as "Current Scenario", "Archived Scenarios", "Historical Scenarios", and "User Scenarios". This helps examine potential investments' compliance not only under current conditions but also after historical and possible future market moves. Simply click on the black arrow next to "Scenario": to select the desirable scenario.

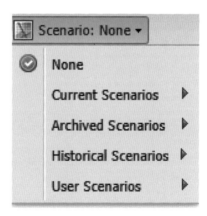

Figure 15.3: Scenario Selection

Once the Portfolios, Products, and Scenario are ready, click the "Run Analysis" button shown in Figure 15.2 to receive the Compliance Analysis results in a table at the bottom of the Workspace. "True" results indicate that at that level of Investable Cash, in that market scenario, the product is in compliance with the portfolio mandate. A "False" result indicates that the investment would breach compliance with the portfolio mandate.

Compliance Analysis Results				
Scenario: Euro Crisis (Pessimistic) ▾				
Product	Asian HNW	Asian Sovereign Wealth	Long Short Equities - Asia	US Multi-Asset Funds
SingTel	False	False	True	True
Aberdeen Asia Bond Insti...	False	False	False	True
PowerShares DB Agricult...	False	False	False	True
Lord Abbett Emerging M...	False	False	False	True

Figure 15.4: Compliance Analysis Results

INVESTMENT ANALYTICS IN THE DAWN OF ARTIFICIAL INTELLIGENCE

16. Data Integrity Validation

16.1 Use Case

Portfolio manager Jack hires several interns to help him compile data in Excel spreadsheets and do data entry into his trading system. However, human data entry also involves a high possibility of errors.

For example, in one of the transactions, one intern accidentally inputs $9.99 instead of $99.99 as the price for a share of one specific stock. Although a mistake like this is easy to detect by a professional based on market knowledge, there are no simple rules that can be used to guide a computer to detect such a mistake automatically, so it can either correct the mistake or send a warning to the user. Obviously, a computer program that automatically detects such errors can improve efficiency and decrease the error rate.

This chapter will show Jack the tools that he needs to detect such erroneous data entries in the process of recording them. Besides error detection, we will also describe effective and realistic ways to fix such errors and give practical examples.

16.2 Defining Data Integrity

The technical view of data integrity mainly involves a whole and complete definition of the data itself and a form of guarantee that the data will not be changed, lost or modified in any other manner when sent and received. If the data is whole and complete, and if the data remains unchanged from the creation time to the reception time, then such data is said to show integrity. Hence, this is a technically precise definition of data integrity.

At a working level, a more practical definition of data integrity is the level of trust assigned by its user. At the most basic level, data integrity depends entirely on trustworthiness. Also, there are four considerations determining the extent to which an enterprise can trust to make complex strategic decisions: timeliness, accuracy, truthfulness associated with its context, and the intention of the data sender.

1. Data **timeliness** means the data is current, timely, up to date and recorded at or very near the time of the event or observation.
2. **Accuracy** means precision and exactness, or freedom from error.
3. The third consideration of the trusted view of data integrity is the **truthfulness** with respect to its context of use, as opposed to data being taken out of context.
4. The final consideration of the trusted view of data integrity is the **intention** with respect to the state of mind of the conveyor of the data, or whether the genuine intention is misrepresent data to fit certain conclusions.

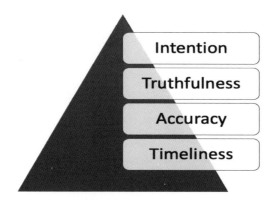

Figure 16.1: Foundation of Data Integrity

Assessing timeliness and accuracy is not difficult, but assessing truthfulness and intention is non-trivial in general, as we will illustrate in the next subsection with a practical example.

16.2.1 A Practical Example

We have chosen PetroChina to give a more specific practical use case. PetroChina Company Limited is a Chinese oil and gas company and is the listed arm of state-owned China National Petroleum Corporation (CNPC). It is the biggest oil producer in China, and its shares are listed in both Hong Kong and New York. This Chinese mainland enterprise announced its plans to issue stocks in Shanghai in November 2007, and subsequently started trading on the Shanghai Stock Exchange with the following tickers:

- PetroChina Company Limited (SHA:601857)
- PetroChina Company Limited (HKG:0857)
- PetroChina Company Limited (ADR) (NYSE:PTR)

16.2.1.1 Data Timeliness

Timeliness is defined as the time delay from data generation and acquisition to utilization. As one example of an income statement based on quarterly data back in 2016, Google Finance was showing PetroChina financials only up until 2012. While there are interesting applications requiring historical financials, outdated data alone is unhelpful to making timely and relevant investment decisions.

In Millions of CNY (except for per share items)	As of 2012-12-31	As of 2011-12-31	As of 2010-12-31	As of 2009-12-31
Sales Revenue	2,195,296.00	2,003,843.00	1,465,415.00	1,019,275.00
Discount and Allowance	-	-	-	-
Net Revenue from Main Operations	-	-	-	-
Less: Cost of Goods Sold	1,634,819.00	1,425,284.00	970,209.00	633,100.00
Sales Tax & Other Charges	246,078.00	258,027.00	177,666.00	129,756.00
Profit (Loss) from Principal Operations	-	-	-	-

Figure 16.2: Sample Income Statement as Published by Google Finance

16.2.1.2 Data Accuracy

Data is used to provide insight. If data accuracy is poor at the start of this process, the insight will be lacking and the decisions made based on the data are likely to be poor as a result. For example, the financials for PetroChina on Yahoo Finance are confusing. The Total Revenue on Yahoo Finance (on the left) is 1,725,428,000 thousand, which is the same number as 1,725,428 million on the 2015 annual report (on the right), only with different units. However, the Net Income on Yahoo Finance is 35,517,000 thousand. Compared to 42,089 million on the annual report, it seems to have used 84.39 as the exchange rate for Chinese Yuan and Hong Kong Dollars, making it quite difficult for any investment professionals to trust these numbers

Income Statement (HKD thousand)

Revenue	As of 2015-12-31
Total Revenue	1,725,428,000
Cost of Revenue	1,056,795,000
Gross Profit	668,633,000
Operating Expenses	
Research Development	.
Selling General and Administrative	.
Non-Recurring	.
Others	.
Total Operating Expenses	1,663,854,000
Operating Income or Loss	61,574,000
Income from Continuing Operations	
Total Other Income/Expenses Net	.
Earnings Before Interest and Taxes	61,574,000
Interest Expense	-24,328,000
Income Before Tax	.
Income Tax Expenses	15,726,000
Minority Interest	.
Net Income from Continuing Ops	.
Non-recurring Events	
Discontinued Operations	.
Extraordinary Items	.
Effect of Accounting Changes	.
Other Items	.
Net Income	
Net Income	35,517,000
Preferred Stock and Other Adjustments	.
Net Income Applicable to Common Shares	.

Annual Report (RMB Million)

Items	As of 2015-12-31
Revenue	1,725,428
Profit from Operations	79,252
Profit before Income Tax Expenses	57,815
Income Tax Expenses	(12,726)
Profit for the Year	42,089
Attribute to:	
Owners of the Company	35,517
Non-Controlling Interest	6,572
Basic and Diluted Earnings Per Share Attributable	
to Owners of the Company (RMB)	0.19
Total Current Assets	349,344
Total Non-Current Assets	2,044,500
Total Assets	2,393,844
Total Current Liabilities	471,407
Total Non-Current Liabilities	578,403
Total Liabilities	1,049,810
Equity	
Attribute to:	
Owners of the Company	1,179,716
Non-controlling Interest	164,318
Total Equity	1,344,034
Other Financial Data	
Capital Expenditures	202,238
Net Cash Flows from Operating Activities	261,312
Net Cash Flows Used for Investing Activities	(215,879)
Net Cash Flows (Used for)/from Financing Activities	(45,439)
Return on Net Assets (%)	3.0

Figure 16.3: Sample Income Statement as Published by Yahoo Finance

when making investment decisions. In Table 16.1, we tried to make the corrections using the exchange rate of 83.78 on 31 December 2015, but the data from Yahoo Finance still did not reconcile.

Table 16.1: Comparison of Income Statement Discrepencies

2015 Income Statement	Annual Report (RMB, millions)	Attempted Correction (HKD, thousands)	Yahoo Finance (HKD, thousands)
Revenues	1,725,428	1,445,563,578	1,725,428,000
Operating Expenses	(1,646,176)	1,379,166,253	(1,663,854,000)
Profit From Operations	79,252	66,397,326	61,574,000
Finance Costs	(22,941)	(19,219,970)	(24,328,000)
Profit Before Tax Expense	57,815	47,177,356	37,246,000
Income Tax Expense	(15,726)	(13,175,243)	(15,726,000)
Net Income	42,089	34,002,113	35,517,000

16.2.1.3   Data Consistency

After confirming the data source is timely and accurate, we turn to data consistency. Data consistency means that the value of data stays the same after different parts in the application access the data, which can lead to both truthfulness and intention. There are standard techniques in computer science used to prevent data from being changed at the same time, resulting in data corruption. Data consistency may include the following aspects:

1. Point in time consistency means that all related data is the same at any given instant. In the event of a power failure, for example, it is important to restore all data as it was right before the moment of failure. In most modern databases, this is guaranteed by the ACID (Atomicity, Consistency, Isolation, Durability) properties of the database.

2. Transaction consistency only exists before the specified set of transactions has been run and after they are completed. During the processing of a transaction, data may not be consistent unless there is a global "lock" on the data entry.

3. Application consistency may involve data from different sources such as databases and individual files. An application involves many transactions, and as such, data is entirely consistent only before and after all transactions have been completed. Controlling simultaneous operations and the ability to handle incomplete transactions are essential to being able to maintain as well as restore data consistency in the event of power failures. In a multi-processor environment, this is typicaly done by reducing the "lock" ownership to a single process, but doing so may also create a processing bottleneck.

16.3   Standard Data Integrity Tests

We have included the descriptions of some standard data integrity tests for the ease of reference:[1]

Allowed character checks

Check to ascertain that only expected characters are present in a field. For example, a numeric field may only allow the digits 0-9, the decimal point and perhaps a minus sign and/or commas. A text field such as a personal name might disallow non-alphabetical characters such as < and >, as they could be evidence of a markup-language-based security attack. An e-mail address might require at least one @ sign and other structural details, and there is plenty of email verification APIs available today. Regular expressions are also effective ways of implementing such checks.

Batch total checks for missing records

It is straightforward to add a numeric field to all the records in the batch. Enter the batch total and the computer can check if the checksum is correct, e.g., adding the "Total Cost" field of all transactions in a record together.

---

[1]Source: see https://en.wikipedia.org/wiki/Data_validation for details.

Cardinality check

Users can check if a record has a valid number of related records. For example, if the Contact record is classified as a Customer, it must have at least one associated Order (Cardinality > 0). If such an order does not exist for such a "Customer" record, then it must be either changed to "Prospect" or the Order must be created. This type of rule can be complicated by additional conditions. For example, if the Contact record in Payroll database is marked as a "former employee", then this record should not have any associated salary payments after the date on which the employee left the organization (Cardinality = 0).

Check digits used for numerical data

An extra digit is added to a number which is calculated from the digits. The computer checks this calculation when data are entered. For example, the last digit of an ISBN for a book is a check digit using modulus 11, i.e., the sum of all the ten digits of the ISBN, each multiplied by its (integer) weight, descending from 10 to 1, should be a multiple of 11.

Cross-system consistency checks

Compare data in different systems to ensure that they are consistent, e.g., the addresses for the customers with the same identity are the same in both systems. The data may be represented differently in different systems and may need to be transformed into a common format to be compared, e.g., one system may store customer name in a single Name field as 'Adams, John Q', while another in three different fields: First_Name (John), Last_Name (Adams) and Middle_Name (Quincy); to compare the two, the validation engine must convert the data from the second system to match the data format from the first system, or be able to identify the most common format.

Data type checks

Check the input data type and give an error message if the input data does not match the selected data type, e.g., in an input box accepting numeric data, if the letter "O" was typed instead of the number zero "0", an error message should be generated.

Limit check

Unlike range checking, data are checked for one limit only, such as upper or lower limit, e.g., a percentage input should not be greater than 100% (<=1).

Logic check

Check if the input does not produce a logic error, e.g., if the input value will be used to divide another value elsewhere in the program, the input value should not be zero.

Presence check

Check that important data is actually present and has not been missed, e.g., customers may be required to have their telephone numbers or the "Contact" record will not be saved.

Range check

Check if the data is within the specified range of values, e.g., the month of a person's date of birth should be between 1 and 12.

Referential integrity

In modern relational databases, the values in two tables can be linked by foreign and primary keys. If the values in the primary key field are not affected by the internal mechanism of the database, then they should be verified. Validation of the foreign key held checks that the referencing table must always refer to a valid row in the referenced table.

16.4   Mitigation Methods

16.4.1   Sample Algorithm to Fill Missing Data: Expectation-Maximization

There are many "data filling" algorithms in use by the financial industry today. We will provide one example here for the purpose of illustration.

The maximum likelihood estimates of parameters in statistical models can be found by expectation-maximization (EM) algorithm. The maximum likelihood estimates (MLE) of the unknown parameters are determined by the marginal likelihood of the observed data:

$$L(\theta;X) = p(X|\theta) = \sum_Z p(X,Z|\theta) \tag{16.1}$$

for a given statistical model which generates a set X of observed data, a set Z of missing values, a vector θ of unknown parameters, and a likelihood function $L(\theta;X;Z) = p(X;Z|\theta)$. However, the marginal likelihood is usually difficult to handle (e.g., if Z is a series of events so that the number of values grows exponentially with the length of the sequence, it will be very difficult to calculate this sum accurately.)

As a workaround, the EM algorithm iteratively applies the following two steps to find the marginal likelihood MLE:

1. Expectation Step (E Step) – based on the distribution of Z conditional on X under current estimates of $\theta^{(t)}$, compute the expected value of the log likelihood function, as follows:

$$Q(\theta|\theta^{(t)}) = E_{Z|X;\theta^{(t)}}[\log L(\theta;X;Z)] \tag{16.2}$$

2. Maximization Step (M Step) – Find the parameters that maximize:

$$\theta^{(t+1)} = \arg_\theta \max Q(\theta|\theta^{(t)}) \tag{16.3}$$

The EM iteration alternates between the expectation (E) step and the maximization (M) step. Note that in typical models to which EM can be applied:

1 The observations of X can be discrete or continuous.
2 The missing values Z are discrete, drawn from a fixed number of values. There is one missing value per observed data point.
3 The parameters are continuous: a) Parameters associated with all data points, and b) parameters associated with a particular missing value.

EM is used to fill in missing data with the predicted values, but it is considered effective only when less than a few percents of data points (usually randomly distributed) are missing. Filling in missing data is a highly specialized research topic in applied statistics, and we cannot cover the various possible solutions here. Other methodologies should be considered when working with asset classes with a higher occurrence of missing data or under a different reporting frequency.

16.4.2 Sample Treatment of Outliers and Influential Cases

This subsection gives one example of how such a validation process is implemented in the real world. To validate data integrity, we retrieve the list of relevant data about product details and price quotes from a database for checking missing price data and abnormal price jumps. Every parameter in our data cleansing mechanism can be adjusted. Users can press "Enter" to use all default values for checking, otherwise to indicate a manual checking. For example, the user can input the start date, which is 2 years from today by default. If the user inputs the end date to search, the default value is today. Also, the start date and the end date are optional as can be set to empty. Users can specify every detailed parameter, such as date, and white-list, by themselves. The information being crawled in our system includes prices, exchange rates, product fundamentals, product news, and interest rates.

A missing quote is defined as price information missing for more than or equal to 5 days. Our detection is highlighting any time-series with missing pieces more than 5 days, excluding holidays and weekend.

For abnormal price jumps, we check for the last available record to the first available date or check the entire time series. We use two algorithms to detect price jumps, as follows:

1 Absolute jumps – Absolute price jumps are that prices increase/decrease more than a given threshold, usually 50%, which would be highlighted in our system.
2 Z-score detection – We calculate the average (μ), the mean daily return, and standard deviation (σ), the variance of the daily return, for each time-series, and then calculate the z-scores, which measures the distance from the mean. $Z = (X - \mu)/\sigma$, where X is the daily return value. Z-score being too large or too small suggests possibly outliers. Typically, for normal distribution, if Z-score is less than -3 or larger than 3, the value could be treated as the outlier. For the fat-tail distribution, if z-score is less than -5 or larger than 5, the value could be treated as the outlier.

16.4.3 Sample Data Integrity Validation Process

Effective testing requires funding collection, creation, validation, and delivery of data with appropriate control measures. Good data is needed to receive good test results. Multiple data sources, missing data, and unverified data will weaken the credibility of the test results.

A key to protecting data integrity is that each user in every job function should depend on the same set of data. Using a single system to manage and test data can solve the conflict method of verifying and preparing data for analysis. The result is the consistency of the entire organization's data integrity. This is the model currently used by HedgeSPA and other major players in FinTech. The steps are shown graphically in Figure 16.4, as follows:

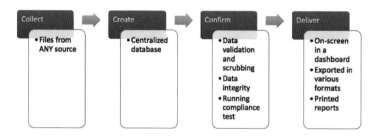

Figure 16.4: Data Validation Flowchart

Collect

Enterprises must first determine the limits to be tested and the data that need to be tested. They must then identify the sources of the appropriate data. Multiple data sources are generally required, including the fund accounting system and other third-party data sources.

Create

Administrators must create data validation rules to confirm the integrity of data, including whether its data set is complete and accurate.

Confirm

Administrators identify, study and resolve data exceptions. After validating the data, compliance tests can be performed.

Deliver

Administrators deliver valid test results. Administrators resolve "garbage in, garbage out" data integrity issues by automating the data management process.

16.5 Conclusion

There is no "one-size-fits-all" approach to validate data integrity. One thing is certain: The amount of readily accessible data will only increase in time. New techniques will be required to handle unstructured data, and it will only get harder to validate data integrity without a professionally maintained platform equipped with the latest algorithms. We trust that this chapter gives readers a taste of the typical data validation techniques involved.

Part V

DEPLOY

INVESTMENT ANALYTICS IN THE DAWN OF ARTIFICIAL INTELLIGENCE

17. Deployment Best Practices

17.1 Use Case

The detailed discussions in the preceding chapters are in a "cookbook" format to allow an expert to define his/her investment analytics workflow. In truth, probably less than 5% of the users will have the time and patience to walk through such details. They will be appointed "administrative users" who will set up the platform for day-to-day use by the rest of his/her investment team. The remaining 95% of the investment team will mainly focus on interpreting the results of such a complex platform, using let's say in a Dashboard format such as the one described in this chapter.

Due to branding reasons, some large institutions may choose to integrate the results of these analyses into their existing web or mobile platforms for end-investors. The HedgeSPA platform also provides a full application programming interface (API) for these large institutions. By contrast, many mid-size institutions need an efficient way for professionals based in multiple locations to grant approvals. The right choice of technology is crucial to success because geographically distributed applications often result in "deadlocks". In this chapter, we would like to illustrate how an institution that focuses on "using" the analytic results can take advantage of user deployment capabilities.

17.2   Dashboard for Investment Teams

The following is a typical flow chart for investment teams monitoring investments:

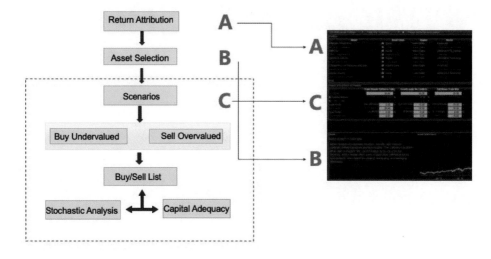

Figure 17.1: Flowchart

Such a Dashboard can be integrated into any existing website as an "iFrame". A magnified picture of the Dashboard can be found below:

Figure 17.2: Dashboard

The top menus allow the selection of investor portfolios:

Figure 17.3: Portfolio Selection

and economic/market scenarios:

Figure 17.4: Economic Scenario Selection

By clicking on the "i" next to each asset name the Dashboard will show its descriptions:

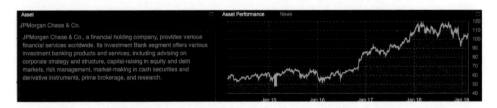

Figure 17.5: Economic Scenario Selection

A. Return Attribution

Once an economic scenario is chosen, the platform will return the portfolio line items where the projected econometric return is higher than the break-even return (an Increase) or vice versa (a Decrease). The size of the threshold to signal an Increase or a Decrease is a user-defined parameter with a default of 3%. This report has been enhanced with tail-risk analytics so that it will work for multi-asset portfolios including emerging market equities, bonds, commodities, and alternative investments.

B. Asset Selection

For each asset that is designated for a potential increase or decrease, we run the asset selection based on its country/sector universe and the user setting. If no user setting exists for that universe, we use a default setting. The idea is that typical investors only want to buy an asset from the top of its universe, or to sell from the bottom of its universe. The thresholds (buy from the top 30%, sell from the bottom 70%) as well as any applicable switching rules are user-defined. Rankings from longer-term factors can be adjusted by rankings from a keyword screen performing sentiment analysis on news and social media, as follows:

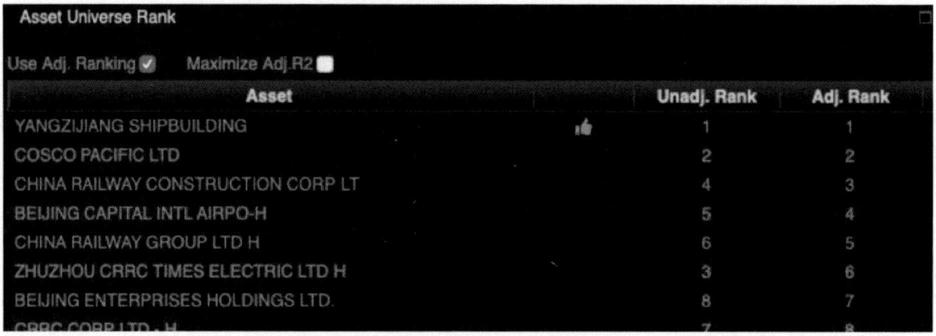

Asset		Unadj. Rank	Adj. Rank
Asset Universe Rank			
Use Adj. Ranking ☑ Maximize Adj.R2 ■			
YANGZIJIANG SHIPBUILDING	👍	1	1
COSCO PACIFIC LTD		2	2
CHINA RAILWAY CONSTRUCTION CORP LT		4	3
BEIJING CAPITAL INTL AIRPO-H		5	4
CHINA RAILWAY GROUP LTD H		6	5
ZHUZHOU CRRC TIMES ELECTRIC LTD H		3	6
BEIJING ENTERPRISES HOLDINGS LTD.		8	7
CRRC CORP LTD - H		7	8

Figure 17.6: Keywords used to Adjust Asset Rankings

The user gets to define how much weight to assign for the long-term vs. the short-term factors for the adjusted rankings. The keywords can be chosen to screen for news items with "Environmental, Social and Governance" keywords, as shown below:

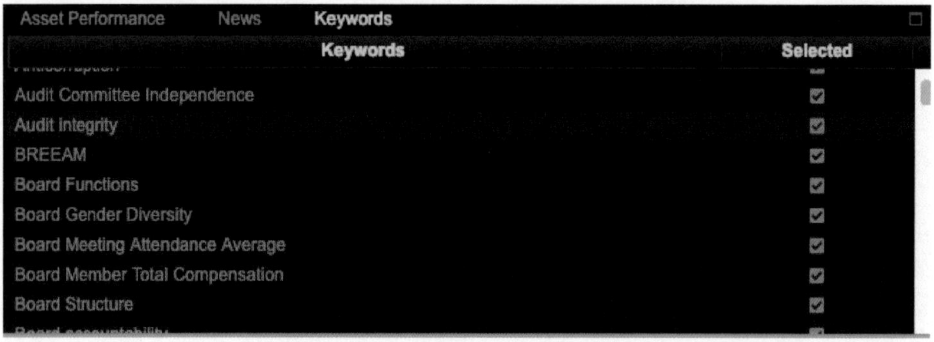

Keywords	Selected
Asset Performance News **Keywords**	
Audit Committee Independence	☑
Audit Integrity	☑
BREEAM	☑
Board Functions	☑
Board Gender Diversity	☑
Board Meeting Attendance Average	☑
Board Member Total Compensation	☑
Board Structure	☑

Figure 17.7: Sample ESG Keywords

C. Scenarios

Now that the buy and sell set has been identified and filtered, by choosing a set of market scenarios with user-assigned probabilities ("Trade Wars" in this example, but the set of scenarios are user-definable) the computer will recommend buys and sells that attempts to improve on the portfolio for all scenarios, including both "up-market" and "down-market" scenarios:

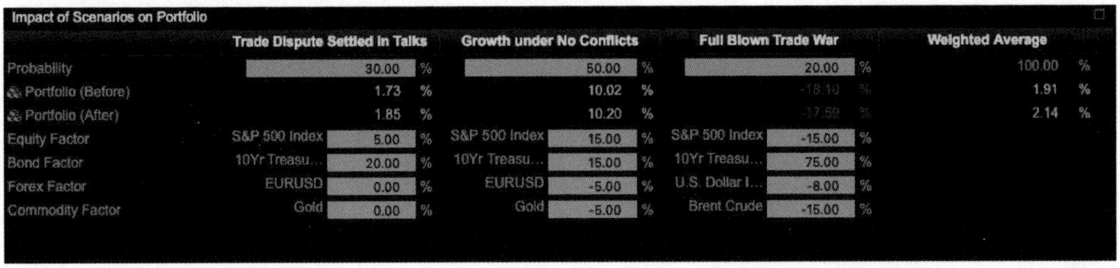

Figure 17.8: Recommendations under Multiple Scenarios

Do note that it is not always mathematically feasible to have an improvement for all scenarios. Unlike the traditional approach which only gives you the result of the best-case scenarios, however, our goal is to optimize for as many scenarios as feasibale. Moreover, the user can add additional manual buys and sells to the list (for instance, these can be specific instructions given by the end-investors) and the system will make the best recommendations based on the remaining tradeable assets:

Figure 17.9: Recommendation with Manual Buys and/or Sells

What we have shown above is one way by which an inevstor can view the rather complicated analytic results computed by the core investment platform using a simple one-page format. Once the parameters are set for an institution (based on the detailed "cookbook" explanations in the preceding chapters), our experience is that 95% of the investors prefer this kind of simple format on a day-to-day basis.

17.3 API for End-Investor Access

The Dashboard is one of the many examples of how these analytics may be deployed in the real world. Some institutions prefer to preserve the branding of their existing web portals and choose to communicate the analytics results to clients in a format consistent with their own branding. These institutions may like to access the Application User Interface (API) directly. Every function supported by the HedgeSPA core investment platform is based on an API call (which is a delivery format similar to that of IBM Watson). On the next page, we have provided one example of an API call for Stochastic Analysis in JavaScript Object Notation (JSON) format, as follows:

```
Request:

https://server1.hedgespa.com/api/getBlackLittermanAnalysis

portfolioId:  4212
showActiveReturns:   false
valuationDate:   2019-04-18T00:00:00+08:00
period:  1
includeCash:  false
frequency:  0
minTau:  0.005
maxTau:  0.1
minLambda:  0.5
maxLambda:  4
scenarioIds:  220,221,222
confidenceLevels:  0.5,0.2,0.3
fixedIds:
productIds:  1002062,1002065,1002066,1002123,1009450,1009107,1002278, 1009939,1009111
upperBounds:  1,1,1,1,1,1,1,1,1
lowerBounds:  -1,-1,-1,-1,-1,-1,-1,-1,-1

Response:

{

"productIds":[

1002062,

1002065,

1002066,

1002123,

1002278,

1009107,

1009111,

1009450,

1009939

],

"scrBefore":0,

"scrAfter":0,

"success":true,
```

```
"returns":[
0.006997956814022944,
0.007688088835994153,
0.006911319179898056,
0.002270422860214477,
0.00472959994274851,
8.093009544054066E-4,
0.006873424273456296,
0.012710280973211151,
0.006383530301116688
],
"originalWeights":[
0.044821681674264875,
0.03612123099502638,
0.016956911216401815,
0.05443268837692675,
0.06311808853783604,
0.20431978327764846,
0.3712129254573257,
0.12351680981057861,
0.08549988065399135
],
"weights":[
0.05030364283759858,
0.04039698788856005,
0.017875856848492952,
0.046964049821340295,
0.06683708900445406,
0.20853743006201148,
0.3780158072519113,
0.10882366598436707,
0.08224547030126438
],
"status":0
}
```

17.4   Management Approval Panel

Imagine the following use case scenario. There is plenty of demand for the time of the CEO/CIO of an investment operation. He/she simply won't be able to review and approve every decision made by the portfolio teams at the level of details provided by the Dashboard. However, it is quite common that he/she only wants to sign off on major decisions and more importantly monitor the top-10 or 20 contributors to portfolio tail risk and negative P&L's every trading day. Also, it is not necessary to share all the portfolio details with each level of senior executives so he/she wants to have a reasonable way to control the amount of information to disseminate at each level. The following is a typical flowchart of such a workflow:

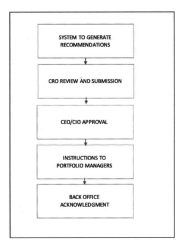

Figure 17.10: Management Approval Flowchart

A typical way to control the distribution and access of reports will be a panel such as the following:

Figure 17.11: Report Distribution and Access Panel

The following is a typical Approval Panel where each level of staff will be given an approval code (which can incorporate two-factor authentication if required) to ensure that a proper flow of instructions from one level of management to the next:

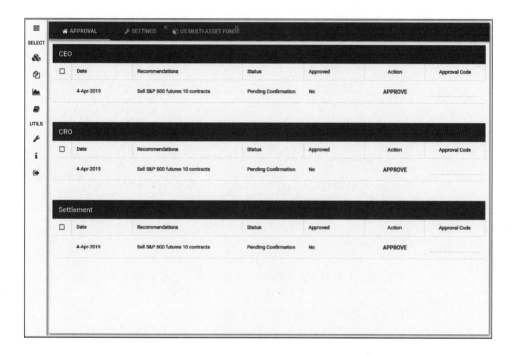

Figure 17.12: Typical Management Approval Panel

We should note that the choice of technology to construct these panels can be quite important to any successful deployment, depending on the context of the customer use case. The specific example given above is constructed using REACT, a JavaScript library for building user interfaces known for speed, which is maintained by Facebook and a community of individual developers and companies.[1] A careful choice of robust, scalable technology is important because many mid-size organizations today are distributed across multiple timezones. An inappropriate choice of technology may result in users being frustrated by the delayed response time of the application (known as "deadlock" in computer science) and eventually finding a workaround to the workflow control, thereby defeating the purpose of a user deployment in the first place.

---

[1]See https://reactjs.org/ for details.

INVESTMENT ANALYTICS IN THE DAWN OF ARTIFICIAL INTELLIGENCE

18. Implications of a Post-IA+AI Society

In this chapter, we will explore the social and policy implications of a world after a meaningful number of IA+AI solutions similar to the one illustrated by this book have been adopted. We will explore questions such as:

1. Who will be the likely winners and losers after the IA+AI evolution?
2. Will IA+AI help eliminate global poverty?
3. Will IA+AI accelerate changes in global wealth distribution?
4. Will IA+AI encourage a new wave of financial crimes or make it easier to detect at least some financial crimes?
5. Finally, will IA+AI lead to more global coordination of financial regulations?

These are important and not purely hypothetical questions. Deploying smarter technology in finance can add more "lubricants" to the global economy so as to identify and support the most value-creating, innovative investment ideas. When the global economic pie grows bigger, conventional wisdom suggests that there should be more resources available to lift the poorest members of society above the poverty line. However, throughout history, technology serves as a means to an end: the global production of tangible goods and services will not double simply because a computer virus suddenly multiplies the units of wealth at every bank and brokerage account globally by two. The distribution of global wealth and thus the dynamics of the global economy will change if a computer virus can do so selectively by targeting the accounts of the poorest members of society or, vice versa, only well-off members of society and large institutions. Ultimately, who has access to what investment technology may change the global distribution of wealth.

18.1 Winners and Losers

Trading is a zero-sum game. One trader can win only by making a profit from trading with the next trader. Hence, trading alone cannot create sustainable long-term wealth for society. To be clear, the discussion in this chapter is about investing to create value, not trading. When computers can invest automatically and intelligently, index investors will become the net "losers" because they have chosen to avoid the most exciting part of the investment return curve in the venture capital stage. This is how index investors are "paying" for expensive investment research to select those assets that eventually become larger capitalization index constituents. The most innovative net creators of wealth will find a way to win, even if most investors in the world may stick to low fees by following indices. With better investment technology that only institutions and the well-to-do can access today, the global distribution of wealth may become more polarized, but it also becomes more "democratic" in that it may be difficult for everyday investors to outperform each other. Thus, it becomes politically feasible for governments in such a world to offer a safety net against the poverty line. This outcome will fit Mark Zuckerburg's vision of wealth distribution, to provide a living, minimum wage for participants in innovation. Many innovative ideas will fail, but a handful will turn into future Dow Jones Industrial components. Countries that fail to emphasize science and engineering education are likely to be the net losers. These countries will be left behind in both the ability to carry out tangible innovations and the investment expertise to evaluate new innovations.

18.2 Enlarging the Overall Pie in the Fight against Poverty

If Bill Gates had kept Microsoft private and continued to run it as a privately held company, Microsoft would still have the "dry powder" to crush some emerging competitors. Eventually, a powerful but privately held Microsoft would run into a problem: Since Microsoft would not be available as an investment (thereby encouraging other technology giants to follow the practice) and it was also dominating the growth of information technology on the internet, there would be a relatively static number of people in developed countries who could afford Microsoft's software. Microsoft and other emerging technology companies may have a difficult time in attracting the best engineers without their employee stock options programs, typically tied to listed companies, while the high technology sector would stay dominated by the "blue suits" working for the likes of IBM, AT&T, and Digital Equipment Corporation. The miracle of Silicon Valley today owes its fair share of credits to modern finance.

While it makes business sense for large institutions and the well-to-do to make sure that the rest of the society can keep consuming, what will be the mechanism to allow entire societies to benefit from IA+AI evolution? Most of the middle class will have some form of pension/retirement funds that can benefit from lower fees and better returns from the IA+AI evolution. The more pressing policy issue is how can the IA+AI evolution help those in extreme poverty[1] and those who are barely getting by, who are not expected to have a meaningful amount of savings to invest. We need constructive ways to avoid the politically unsustainable and socially destabilizing outcome where only the rich get richer and the poor become poorer. Even the super-rich are increasingly uneasy about the social and political outcome under such a scenario.[2]

IA+AI technology can help in wealth creation and preservation, but no matter how much productive activities can be automated by society, today's technology is still far from creating a world of abundance. We work backward from the undesirable scenario where the lack of access to IA+AI tools can turn into a significant barrier to stop certain societies or segments of societies from escaping poverty. These are some known policy options to avoid highly negative outcomes:

1. Thanks to the IA+AI evolution, the financial sectors of developing countries can now leapfrog a few generations of IA tools, especially if they do so under effective government policies.
2. Governments in developed countries can offer free or highly subsidized access to IA tools to encourage the poorest among their populations to start saving and investing.
3. Finally, the key step in eradicating poverty comes down to educating the younger generation on saving and investing based on such IA tools to improve financial literacy.

Countries with more proactive FinTech policies and smarter execution will more likely become the winners. Locally-focused players trying to resist change and protect incumbents will more likely become the losers.

18.3   Changing Global Asset Management Landscape

Today, it is not uncommon for many leading professional managers in the developed world to have more than half of their assets under management coming from Asian and Middle Eastern sources. Asian and Middle Eastern sovereigns and institutional investors are used to allocating their wealth to America and Europe-based asset managers, citing "best interest" for their beneficiaries under fiduciary duties. The reality is that, with government funds or other centrally controlled pools of money, such a strategy helps career civil servants or former civil servants with no private

---

[1]Defined by the United Nations as roughly 10% of humanity. See https://www.un.org/sustainabledevelopment/poverty/.

[2]8 July 2018, *Medium*, https://medium.com/s/futurehuman/survival-of-the-richest-9ef6cddd0cc1.

sector experience avoid being blamed for potential mistakes. Risk aversion is a common culture among civil servants globally, more so for typical bureaucrats from Asian and Middle Eastern countries who see limited upside in trusting in any upstart local asset manager as supposed to a proven global one.

With smarter IA+AI tools, these countries now have increased abilities to run money with their own local talents. Adoption will likely be first driven by the public sector or under certain guidance by the public sector, and their private sectors will catch on eventually. With the help of smart technology, their performance can be as competitive as western asset managers', if not better, so eventually, there will be public pressure to go local instead of "overpaying" for "underperforming" global managers.

With further adoption, they will attract proven local players and also seed rising local players. One unintended consequence of adopting IA+AI is that it will spark the gradual migration of a Western-centric asset management industry to the East, with a bigger technology and analytics oriented focus favored by asset sponsors in the East.

18.4 More Frauds Initially Until Robust Solutions Stand Out

Suppliers in the financial services, even the more recognized names, will claim that they have smart IA+AI tools. The current hype in IA+AI will make it easier to defraud unsuspecting investors, especially retail, unsophisticated ones.

While supporters of IA+AI claim to have discovered a new way to empower the developing world, history has shown that certain less successful players in developed markets, unattractive to clients in the developed world, may prey on less sophisticated investors in Asia and the Middle East with unsound or even fraudulent schemes.

Not every solution available to investors will be legitimate. This phenomenon is less about outright frauds but is caused by solutions that are unsuccessful in delivering what they claim to do in aggressive advertizing campaigns. It is impor-tant that regulators recognize this reality and find effective ways to protect retail investors without choking off all innovations. Eventually, investors will catch on as well: problematic providers in the retail space will die out after highly publicized investment losses, but the opportunists will still find creative ways to profit from the ecosystem of unsuspecting investors.

Blatant and simplistic corruption will also be discouraged by the deployment of IA+AI tools in investing, in that an unattractive investee company can no longer pay off a research analyst to write a glowing investment recommendation if the analysis from IA+AI tools using its financial releases and other objective facts simply does not support the claim of a justifiable investment.

18.5   Steady-State Outcomes

In this final section of the book, we will analyze the steady-state outcome of the
IA+AI evolution. For instance, what may happen when one jurisdiction tries to
dictate rules that differ from the other jurisdictions'? In the era of cross-border
hosting of internet-based services, some global coordination of financial regulations
will be required and agreed on.

Major economies such as the US and China will pursue their own policies because they do have some ability to enforce their unilateral rules on out-of-jurisdiction
activities, at least against operators who are keen to stay in their massive domestic
markets. Eventually, regulators from other jurisdictions will have to agree with those
one or two countries.

Issues that will also be discussed in this section include:

1. Where is the correct line to draw between individual, retail investors versus
   institutional and high-net-worth assets, which obviously will be different from
   one market to the next?
2. What rules will be applicable to each group?
3. What investment activities will be regulated?
4. How to define such activities? For instance, definition simply based on fee
   structure, as in whether fees are charged on AUM, will go against industry practice, since many generally unregulated activities such as custodian
   software are charged by AUM.
5. How to ensure that regulations are applied consistently across borders? If
   certain activities were unregulated or lightly regulated in the past, simply
   because newer technology is used, it will be difficult to argue that they should
   be subject to significantly more regulations than their more manually driven
   counterparts.

18.5.1   How may the Steady-State Outcome Impact the Industry?

Paraphrasing Bill Dally, Chief Scientist at hardware vendor NVIDIA and formerly a
computer science professor at Stanford University (where he was also Chairman of
the Computer Science Department), MIT and Caltech:[3]

> AI algorithms are not new. They have been in use since the 80's. It is
> also true that machines can now surpass human capacity in a certain type
> of applications that involve pattern classification and recognition. The
> key determinant to success in applications to other areas is the massive

---

[3]31 January 2018, *SG Innovate*, "In Conversation with Bill Dally", https://www.
eventbrite.sg/e/sginnovate-presents-in-conversation-with-bill-
dally-nvidia-chief-scientist-tickets-41999913873.

volume of data for the AI algorithms to learn from, and whether the algorithms can adapt and improve over time.

The likely outcomes from the investment industry's inevitable adoption of AI-driven analytics in the current era of AI infatuation may include:

1. Gradually, AI will gain the public's trust and eventual acceptance, but probably only after its many unhealthy myths are disputed. AI can add value in that computers can process a massive amount of data, recognize higher-dimensional patterns beyond the three dimensions that human brains are evolved to perceive, and do so with processing speed that human brains cannot match.

2. IA+AI applications are proven, in that similar techniques are already in use by pioneers in the financial industry. However, investment industry players with successful IA+AI applications often do not want to reveal their use, because doing so may "thin out" the finite amount of alpha available, and attract unwanted regulatory attention. The likely outcome of wider adoption will be further disintermediation of the investment industry and fewer middlemen.

3. Since the prerequisite to success lies in data availability, many asset management firms will find themselves being squeezed from both ends, as in they lack both the big budgets of large asset managers, and the agility of more specialized boutiques who have been doing something comparable for quite some time.

18.5.2   How may the Steady-State Outcome Manifest in Time?

1. **Stage 1.** Some of the largest asset managers with significant budgets for data infrastructures will lead by cutting investment management fees. Doing so is an anti-competition tactic so that smaller managers who are "stuck" with higher cost from human resources (due to their lack of automation) will eventually become unprofitable. However, the strategy also means that large asset managers must retool so-called "legacy" systems, usually ones that were built decades ago. Doing so is a massive challenge because in software engineering a single software "patch" often results in many unintentional dependency programming errors elsewhere in legacy systems, after most if not all original programmers have left the team. Retooling legacy platforms with AI will be a significantly more formidable challenge than performing regular maintenance on such platforms, even more so than rebuilding from scratch. In short, these large asset managers' ambitions may become bigger than their ability to execute.

2. **Stage 2.** Sensing a potential opening from traditional investment firms being disrupted by IA+AI, technology firms successful in data science will try

to get into the game. Some will succeed, but most will lack the domain expertise to comprehend the much deeper challenges faced by the other more sophisticated areas of finance. Payment is a logical extension of retail sales. However, going into the more sophisticated areas of finance may require more than pure technical know-how; as in all things finance-related, there will be an element of art in crafting solutions. For instance, there is quite a large collection of financial information and wealth management websites in China today, although their qualities vary. Why did Alibaba's Jack Ma choose to invest in such a venture in Hong Kong instead?[4] In particular, this team focuses on a technique used to be called "grass root research" in the US, using data mining to automate how traditional financial players identify alpha opportunities, when the technique itself is not known for impressive hit rates, and the automation may not necessarily work well for multi-byte-sized data in Asian languages.

3. **Stage 3.** Teams with depth in both finance and technology will take over the landscape. Some existing firms, such as DE Shaw, Citadel and Renaissance Technologies, have existed for decades and are highly profitable. These firms have not shared and are unlikely to share finite alpha opportunities with society at large. Thus, we predict that there should be a disruptive change in the incentive model in global finance to entice those teams with the capabilities to step up and meet this challenge.

One common speculation among asset management industry professionals is that the industry must save itself from "Uberization." The concern was significant enough that the CEO of one sizeable player felt the need to defend the value added by his colleagues in the press.[5] The term "Uberization" means that existing financial firms will turn into what taxi companies are to Uber – i.e., increasingly, they will become client facing distribution channels and outsource both know-how and technology. Conducting a public debate on such a topic would be unthinkable only a few years ago but is not surprising today, because even the handful of investment firms that focus on quantitative analysis and technology are struggling to keep up with the speed at which they are being disrupted by new and emerging FinTech firms. The potential implications for the investment industry are:

1. There will be less alpha to go around for every market participant. With new and faster IA+AI tools and thus more transparent access to whatever financial data available on investments, most investment portfolios will be

---

[4] 5 January 2018, *Nikkei Business Insight,* https://asia.nikkei.com/Features/Business-Insight/Jack-Ma-puts-his-data-magic-to-work-at-a-Hong-Kong-brokerage.

[5] 19 November 2017, *Financial Times,* "RBC GAM: blockchain will prevent us being Uberised", https://www.ft.com/content/4fbb78d4-bf1d-11e7-9836-b25f8adaa111.

reasonably efficient and it will become more difficult to outperform. However, the selection of new companies and new investment ideas will still be done by savvy human investors for years to come, because these new investment opportunities do not have data to train machine learning algorithms on.

2. With asset selection driven by IA+AI, asset allocation will increasingly dominate the activities employed by the investment industry. Gradually, investing will become a "personal" balance sheet allocation exercise customized for each person, as in how some technology sector workers want to choose retirement portfolios that hedge against a potential downturn in the technology sector.

3. While the "known-known" and "known-unknown" risk can be addressed with IA+AI tools, under the increasing accessibility of financial data on the internet, investors are more exposed to the so-called "unknown-unknown" risk: by promoting the power to predict the future, the irony is that the unpredictable future elements often turn more extreme. For example, if an Electromagnetic Pulse (EMP) attack from a hostile country shuts down the US electricity grid, US exchanges and their clients will be unable to trade in the financial markets. Such an unprecedented economic shock may make the 9-11 attacks look relatively mild. No data will be available to train AI engines or to model any hedging solution against such an extreme scenario. With the increased reliance on tools, investors are less prepared to handle entirely unexpected surprises; the overall market risk turns systematic for every investor.

18.5.3 How may the Steady-State Outcome Manifest Geographically?

1. **Small, Wealthy Countries.** Imagine any country with a relatively small population such as Norway, Singapore, or Switzerland. They are generally rich, endowed with a number of successful, nationalized companies and publicly managed retirement plans. Some of the key outcomes for them to adopt IA+AI technologies in investment management may include:

    (a) Asset allocation will increasingly drive most public investment decisions, already the case in Norway today, especially when AI can be used to eliminate human bias in asset selection, which may be considered desirable for public investments.

    (b) Their private sectors will begin to adopt IA+AI technologies in offering higher value-added services without policy complications, such as private banking services for UHNW individuals

    (c) As their governments are partially funded by investment returns, there is no need to impose high tax rates. Doing so will free up more human capital to engage in entrepreneurship, feeding a positive feedback cycle.

2. **Other Western Countries.** Will such a model work for other Western countries? Among traditional Western economic powers such as the US and the UK, there is an abundance of asset managers all fighting for a piece of the pie. The political objection against any centralized pension system will be difficult to overcome. Still, Western countries should encourage the adoption of IA+AI tools to help reduce management fees and prevent monopolistic practices from taking root. The promotion of direct access by investors is likely to encourage savings across all income groups and reduces the need for social safety nets. IA+AI tools will not change their asset management industries overnight. Instead, successful tools should be as simple and friendly as possible and should function like a non-intrusive tool that does not impact the branding of the incumbent asset managers.

3. **Large Asian and Central Asian Countries.** In any centralized social and political system such as China's, IA+AI tools can be used to lower public concerns about potential abuse and corruption, whether the concern is legitimate or not. However, the likely outcome of adoption will be either a Government-led effort or one driven by a handful of players with strong Government ties. For any such effort to be accepted by the public, the proposed platform must be built with a sound data privacy policy that does not allow arbitrary "commandeering" of private investment data for non-investment purposes.

4. **Other Countries.** Japan can be used as a helpful example here. It is wealthy but has a stagnating economy and inverted population pyramid. IA+AI tools can be used to help invest some of Japan's massive savings out of Japan, achieving global diversification and higher returns (generally a challenge in an aging society), as there is a smaller supply of investment professionals in Japan with deep expertise in non-Japanese markets. Doing so will help restore its balance of payments and lower inflation, while the savings can be invested in more strategic projects to complement known weaknesses in the Japanese economy, such as the liquefied natural gas sector. In addition, Japan's retiring population is looking to invest in other faster-growing Asian economies, but they demand to invest in companies with Environmental, Social and Governance (ESG) standards that they are accustomed to, so IA+AI tools can be used to evaluate ESG factors and keywords in news and social media. Roughly the same logic may be applied to certain mineral-rich Middle Eastern countries facing similar challenges to move their economies away from dependencies in oil revenues.

18.6   Final Conclusion

In summary, IA+AI tools are no longer a myth. The game changer today is data access and the availability of internet-based infrastructure with speed and computational scale to process a massive volume of data from the convenience of a mobile phone or tablet. However, financial data formats are still highly fragmented today. A platform that can automatically collect, integrate and clean data from all relevant sources available on the internet adds significant value to investors, but that alone does not necessarily mean better investment decisions. Like all things finance-related, there will always be an element of art in crafting a few solid IA+AI platforms that will successfully transform the investment industry over the next decade.

Bibliography

[1] "A Discussion of Tau." BlackLitterman.org, www.blacklitterman.org/tau.html.

[2] Ang, Andrew, et al. Review of the Active Management of the Government Pension Fund Global. 20 Jan. 2014, www0.gsb.columbia.edu/ faculty/aang/papers/AngBrandtDenison.pdf.

[3] Berk, Jonathan, and Richard Green. "Mutual Fund Flows and Performance in Rational Markets." Journal of Political Economy, vol. 112, no. 6, Dec. 2004, doi:10.3386/w9275.

[4] Corwin, Shane A, and Paul Schultz. "A Simple Way to Estimate Bid-Ask Spreads from Daily High and Low Prices." Journal of Finance, Volume 67, Issue 2, April 2012, pp. 719–760.

[5] Chekhlov, Alexei, et al. "Portfolio Optimization with Drawdown Constraints." SSRN Electronic Journal, 8 Apr. 2000, doi:10.2139/ssrn.223323.

[6] Dionne, Georges, and Louis Eeckhoudt. "Self-Insurance, Self-Protection and Increased Risk Aversion." Economics Letters, vol. 17, no. 1-2, 1985, pp. 39–42, doi:10.1016/0165-1765(85)90123-5.

[7] Dionne, Georges. "Risk Management: History, Definition, and Critique." Risk Management and Insurance Review, vol. 16, no. 2, 2013, pp. 147–166, doi:10.1111/rmir.12016.

[8] Egloff, Daniel, Markus Leippold, and Liuren Wu, 2009, Variance risk dynamics, variance risk premia, and optimal variance swap investments, *EFA 2006 Zurich Meetings Paper*, November 16, 2007.

[9] Ehrlich, Isaac, and Gary S. Becker. "Market Insurance, Self-Insurance, and Self-Protection." Journal of Political Economy, vol. 80, no. 4, 1972, pp. 623–648., doi:10.1086/259916.

[10] Huang, Yuqin, and Jin E. Zhang, 2010, The CBOE S&P 500 three-month variance futures, *Journal of Futures Markets* 30, 48–70.

[11] Higgins, Tim. "Elon Musk Lays Out Worst-Case Scenario for AI Threat." The Wall Street Journal, Dow Jones & Company, 15 July 2017, www.wsj.com/articles/elon-musk-warns-nations-governors-of-looming-ai-threat-calls-for-regulations-1500154345.

[12] LaFrance, Adrienne. "An Artificial Intelligence Developed Its Own Non-Human Language." The Atlantic, Atlantic Media Company, 15 June 2017, www.theatlantic.com/technology/archive/2017/06/artificial-intelligence-develops-its-own-non-human-language/530436/?utm_source=mitfb.

[13] Lee, Bernard, and Youngju Lee, "The Alternative Sharpe Ratio," in: Schachter, B. (Ed.), Intelligent Hedge Fund Investing (ed. B.), Risk Books, London, 2004, pp. 143–177.

[14] Lee, Bernard, et al. "An Analysis of Extreme Price Shocks and Illiquidity Among Systematic Trend Followers." Review of Futures Markets, vol. 18, no. 4, 2010.

[15] Lee, Bernard, "Using Volatility Futures as Extreme Downside Hedges." Proceedings of the 25th Australasian Finance & Banking Conference, December 2012. Available on SSRN: `https://papers.ssrn.com/sol3/papers.cfm?abstract_id=2132558`.

[16] Lee, Bernard, and Nicos Christofides, "Time-Constrained Predictive Modeling on Large and Continuously Updating Financial Datasets." JSM Proceedings, Statistical Learning and Data Science Section. American Statistical Association, Alexandria, VA, 2018, pp. 2831–2837.

[17] Leippold, Markus, et al. "Variance Risk Dynamics, Variance Risk Premia, and Optimal Variance Swap Investments." SSRN Electronic Journal, 2007, doi:10.2139/ssrn.903728.

[18] Mackintosh, James. "Robotic Hogwash! Artificial Intelligence Will Not Take Over Wall Street." The Wall Street Journal, Dow Jones & Company, 17 July 2017, www.wsj.com/articles/robotic-hogwash-artificial-intelligence-will-not-take-over-wall-street-1500304343.

[19] Mackintosh, James. "World's Biggest Pension Fund Wants to Stop Index Trackers Eating the Economy." The Wall Street Journal, Dow Jones & Company, 17 Aug. 2017, www.wsj.com/articles/worlds-biggest-pension-fund-wants-to-stop-index-trackers-eating-the-economy-1502974668.

[20] Mooney, Attracta. "RBC GAM: Blockchain Will Prevent Us Being Uberised." Financial Times, Financial Times, 19 Nov. 2017, www.ft.com/content/4fbb78d4-bf1d-11e7-9836-b25f8adaa111.

[21] Moran, Matthew T., and Srikant Dash. "VIX Futures and Options: Pricing and Using Volatility Products to Manage Downside Risk and Improve Efficiency in Equity Portfolios." Journal of Trading, vol. 2, 2007, pp. 96–105.

[22] Rushkoff, Douglas. "Survival of the Richest." Medium, 5 Jul. 2018, https://medium.com/s/futurehuman/survival-of-the-richest-9ef6cddd0cc1.

[23] Schulte, Paul. "Jack Ma Puts His Data Magic to Work at a Hong Kong Brokerage." Nikkei Asian Review, Nikkei Asian Review, 5 Jan. 2018, asia.nikkei.com/Features/Business-Insight/Jack-Ma-puts-his-data-magic-to-work-at-a-Hong-Kong-brokerage.

[24] Son, Hugh. "Dimon Says JPMorgan Headcount to Keep Rising Despite Automation." Bloomberg.com, Bloomberg, 26 June 2017, www.bloomberg.com/news/articles/2017-06-26/dimon-says-jpmorgan-headcount-to-keep-rising-despite-automation.

[25] Szado, Edward. "VIX Futures and Options-A Case Study of Portfolio Diversification during the 2008 Financial Crisis." Journal of Alternative Investments, vol. 12, 2009, pp. 68–85.

[26] Treynor, Jack, and Fisher Black. "How to Use Security Analysis to Improve Portfolio Selection." Journal of Business, vol. 46, issue 1, 1973, pp. 66–86.

[27] "Goal 1: End poverty in all its forms everywhere." United Nations, https://www.un.org/sustainabledevelopment/poverty/.

[28] Zhang, Jin E., and Yuqin Huang. "The CBOE S&P 500 Three-Month Variance Futures." Journal of Futures Markets, vol. 30, no. 1, 2010, pp. 48–70, doi:10.1002/fut.20400.

Index

P matrix, 166
Q matrix, 167
1-month VIX futures, 85
6-month beta, 18

Accounting, 191
Accounting details, 201
Accounting entries, 191
Accounts payables, 205
Accounts receivables, 205
Accuracy, 213
Adjusted R-squared, 123
Aggregated reports, 188
AI algorithms, 238
Allowed character checks, 216
Alternative Sharpe Ratio, 19, 49, 184
Application programming interface, 225
Asset allocation, 179
Asset class, 179
Asset turnover, 119
Assets, 109

Balance sheet, 109
Bank accounts, 205
Bank non-performing loan to total gross
    loans(%), 120
Batch total checks for missing records,
    216
Bayesian inference, 117
Bayesian information criterion (BIC), 123
Beta, 184
Black-Litterman model, 158, 162, 164
Brinson attribution, 57
Broad money (M3), 120

C-P criterion, 123
Cardinality check, 217
Cash forecast, 202
Cash reconciliation, 191
Changes to assets held, 205
Check digits used for numerical data, 217
Client's need for liquidity, 199
Client's performance goals and risk tolerance, 199

Commodity term structure, 132
Compliance analysis, 209
Composite leading indicator, 120
Conditional value at risk, 19, 30, 184
Conditional value-at-risk at 95%, 46
Confirmation, 190
Consolidated positions report, 177
Consolidated positions reports, 177
Consumer price index, 120
Contributions, 176
Correlation, 187
Correlation matrix, 164
Cross-system consistency checks, 217
Current account balance, 120
Current NAV, 182
Current price, 178
Current ratio, 119
Custom benchmark, 195

Data accuracy, 214
Data consistency, 215
Data integrity, 212
Data timeliness, 213, 214
Data type checks, 217
Debt-equity ratio, 119
Diagonalized matrix, 167
Dividends, 176

Equity, 205
Exchange in and exchange out, 176
Expectation-maximization algorithm, 218
Expected shortfall, 184
Expenses, 205

Factor exposure, 62, 188
Factor set definition, 121
Fat tail, 33
Full report, 192
Full risk report, 188
Full trade report, 188
Fundamental analysis, 108

Fundamental factors, 119

Gains and losses, 176
GDP growth, 120
Gross profit margin, 119

Historical return, 20, 179, 184
Historical simulation, 149

Implied forward variance, 71
Implied return, 179
Income, 205
Income and benefits accruing from the
    assets, 205
Income statement, 183
Intention, 213
Interest rate term structure, 132
Investments, 205
Investor summary, 174

JSON, 230

K-means clustering, 118
Kurtosis, 20, 184

Leptokurtosis, 32
Liabilities, 109
Limit check, 218
Linear regression, 112
Linear regression model, 110
Logic check, 218
Long stock portfolio, 177
Long/short exposures, 12

Macro factors, 120
Marginal distribution function, 34
Mark-to-market value, 82
Maximum Drawdown, 21, 31, 184
Maximum Sharpe Ratio, 48
MCTRet, 186
MCVaR, 185

Minimum 95% conditional value-at-risk, 46
Minimum 95% value-at-risk, 44
Minimum absolute residual, 41
Minimum expected shortfall, 46
Minimum peak-to-trough maximum draw-down, 42
Minimum potential loss, 44
Minimum variance, 41
MVaR, 185

Naïve modelling, 161
Net asset value, 180
Neural networks, 112
Normal distribution, 33
Nostro, 191

Options implied volatility, 130
Options pricing model, 129
Out-of-the-money, 80

PCTR, 179
PetroChina Company Limited, 213
Poisson distribution, 34
Portfolio gauges, 17
Portfolio optimization, 161
Portfolio rebalancing, 137
Portfolio statistics, 184
Portfolio summary, 177
Prepayments, 205
Presence check, 218
Prime broker and/or brokers, 205
Product attributes, 12
Product benchmark, 198
Product fundamentals, 126
Product statistics, 22
Product tree, 10
Profit & loss, 178, 179
Purchase price, 178
Purchases, 176
Purchasing power parity, 120

Range check, 218
Range of securities to invest in, 199
Rank correlation, 123
Ranking, 186
Realized variance, 71
Rebalancing, 137
Records of distribution of capital, income, or dividend to investors, 206
Records of any performance related to fees due to the manager, 206
Records of assets held, 205
Records of fees and expenses, 205
Records of the purchase and sales of units or shares in the fund by investors, 206
Redemption, 202
Referential integrity, 218
Return attribution, 54
Return level, 30
Reversed portfolio optimization, 161
Risk and return, 185
Risk attribution, 53
Risk management, 28
Risk-adjusted return, 197

Scenario analysis, 146
Semi-deviation, 21
Sentiment analysis, 116
Settlement, 190
Sharpe Ratio, 19, 48, 161, 184
Short stock portfolios, 178
Skewness, 20, 184
Stochastic analysis, 157, 158, 230
Subscription redemption details, 202
Subscriptions, 202

Tax situation pertaining to the fund, 206
Today's change, 178
Total gain/loss, 178
Total value, 178
Tracking error, 197

Trade capture, 189
Trading lifecycle, 188
Transactions, 176, 191
Truthfulness, 213

Valuations of the total assets of the fund,
        206
Value-at-risk, 18, 29, 184
Value-at-risk at 95%, 44
Variance futures, 71
Vector autoregression model, 117
Verification, 190

VIX futures, 68
VIX Index, 67
Volatility, 18, 184
VT, 67

Weight, 179
Withdrawals, 176

Yield curve, 132

Z-Score, 110, 220